CUTTING
EDGE

THIRD EDITION

PRE-INTERMEDIATE

STUDENTS' BOOK

WITH DVD-ROM

SARAH CUNNINGHAM PETER MOOR
AND ARAMINTA CRACE

CONTENTS

CONTENTS

01

LEISURE AND SPORT

IN THIS UNIT

- **Grammar:** Revision of questions; Present simple and frequency phrases

- **Vocabulary:** Leisure activities; Sports and games

- **Task:** Do a 60-second interview

- **World culture:** Unusual sports

Speaking and vocabulary
Leisure activities

1a Work in pairs and discuss.

- Which activities in the box can you see in the photos?
- Which activities do you do every day?

go to the cinema	listen to the radio	watch live music
go out with friends	use the internet	play computer games
listen to music	play a musical instrument	go to the gym
go to evening classes	play sport	watch TV

b 🎧 1.1 Listen to the phrases. Practise saying them aloud.

2 Read the results of the leisure time survey and answer the questions.

1 Where was the survey?
2 What is it about?

KEY FACTS

LEISURE TIME SURVEY OF YOUNG ADULTS IN THE UK

In our online poll, we asked 1,000 young adults aged between 16 and 24 'How do you spend your free time?' Here are the results:

- [1]_____ percent of young adults use the internet every day.

- The most popular leisure activity is going to the cinema: [2]_____ percent say it is their favourite evening activity.

- 82 percent of people say they watch TV for more than [3]_____ hours a week, but only [4]_____ percent listen to the radio.

- 38 percent of young people watch live music, but only [5]_____ percent can play a musical instrument.

- Only [6]_____ percent of young adults play sport. Football, swimming and cycling are the most popular sports.

3a 🎧 1.2 Listen to a radio news report about the results of the survey. Before you listen, try to guess where the numbers in the box go in the survey.

10   23   30   32   42   87

b Listen again and check your answers. Then work in pairs and compare your answers.

4 Jay and Tina both took part in the leisure time survey. Complete what they say with the correct verbs from exercise 1a.

JAY

My computer is very important for me. I'm a student at Manchester University, so I ¹_____ the internet a lot for my studies and my friends and I ²_____ a lot of computer games. I don't ³_____ any sport. I ⁴_____ to evening classes twice a week; it's a course on Computer Skills. On other nights, I ⁵_____ out with friends – we usually ⁶_____ to the cinema.

TINA

I'm a professional musician, so music is my life! I ⁷_____ to the radio nearly all day – mainly classical or jazz. When I ⁸_____ TV, it's always a music channel. I even ⁹_____ to music when I ¹⁰_____ to the gym! I ¹¹_____ the piano and the saxophone. And I ¹²_____ a lot of live music in my free time.

5a Work in pairs and ask and answer questions using the verbs in exercise 1a. Make a list of three activities your partner does and three activities he/she doesn't do.

> Do you go to evening classes?

> Yes, I do … I study English!

> Do you play a musical instrument?

> No, I don't. How about you?

b Compare your ideas. What are the most popular leisure activities? What other things do people do in their free time?

> Do you go to the gym?

> No, I don't. I hate it!

Grammar focus 1
Revision of questions

1 Work in pairs. Look at the games in the photos and discuss the questions.

- Which are board games? Which are puzzles?
- Which do children often play?
- Which have the same name in your language?
- Which of the games do you play? Which are your favourites? Why?
- Which of these do you usually prefer? Why?
  - word games (e.g. Scrabble®)?
  - number games (e.g. sudoku)?
  - games of strategy (e.g. chess)?
  - games of chance (e.g. Snakes and Ladders)?
- What other games like these do you play?

2 Work in pairs. Read the games quiz and try to answer as many questions as you can in five minutes. If you don't know the answer, try to guess.

3 🎧 1.3 Listen and check your answers. How many questions did you answer correctly?

GRAMMAR

Question words

1 Look at the question words in bold in exercise 2. Which question word(s) do we use to talk about:

1 a person? __who__
2 a place? _____
3 a thing? _____ / _____
4 a time? _____
5 the reason for doing something? _____
6 the way you do something? _____
7 a period of time? _____
8 the number of times you do something? _____
9 the class or type of thing? _____
10 the number of people or things? _____

Word order in questions

2 Put the words in the correct order to make questions.

1 good at / Is / James / playing chess ?
2 computer games / play / your friends / Do ?
3 start / the game / does / When ?

> **IT'S A FACT!**
> The longest recorded game of Monopoly® is 1,680 hours – that's 70 days!

GAMES QUIZ

01 **When** was the first Mario Brothers computer game?

02 **Who** starts in a game of chess: the black player or the white player?

03 **What** are marbles usually made of?

04 **Where** did the game mahjong originate?

05 **What kind** of game is Snakes and Ladders?

06 **Why** are there 52 cards in a normal pack?

07 **How** do you do a sudoku puzzle?

08 **What colour** are the pieces on a backgammon board normally?

09 **Which** two letters have the highest score in the English version of Scrabble®?

10 **How many** spots are there on a dice?

11 **How often** do the World Dominoes Championships take place?

12 **How long** does an average game of Monopoly® last?

PRACTICE

1 Match questions 1–4 with answers a–d in parts A, B and C below.

A
1 **When** do you **play football**?
2 **Who** do you **play football with**?
3 **Where** do you **play football**?
4 **Why** do you **play football**?

a My friends from college.
b On Sunday mornings.
c Because it's fun and it's good exercise.
d In the local park.

B
1 **How often** do you **have English lessons**?
2 **How long** are the **lessons**?
3 **Which days** do you **have lessons**?
4 **How many teachers** do you **have**?

a Two.
b Twice a week.
c Tuesdays and Thursdays.
d 90 minutes.

C
1 **What time** is it?
2 **What time** does the **train leave**?
3 **What day** is it?
4 **What date** is it **today**?

a 16th May.
b Monday.
c Nearly three o'clock.
d Five forty-five.

PRONUNCIATION

1 🎧 1.4 **Look at the list of questions in exercise 1. Notice the words which are stressed (these are in bold). Listen and practise the stressed words.**

2 🎧 1.5 **Listen and practise saying the complete questions.**

2 Complete the questions.

1 Where _____ you live?
2 Who do you live _____ ?
3 How _____ do you drink coffee?
4 What _____ your favourite food?
5 When do _____ have lunch?
6 _____ you watch TV a lot?
7 _____ many pets have you got?
8 _____ you speak French?
9 _____ would you like to do this weekend?
10 What time _____ it now?

3 Write the questions for the answers below.

I get up at **seven o'clock** at the weekend.
What time do you get up at the weekend?

1 I get up **at six o'clock** in the week.
2 I go to the cinema **once a month**.
3 I come to school **by bus**.
4 My birthday is **in August**.
5 I play **basketball**.
6 My favourite colour is **blue**.
7 There are **five people** in my family.
8 My journey to school takes **about half an hour**.
9 I'd like to visit **India and Australia**.
10 I like **rock and jazz**.

4 Work in pairs. Take turns to ask and answer the questions in exercises 2 and 3.

> What time do you get up at the weekend?

> About seven o'clock.

> Seven o'clock! Why do you get up so early?

> Because I always go to the gym before breakfast.

Unit 1, Study & Practice 1, page 138

Reading and vocabulary

Sports and games

1 Work in pairs and make a list of six sports that are popular in your country. Which sports do you play? Which ones do you watch?

2 Read the article and answer the questions.

Which sport:
1 is good for playing with friends?
2 can you play in a park?
3 do you do on your own?
4 is similar to dancing in some ways?
5 is likely to result in injuries?
6 can you play in many different countries?

3a Complete the questions below with one word.

1 _____ 's the name of the world's best-selling computer game?
2 _____ do you hit the ball when you play Wii-tennis?
3 _____ old is the game of golf?
4 How _____ Disc Golf courses are there in the world?
5 _____ is John Farnworth?
6 _____ long did it take John Farnworth to run the London Marathon?

b Work in pairs. Take turns to ask and answer the questions using the phrases in the box.

....

by moving your arm and pressing a button
more than 1,000
he's a freestyle football champion
12 hours 15 minutes   Wii Sports
250 years old

....

4 Look at the words in the box and put them into three groups: things you need, verbs and people.

....

ball	racket	games console	equipment
hit	throw	winner	player
team	kick	score	champion

....

5 Work in pairs and discuss.

• Which of the three sports do you think is the most difficult / least difficult? Why?
• What other unusual sports do you know?

NEW WAYS WITH OLD SPORTS

Can you play golf without a ball? Or tennis without a tennis racket? These days the answer is 'Yes you can'. Here are some 21st century ways of playing our favourite traditional sports.

1 WII SPORTS

Nintendo's Wii Sports is the best-selling computer game of all time. You can play tennis, baseball or golf, go bowling or do boxing. You don't run around or get tired, however. You do everything by moving your arm and pressing a button on your games console. It's also a good social activity and many people organise gaming parties with their friends. But there is a downside; at least ten people in the UK injure themselves playing Wii Sports every week and have to go to hospital. There are also hundreds of cases of broken furniture, broken windows and injured pets! Some people call this new 21st century problem 'Wii-it-is'.

2 DISC GOLF

The game of golf is more than 250 years old. But for the 21st century version of the game, you don't need any expensive special equipment. Players don't hit a ball; they throw a plastic disc towards the 'hole' – which is actually a metal basket. The winner is the player who reaches the 'hole' with the lowest number of throws. More than half a million people around the world now play the game. There are more than 1,000 disc golf courses in 40 countries, many of them in public parks. It's a great way to get exercise in the fresh air.

3 FREESTYLE FOOTBALL

In Freestyle football there are no teams, you don't kick the ball and you never score a goal. Freestyle footballers try to keep the ball in the air using any part of their body. Some people describe it as a mixture of breakdancing and football. Judges give points for ball control and original moves. John Farnworth, from Lancashire in the north of England, was the world's first Freestyle champion: in 2011 he ran the London Marathon (42 km) in 12 hours 15 minutes, keeping a ball in the air all the way!

Grammar focus 2
Present simple and frequency phrases

1 Work in pairs. Look at the photos of two sports people and guess who:

1 swims for at least five hours every day.
2 is a Goodwill ambassador for UNICEF, the World Children's Charity.
3 has 4 million followers on Twitter.
4 consumes 12,000 calories a day, and often eats burgers and other fast food.
5 makes pop records.
6 gets up at 5 a.m. to go to the swimming pool.
7 weighs 100 kg.
8 has the nickname 'The Fish'.
9 lives in Los Angeles, California.
10 earns about $10 million a year.

2 🎧 1.6 Listen and check your answers. Whose life do you think is more interesting? Why?

Michael Phelps, world champion swimmer from Baltimore, USA

Yu-na Kim, world champion ice-skater from Bucheon, South Korea

GRAMMAR

Present simple

1 Which of the following examples describes:
- a habit?
- something that is always true?
1 He trains for five to six hours every day.
2 She comes from Bucheon, South Korea.

2 Put each sentence into:
- the question form
- the negative form

Frequency phrases

3 Underline the phrases below which answer the question *How often ... ?* Where in the sentences do the phrases go?
1 He sometimes eats burgers and other fast food.
2 She often gives money to charities.
3 He does at least five hours of training every day.
4 She has English classes three times a week.

4 Number these words from 1 (most often) to 6 (least often).

sometimes   often   usually
always   never   occasionally

PRACTICE

1 Write the frequency phrases in brackets in the correct place in the sentences.

1 Michael sends messages on Twitter. (five or six times a day)
2 He swims for five or six hours. (every day)
3 He misses breakfast. (never)
4 He goes to fast food restaurants. (sometimes)
5 He goes to the swimming pool in the mornings. (always)
6 Yu-na works for children's charities. (often)
7 She studies English. (three times a week)
8 She eats fast food. (never)
9 She skates for several hours. (every morning)
10 She sings in English. (occasionally)

2a Complete the sentences with a frequency phrase in the box below to make them true for you.

always   occasionally   sometimes   usually   never
every day/week/month/year/two years, etc.
once/twice/three times a day/week/month/year

sometimes
I ^ watch TV in bed.
1 I go out with my friends.
2 I am late for school/work.
3 I play games on my phone.
4 I listen to the radio in the morning.
5 I go to the opera.
6 I watch TV in the afternoon.
7 I go to bed after midnight.

b Work in pairs and compare your answers.

Unit 1, Study & Practice 2, page 138

11

Task

Do a 60-second interview

Preparation Reading

1a Work in pairs and look at the photos. Do you know who the woman is? Why do you think she's famous? Where do you think she is from?

b Work in pairs and write five questions to find out more about Freida Pinto.

Where was she born? Is she an actress?

c Read the 60-second interview about Freida Pinto and find the answers to your questions.

2 Work in pairs and answer the questions.

1 What is the most interesting thing you learnt from the interview?
2 Have you seen any of her films?
3 What do you have in common with Freida Pinto?

3a 🎧 1.7 Listen to two students, Marek and Laura, doing a 60-second interview. Tick the questions you hear in the Useful language box. How many questions does Marek ask?

b Listen again and make a note of Laura's answers.

60-SECOND interview with

Freida Pinto

Q1 What's your full name?
Freida Pinto.

Q2 Have you got a nickname?
Fro.

Q3 Where and when were you born?
On 18th October 1984, in Mumbai, India.

Q4 Tell me about your family.
My mother, Sylvia, is a head teacher at a high school and my father, Frederick, is a bank manager. I've also got an older sister, Sharon. She works for a TV news company. She's my best friend.

Q5 What was your first acting job?
In 2008, I played Latika in the film *Slumdog Millionaire*. I don't have any acting training so I did a three-month acting course to prepare for the film. My other films include *Trishna, You will meet a tall dark stranger, Miral, Rise of the Planet of the Apes* and *Immortals*.

Q6 Where do you live?
I live in three suitcases! I come from Mumbai and sometimes I live there. But I also spend time in London and New York, and lots of other places. Right now, I don't mind moving around a lot.

Q7 What do you do in your free time?
I do yoga regularly and I read books. I don't do much sport, but I have a lot of different hobbies! I like dancing, especially Indian dance and Salsa. I cook different kinds of food, especially Italian. Also, I collect boarding passes! I travel by air a lot for work, and also with my friends, so I've got a lot of them now!

Q8 Are you scared of anything?
I'm scared of water and I can't swim very well! I want to learn to swim properly so I don't feel so scared.

Q9 What's your favourite possession?
Shoes! And my Chanel bandana bag!

Q10 What's your favourite weather?
I like rain. I love the monsoon season in India when it rains a lot!

Q11 Who is your favourite actor?
I've got lots of favourite actors: Aamir Khan, Madhuri Dixit, Nicole Kidman and Johnny Depp. And my favourite singer is Sting.

Q12 What are your ambitions for the future?
I want to continue acting in films. I also want to open a school for poor children in India.

Task Speaking

1 You are going to interview each other. First, decide on 12 questions you want to ask, using the Freida Pinto interview and the Useful language box to help you. You can also add questions of your own. Ask your teacher for any words/phrases you need.

2 Then, spend some time preparing your answers to the questions in the Useful language box. Look at the answers in the Freida Pinto interview to help you and ask your teacher for any words/phrases you need.

> Useful language a, b and c

3 Work in pairs and take turns to interview each other. Make brief notes of the answers. Check the time at the beginning of the interview and try to complete it in exactly 60 seconds.

60-SECOND interview with

Q1 _____   Q7 _____
Q2 _____   Q8 _____
Q3 _____   Q9 _____
Q4 _____   Q10 _____
Q5 _____   Q11 _____
Q6 _____   Q12 _____

SHARE YOUR TASK

Practise your interview questions until you feel confident.

Film/Record yourself interviewing your partner.

Share your film/recording with other students.

WORLD CULTURE

UNUSUAL SPORTS

Find out first

1a Work in pairs and discuss. How much do you know about New York City? Try to answer the questions below.

   1 What is:
- the Big Apple?
- The Bronx?
- the Latin community?

   2 What is the approximate population of New York City?

   3 What sports do you associate with New York or the USA?

b Go online to check your answers or ask your teacher.

Search: New York City / Big Apple / The Bronx

View

2a You are going to watch a video about stickball, a popular sport in New York City. Before you watch, check you understand the meaning of the words/phrases in the glossary below.

GLOSSARY

broom	a brush that you use to clean floors
handle	the part of the broom that you hold
immigrants	people who come to a country to live
huge	very big
brawling	fighting

b ▶ Look at the sentences/phrases below. Then watch the video and number them (1–8) in the order you hear them.

   a ... the first stickball leagues began.

   b The Emperor League helped to bring different communities together.

   c New York is also an important sporting city.

   d Stickball in the Bronx has a rich history.

   e I love coming here every Sunday ... playing around with my friends ...

   f The first people to play stickball were immigrants ...

   g ... the Latin community played stickball ...

   h ... played with old broom handles and a ball ...

3 Watch again and choose the correct answers.

   1 The population of New York is more than *8 / 18* million.

   2 People began playing stickball about *seven / seventy* years ago.

   3 People play stickball *all over New York / only in the Bronx*.

   4 The Emperor Stickball League began in *1985 / 1995*.

   5 Stickball is popular *only in the Latin community / in many different communities*.

   6 Ray Justin *only plays stickball / plays more than one sport*.

World view

4a Look at the statements below. Tick the statements you agree with and cross the statements you disagree with.

> I don't understand why people get so excited about sport.

> I prefer playing computer games to playing real sports.

> I prefer individual sports like tennis to team sports like volleyball or hockey.

> Sportsmen and women get too much money – they should all give 20 percent of their money to charity.

> I think global sports are good for international relations.

> Large sporting events are a waste of money.

> I think governments should pay for young people to take part in sport.

b Work in pairs and compare your ideas.

FIND OUT MORE

5a Choose one of the sports in the box below (or another sport you want to know more about).

stickball   Australian Rules football   baseball
curling   kabaddi   snooker

b Go online to find out more about the sports and answer the questions.

1   When did it start?
2   Where is it popular?
3   How many players are in a team?
4   What equipment do you need?
5   What is the name of an important league or player of this sport?

Search: stickball / Australian Rules football / baseball / curling / kabaddi / snooker

Write up your research

6 Write a paragraph about the sport you chose. Use the prompts below to help you.

People started playing _____ (name of sport) about _____ ago (when?).
The sport is now popular in _____ (names of countries).
There are _____ (how many?) players in a team.
To play _____ (name of sport) you need _____ (equipment).
_____ (name) is a famous _____ (name of sport) player.

02

FIRSTS AND LASTS

IN THIS UNIT

- **Grammar:** Past simple – positive and negative; Past simple – questions

- **Vocabulary:** Time phrases: *at, on, in, ago*; Words to describe feelings

- **Task:** Describe a first or last time

- **Language live:** A narrative; Travel questions

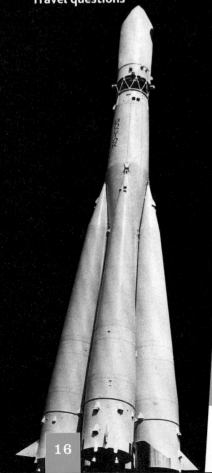

Reading

1 Work in pairs and discuss.

- How often do you watch television? When and where do you usually watch it?
- Which programmes and TV channels do you prefer? Why?

2 Read the article quickly and decide which of these titles fits best.

a The first television programmes
b Television – past and future
c Firsts in television technology

Everyone knows that Scotsman John Logie Baird invented the first television: in the early 1920s, he made a basic television which transmitted pictures, but he didn't develop his idea further. But not many people know that Vladimir Zworykin, a Russian inventor, invented the first 'electronic' television in 1929. People often call him 'the father of television' as his invention became the basis of all modern televisions.

The BBC (the British Broadcasting Corporation) made its first TV programmes in 1936. Most people didn't watch, as there were only about 100 television sets in Britain at that time. There were programmes for only two hours a day – except Sundays, when they didn't show any programmes at all! As well as news and sports, cookery programmes were popular even in the 1930s: Frenchman Marcel Boulestin became the first TV chef in 1937. The first TV advert, in 1941, was for a Bulova clock: it lasted 20 seconds and the company paid just $9 to show it during a baseball game in New York. Technology started to develop faster and faster in the second half of the 20th century. Colour TV came to the USA in the 1950s, to Japan in 1960 and to Europe and South America in the late 1960s and early 1970s. Meanwhile, in 1967 people all over the world watched as The Beatles sang on the programme *Our World*, the first-ever satellite TV programme. The world's first video recorders came from Japan in the mid-1970s, but DVD players didn't appear until November 1996, also made by Japanese companies.

From 2005, it became possible to watch TV on your mobile phone, thanks to 3G technology. The first country to change from analogue to digital television was the USA in June 2009. Canada and Japan did the same in 2011. People watched the first TV programme nearly 80 years ago. After the huge changes in television broadcasting in the 20th century, who knows what the next 80 years will bring?

The Beatles

Vladimir Zworykin

3 Read the article again and match the information with a number or date in the box.

the early 1920s	1929	1936	100	$9
1967	1996	2005	2009	

1 the number of TVs in Britain in 1936
2 the first BBC TV programme
3 the last analogue TV broadcast in the USA
4 the cost of the first TV advert
5 the first basic television
6 the first TV programme on a mobile phone
7 the first satellite TV programme
8 the first electronic television
9 the first DVD player

Grammar focus 1
Past simple – positive and negative

1 Look again at the text on page 16. Underline five verbs in the Past simple. Which of the verbs are regular and which are irregular?

GRAMMAR

1 Write down the infinitive forms of the regular verbs you underlined. How do we form the Past simple of regular verbs?

2 Write down the infinitive forms of the irregular verbs you underlined.

3 What are the past forms of the verb *be*? Look in the text to help you.

4a Put these sentences into the negative form. Look in the text to help you.
  1 He **developed** his idea further.
  2 Most people **watched**.

b Then find two more negative past forms in the text.

PRACTICE

1a Complete the extracts with the correct past forms of the verb in brackets.

1 German car company Benz ¹_____ (begin) producing cars on a large scale in the 1890s. Their first car ²_____ (be) the 'Benz Velo' in 1894. It ³_____ (not go) very fast – in fact, it ⁴_____ (have) a top speed of just 20 kilometres per hour!

2 Bridget Driscoll was the first person to die as a result of a car. The accident ⁵_____ (happen) on 17th August 1896. She ⁶_____ (walk) into the path of a car, travelling at just over 6 kilometres per hour. The car ⁷_____ (not stop) – it hit her and she ⁸_____ (die).

3 Italian engineers ⁹_____ (be) the first in the world to build a motorway. On 21st September 1924, the first car ¹⁰_____ (drive) from Milan to Varese on the Autostrada A9 – a distance of about 50 kilometres.

b 🎧 2.1 Listen and check your answers.

PRONUNCIATION

1 🎧 2.2 Listen to the pronunciation of the past forms. Notice the different pronunciation of the -ed endings.
  a /d/ called appeared
  b /t/ looked worked
  c /ɪd/ ended lasted

2 🎧 2.3 Listen to the pronunciation of some more past forms. Write the verbs you hear in the correct group above (a, b or c).

3 Practise saying the verbs.

2a Write one sentence about each of the following. Write three true and three false sentences.

1 a TV programme you watched last night/week
2 somewhere you went last year
3 someone you saw last week
4 something you bought last week/month
5 someone you didn't know five years ago
6 something you didn't like when you were a child

b Work in pairs and compare your sentences. Guess which are true and which are false.

Last night, I watched a programme about dinosaurs.

I don't believe you!

Unit 2, Study & Practice 1, page 140

Vocabulary

Time phrases: *at, on, in, ago*

1a Read the sentences below and decide if they are true (T) or false (F).

   1 John Logie Baird made the first television in the 1940s.
   2 The first TV programme was nearly 100 years ago.
   3 The world's first motorway opened in Italy on 21st September 1934.
   4 The first British motorway opened in 1958.
   5 I watched three hours of TV yesterday afternoon.
   6 I first went abroad in July 1995.
   7 I was in bed at 8 o'clock this morning.
   8 The weather was hot last weekend.
   9 I had an English lesson on Monday morning.
   10 My teacher was born in the 19th century.

b Number the time phrases in the box (1–10), starting with the most recent.

in the 1940s	100 years ago	on 21st September 1934
in 1958	in July 1995	yesterday afternoon
at 8 o'clock this morning		last weekend
on Monday morning		in the 19th century

2 Choose six of the sentences in exercise 1a and rewrite them so they are true for you. Compare your new sentences in pairs.

Grammar focus 2

Past simple – questions

1a Work in pairs. Look at the photos and read the quiz. Can you guess any of the answers?

b 🎧 **2.4** Listen and check your answers.

GRAMMAR

Look at the quiz again and answer the questions.

1 In question 3, the question word (*Where* ...) refers to the object in the question. What is the correct word order in this type of question?

   1
   base form of verb / *did* / Question word / subject

2 In question 5, the question word (*Which* woman ...) refers to the subject in the question. What is the correct word order in this type of question?

   past form of verb / question word

3 Look at questions 4 and 6. Does the question word in each case refer to the object or the subject in the question?

PRONUNCIATION

1 🎧 **2.5** Listen to the sentences. Notice the pronunciation of *was* and *were*.

2 Practise saying the sentences.

Important firsts

1 **Who was the first woman to win a Nobel Prize?**

   ○ **a** Aung Saan Suu Kyi
   ○ **b** Marie Skłodowska Curie
   ○ **c** Mother Teresa

2 **Why were the Williams sisters famous in the 2000s?**

   ○ **a** They were the first sisters to win the US Open Tennis.
   ○ **b** They both won an Olympic gold medal.
   ○ **c** They were the first women professional footballers.

3 **Where did women get the right to vote for the first time in 1918?**

   ○ **a** New Zealand
   ○ **b** United Kingdom
   ○ **c** The United States

4 **Why did Anousheh Ansari become famous in 2006?**

   ○ **a** She won the first *Britain's Got Talent* TV programme.
   ○ **b** She was the first Asian woman to win an Academy award.
   ○ **c** She became the first female space tourist.

PRACTICE

1a Read about Boa Sr. Why was she famous?

An important last

When Boa Sr died in 2010 at the age of about 85 (no one was sure exactly how old she was) something died with her – one of the oldest languages in the world. Boa Sr lived in the Andaman Islands off the Bay of Bengal in India. She was the last person to speak a language called Bo as a mother tongue. As she had no one to talk to, she often felt lonely so she learnt Hindi (one of the main languages in India) and another local language. She lived through World War II, and escaped the 2004 Indian Ocean tsunami by climbing up a tree. After her death, Stephen Corry of Survival International said about Boa Sr: 'Part of human society is now just a memory.'

b Make questions about Boa Sr using the prompts. Then write the answers using information from the text.

1 When / Boa Sr / die?
2 How old / she / when she died?
3 Where / she live?
4 What / her mother tongue?
5 How many / other languages / she / speak?
6 What / happen / to her / in 2004?
7 Who / say / 'Part of human society is now just a memory'?

2a Complete the questions with the words in the box.

did   started   study   was (x2)   were

1 How old _____ you when you _____ learning English?
2 When _____ your first English lesson?
3 Where _____ you first study English?
4 What _____ the name of your first English teacher?
5 What did you _____ in your last English lesson?

b Work in pairs. Take turns to ask and answer the questions.

Unit 2, Study & Practice 2, page 140

---

5 Which woman flew into space in 1963 for the first time?

○ **a** Valeria Mata
○ **b** Valentina Tereshkova
○ **c** Shirley Valentine

6 What happened to Pratibha Patil on 25th July 2007?

○ **a** She became the first female President of India.
○ **b** She became the first female President of Pakistan.
○ **c** She became Secretary-General of the United Nations.

7 Who was the first woman to climb to the top of Mount Everest on 16th May 1975?

○ **a** Junko Tabei from Japan
○ **b** Wanda Rutkiewicz from Poland
○ **c** Stacey Allison from the USA

8 Who was the first woman to win an Oscar for Best Director?

○ **a** Lucrecia Martel in 2008
○ **b** Jane Campion in 2009
○ **c** Kathryn Bigelow in 2010

Vocabulary
Words to describe feelings

1 Read about emoticons and answer the questions.

  1 What are they?
  2 Who invented them? When?

Emoticons are special signs used in electronic communication to show the writer's feelings. Scott Fahlman designed the first one in 1982. It is ;-) .

2 Match the emoticons with the words in the box.

surprised angry embarrassed in a good mood
scared worried

In a good mood in a bad mood Worried stressed

Scared excited angry relaxed

Surprised disappointed Embarrassed bored

3a Answer the questions below using the words from exercise 2.

How do you normally feel: Excited
  1 if there's football on TV?
  2 just before an important exam? stressed, Nervous
  3 if you can't remember someone's name? embarrassed
  4 with people you don't know well? Nervous, w
  5 when you finish school/work? In a good m
  6 if you lose your mobile phone? worried, stre
  7 if you go to watch a big rock concert? in a good m
  8 if you're late for school/work? worried, Nerv
  9 if you see a big spider? Scared, excited
  10 if your English lesson is cancelled? angry

b Work in pairs. Take turns to ask and answer the questions in exercise 3a.

PRONUNCIATION

1 🎧 2.6 Listen to the words and mark the stress. (Words with one syllable e.g. *bored*, *scared*, *stressed* do not have any stress).

2 Practise saying the words.

Task

Describe a first or last time
Preparation Listening

1a Read the list of important firsts and lasts. Tick the things you remember.

- the first time you drove a car
- your last holiday
- your first English lesson
- the last time you stayed up all night
- the last time you went to a wedding ✓
- your first pet
- the first time you went abroad ✓
- the last time you felt really scared

b Work in pairs and compare your answers.

2a 🎧 2.7 Listen to Helen and Mark talking about the first time they did something. Which of the important firsts in exercise 1a do they talk about?

b Listen again. For each story write down the answers to questions 1–4.

  1 Where and when did it happen?
  2 Who else was in the story?
  3 How did they feel?
  4 What happened in the end?

3 Listen again and tick the phrases you hear in the Useful language box.

Task Speaking

1 You are going to talk about the first or last time you did something. Choose one or two important firsts or lasts from Preparation exercise 1a. Think about these questions and make a note of your answers.

- Which important 'first' or 'last' are you describing?
- Where/When did this happen?
- How old were you at the time?
- Who was with you?
- How did you feel before/after?

2 Look at the Useful language box and decide which phrases you want to use. Ask your teacher for any other words/phrases you need.

> Useful language a, b, c and d

3a Work in small groups. Practise telling your stories to each other.

b Think about the stories you have heard.

Which was:
- the funniest story?
- the saddest story?
- the strangest story?

Writing
A narrative

1 Work in pairs and discuss.

- Which is your favourite / least favourite way of travelling? Why?
- Which is the best way for meeting new people?

2 Read about Jack's first trip abroad and answer the questions.

1 Who did Jack go to Australia with?
2 Who did he meet?
3 Did he enjoy his holiday?

My first trip abroad was to Australia. It was five years ago **and** I went with two friends. The plane tickets were really expensive, **so** before we went, we worked in a restaurant to save up enough money. It was a long flight – about 20 hours – **but** we didn't mind. We were all very excited **because** it was our first time abroad.

We stayed in Sydney for a few days, in a hotel near the city centre. In the mornings, we went sightseeing; **then** we went to the beach in the afternoons. My friends travelled to Byron Bay by coach, but I stayed in Sydney because I wanted to spend more time there.

In Sydney, I met a young man called Daniel and he introduced me to some of his friends. Then Daniel asked me to stay with his family in Sydney so in the end, I stayed with them for two months. It was the best holiday of my life!

3a Look at the linking words in bold in the text in exercise 2. Decide which is:

1 used to talk about a reason
2 used to talk about a consequence
3 used to talk about something that comes after
4 used to add similar information
5 used to add different or contrasting information

b Find one more example of each linking word in the text.

4 Choose the correct answers.

1 It was my first flight **then** / **so** I was really excited and I didn't sleep at all.
2 My first pet was a dog. He was a black Labrador **and** / **because** his name was Mister.
3 I was really worried on my first day at school **but** / **because** I didn't know anyone.
4 In my last exam, first I was late – **then** / **but** I couldn't find the exam room.
5 The last time I went to a restaurant the food was lovely **so** / **but** it was really expensive.
6 I fell over **and** / **because** broke my arm the last time I went running in the park.

5a You are going to write a narrative about the first time you went on a long journey. Think about the answers to these questions.

1 Where did you go?
2 When did you go there?
3 Who did you go with?
4 What did you do before the journey?
5 How long was the journey?
6 How did you feel before/during/after the journey?
7 What did you do when you got there?
8 How long did you stay?
9 What happened in the end?
10 How do you feel about it now?

b Complete the phrases below with information about your journey.

1 My first trip abroad / long journey was to _____ .
2 It was about _____ years ago .
3 I went with _____ .
4 Before I/we went, I/we _____ .
5 I/We were very _____ because _____ .
6 We stayed in _____ .
7 We went to _____ .
8 I met _____ .
9 In the end I/we _____ .
10 It was the best/most _____ of my life!

6 Use your answers to write a paragraph about your journey. Write about 100–120 words.

Speaking
Travel questions

1 Work in pairs and discuss.

- How do you feel before a plane journey?
- What things do you usually take with you?
- What things do you always put in your hand luggage? Why?
- How do you usually travel to and from the airport? Why?
- What kinds of things do you usually buy in the airport before your flight?
- What do you usually do while you wait for your departure?

2a ▶ Watch the video and number the situations (a–d) in the order you see them. You do not need to use one of the situations.

- **a** Booking his ticket for a plane journey
- **b** Answering questions with an immigration officer
- **c** Checking he's got everything he needs before going to the airport
- **d** Phoning his partner after he arrives back at the airport

b Watch again and answer the questions.

1 Which of these things does the man check he's got? Tick the words.
- passport
- money
- credit card
- ticket
- time of taxi
- time of arrival
- mobile phone

2 Is the man on holiday or on a business trip?

3 Did he buy a present for his partner? What do you think he's going to do?

3a Match the questions below with the answers in the box.

....
9:15   Yes. Here it is   10 a.m. local time   Yes, brilliant
Yes, it is   Fine   At The Grand Hotel   No, I'm on holiday
....

1 Have you got your passport/ticket?
2 What time's your taxi?
3 What time do you arrive?
4 Is this your first time here?
5 Are you here on business?
6 Where are you staying?
7 Did you have a nice time?
8 How was your flight/journey?

b ▶ Watch and listen to the key phrases and check your answers.

PRONUNCIATION

1 Watch and listen again to the key phrases.

2 Practise saying them.

4a Work in pairs. Choose one of the situations below. Prepare and practise a short conversation using the words/phrases from exercise 3a and your own ideas.

- before your journey (you and a friend)
- arrival at the airport (you and an immigration officer)
- after your holiday/trip (you and a friend)

b Compare your conversations with other students.

AFTER UNIT 2 YOU CAN ...

Ask and answer questions about past activities.

Say how you feel in different situations.

Write a story about something that happened to you.

Ask useful questions about personal and practical information.

03

WORK AND REST

IN THIS UNIT

- Grammar: *should, shouldn't*; *can, can't, have to, don't have to*

- Vocabulary: Daily routines; Jobs

- Task: Decide on the best job

- World culture: Amazing trains

Vocabulary
Daily routines

1 Work in pairs and discuss.

- On weekdays is your routine the same or different every day?
- In what ways is your routine different at the weekend?
- Do you find it easy to sleep during the day? How often do you do it?
- Do you ever sleep on public transport (e.g. bus, train, plane)? Why / Why not?

2 Look at the verb phrases below. Write the time(s) of day when it usually happens for you by each phrase. (This may happen at several different times of the day.)

1 I fall asleep.
2 I have a nap.
3 My alarm clock goes off.
4 I feel energetic.
5 I feel tired.
6 I have a cup of tea/coffee and something to eat.
7 I go to bed.
8 I get up.
9 I have a bath/shower.
10 I relax at home.
11 I finish school/work.
12 I wake up.

3 Work in groups. Find someone who:

... gets up at the same time as you. *Gabriela*
1 usually feels energetic in the morning.
2 goes to bed after 11 p.m.
3 has a cup of tea in the morning.
4 usually has a nap in the afternoon.
5 has a shower before he/she goes to bed.
6 wakes up without an alarm clock.
7 has something to eat after 9 p.m.

'Short sleeper' or 'long sleeper': Which is healthier?

Dentist Dr Uchenna Okoye gets up every day at 4:30 a.m., weekends and holidays included. It's not because she's a bad sleeper. And it's not because she starts work early – her dental surgery doesn't open until 8:30. And she's not one of those people who are always in bed by ten – in fact, she usually goes to bed after midnight. She gets up at this time because she's a 'short sleeper' – a person who can live happily on much less than the seven or eight hours of sleep that most of us need. And, amazingly, Uchenna is energetic all day. Dr Okoye works eight hours at her dental surgery 'London Smiling', she appears regularly on the TV programme Ten Years Younger, she does regular work for charity and she even has time for piano lessons! 'People are often surprised when they get emails from me late at night, or early in the morning … but I never need much sleep, and I always feel good on it. It's just the way I am,' says Uchenna, 41.

Many short sleepers, like Dr Okoye, are energetic and successful in life. Famous short sleepers include Leonardo da Vinci, John F. Kennedy and Madonna. Being a short sleeper has other advantages too – you have 15–20 percent more time to do things, and short sleepers are often slim too. But here's the bad news. Only about 3 percent of people are short sleepers – for most of us, sleeping for only three or four hours a night just isn't enough.

In contrast, there are 'long sleepers' – people who regularly sleep ten hours or more a night. (In fact, before the invention of electric light in the 19th century most people slept for ten hours.) Babies are the biggest long sleepers – they sleep up to 18 hours a day in the first few weeks of life. Teenagers also typically need ten hours' sleep. Many people believe that long sleepers are less healthy than short sleepers. But the latest research shows there are no important differences in health or personality between the two groups.

> **IT'S A FACT!** The average person spends six years of their life dreaming – that's about two hours each night.

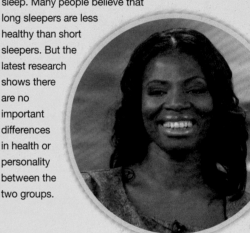

Reading and speaking

1a Work in pairs and discuss.

- How do you usually feel when you wake up? What helps you to wake up?
- What helps you to fall asleep? Do you ever have problems falling asleep?
- What do you think is the perfect number of hours' sleep for you? How often do you get that?

b Work in pairs and read the text quickly. Discuss which is better: a 'short sleeper' or a 'long sleeper'?

2a Read the text again and decide if the statements are true (T) or false (F).

1 Dr Uchenna Okoye gets up at the same time every day.
2 She doesn't go to bed late.
3 She often feels tired during the day.
4 Dr Okoye has more than one job.
5 97 percent of people are 'long sleepers'.
6 Nowadays, people sleep less than they did in the 19th century.
7 Babies sleep more than teenagers.
8 There are important differences between long sleepers and short sleepers.

b Work in pairs and compare your answers.

3 Underline two pieces of information in the text you find interesting. Compare your answers in groups.

4 Work in pairs and read the quotes. Decide which you think are the most relevant to you. Which do you completely disagree with?

> " Without enough sleep, we all become two-year-olds.

> " *The worst thing in the world is to try to sleep, and not to.*

> " People who say they sleep like a baby usually don't have one.

> " *For me, sleeping is waste of time when I could be living.*

> " Dreams are thoughts that we don't have time to think during the day.

Grammar focus 1
should, shouldn't

1 Read the web page and answer the questions.

  1 Why is Alice asking for advice?
  2 What advice do people give her?

> ### Q How can I revise effectively?
>
>  **Help! I have some important exams next week and I'm studying 12 hours a day. The problem is … it's difficult to concentrate! What should I do?**
> **Thank you ;) Alice**
>
> ....
>
> You should find a 'study buddy' – someone who is studying for the same exam. It's usually more fun when you have someone to talk to about your studies. Why don't you revise together and then test each other?   Will
>
> ....
>
> You shouldn't study for so many hours – 12 hours a day is too much! Try working non-stop for an hour and then have a break. Then work for another hour and have another break ... and so on! And you should give yourself a reward at the end of the day.   Molly
>
> ....
>
> You should make a revision timetable and make sure you include lots of variety. You should start with a difficult subject, then do an easier subject. And you shouldn't always revise in the same place. Why don't you start at your desk and then move to a different room?   Sam

2 Read the three pieces of advice above again. Underline four examples of *should* and two examples of *shouldn't*.

GRAMMAR

1 Choose the correct answer to complete the rules.
  1 We use *should* when it **is** / **isn't** a good idea to do something.
  2 We use *shouldn't* when it **is** / **isn't** a good idea to do something.

2 We use *should/shouldn't* to give or ask for advice.
  You should find a 'study buddy'.
  You shouldn't study for so many hours.
  What should I do?

3 We can also give advice like this:
  Why don't you get up earlier?
  Try getting up earlier.

PRACTICE

1a Read the list of things some other people do during their study time. Decide which of them you should/ shouldn't do.

  • send text messages to your friends *shouldn't*
  • listen to loud music *shouldn't*
  • make a list of things to do *should*
  • find somewhere quiet to study *should*
  • watch TV *shouldn't*
  • start work as early as possible *should*
  • take breaks sometimes *should*
  • use social-networking sites *shouldn't*

b Work in pairs and compare your ideas.

c 🎧 3.1 Listen and check your answers.

PRONUNCIATION

1 Listen again. Notice the pronunciation of *should* and *shouldn't*.

2 Practise saying the sentences.

2a Work in pairs. Read about the situations below and discuss what each person should and shouldn't do.

> ### Q What should I do?
>
> **My boyfriend Chris recently started a new job. The money is good, but he works very long hours – sometimes late at night. We never go out anymore. He always says he's too tired and at the weekend, he just stays at home and watches DVDs. What should I do?**
> **from Carla**

> ### Q I need some advice!
>
> **I'm not sure what to do about my daughter. She is 17 and she spends every evening on the computer – on social-networking sites. She doesn't study enough and she goes to bed really late. I'm worried about her exams. I need some advice!**
> **from Oliver**

b Write a similar short paragraph describing a situation you want advice for.

c Work in pairs and swap your papers. Look at what your partner has written and write a reply.

> Unit 3, Study & Practice 1, page 142

Listening
An unusual job

1 Work in pairs. Look at the poster and discuss the questions.

- What kind of tour is it? Where is it? What do you think happens on the tour?
- Do you like going on ghost tours or other guided tours in cities?
- What different guided tours do you have in your town or city?

2 3.2 You are going to listen to an interview with Kirsty about her job. Listen to the first part of the interview and answer the questions.

1 What is Kirsty's job?
2 Which city or cities does she work in?

3 3.3 Listen to the second part of the interview and number the things Kirsty talks about in the order you hear them.

a languages that Kirsty speaks
b Kirsty's favourite tour
c clothes you wear for the job
d qualifications you need for the job 1
e personal qualities you need for the job
f real ghosts Kirsty has seen/heard
g types of visitors who come on the tours

4 Work in pairs and discuss. Would you like Kirsty's job? Why / Why not?

Grammar focus 2
can, can't, have to, don't have to

1a Complete the sentences with *can, can't, have to* or *don't have to*.

1 You _____ have any special qualifications.
2 You _____ be a good story-teller.
3 I _____ speak French and Spanish.
4 You _____ see anything at all!

b Then look at audio script 3.3 on page 167 to check your answers.

GRAMMAR

1 What form of the verb follows *can, can't, have to* or *don't have to*? Look again at the sentences in exercise 1.

2 Complete the sentences below with *can, can't, have to* or *don't have to.*

1 _____ means that something is necessary.
2 _____ means that you are able to do something.
3 _____ means that something is not necessary.
4 _____ means that you are not able to do something.

PRONUNCIATION

1a 3.4 Listen to four sentences. Does each speaker say *can* /kæn/, *can* /kən/ or *can't* /kɑːnt/?

b Listen again and practise saying the sentences.

2a 3.5 Listen to four sentences. Does each speaker say *have to* /tuː/ or *have to* /tə/?

b Listen again and practise saying the sentences.

PRACTICE

1a Read the list of activities below. Think about a normal day for you. Write sentences with *can, can't, have to* or *don't have to.*

1 catch the bus or train
2 make my own breakfast
3 study in the evening
4 send emails
5 cook a meal for my family
6 work in the evening
7 stay out after 11 p.m.
8 work at a computer
9 go to the supermarket

b Work in pairs and compare your answers.

Unit 3, Study & Practice 2, page 142

Vocabulary

Jobs

1 Match the pictures with the words in the box.

> accountant doctor plumber nanny cook
> translator judge taxi driver

2 Work in pairs and read the sentences. Which job(s) do you think each one refers to?

1 You sometimes have to work at night in this job.
2 You can make a lot of money doing this job.
3 This job can be dangerous.
4 You have to study for a long time to do this job.
5 You can work at home in this job.
6 You have to be very patient to do this job.
7 You can really help people in this job.
8 You have to be good at languages to do this job.
9 You don't have to wear a uniform.
10 You have to be very good with people to do this job.

Task

Decide on the best job

Preparation Listening

1 Work in pairs. Think of a job, but do not tell your partner what it is. Take turns to describe the job by saying what you can/can't do, and what you have to / don't have to do. Can your partner guess which job you are describing?

> In this job, you can really help people …

> You sometimes have to work at night …

> Is it a nurse?

2a Which of the jobs you talked about in exercise 1 would you like / wouldn't you like? Why?

b Work in groups and compare your ideas.

3 🎧 3.6 Listen to the four people in the photos talking about themselves and make notes about each person's interests and skills.

4 🎧 3.7 Listen to two students trying to decide on the best job for one of the people in the photos. Answer the questions.

1 Which person are they talking about?
2 What job do they agree on?
3 What reasons do they give?

5 Listen again and tick the phrases you hear in the Useful language box.

My Profile

Name: **Annie**
Age: **17**
From: **New Zealand**

Interests/Skills:

science subjects
music

Task Speaking

1 You are going to decide on the best job for each person. First, write down two or three possible jobs for each person. You can look at the jobs on page 28 and think of your own ideas.

2 Make notes about the reasons for your choices. Ask your teacher for any words/phrases you need.

> Useful language a

3a Work in pairs and discuss the best job for each person.

> Useful language a and b

b Discuss. Did you find it easy or difficult to agree on the best job for each person? Why?

4 Work in groups and agree on the best job for each person.

USEFUL LANGUAGE

a Comparing your ideas and giving reasons

I think he/she should be a (doctor/teacher) because he/she's good at ...

I don't think he/she will be a good (lawyer/translator) because he/she can't ...

He/She likes solving problems, so he/she'll be a good (plumber/accountant) ...

Perhaps he/she should be a (doctor/journalist) because he/she likes ... (he/she's good with) ...

b Agreeing and disagreeing

Do you agree?

What do you think?

Yes, I agree.

That's true.

I don't think so.

I'm not sure.

My Profile

Name: **Jem**
Age: **32**
From: **England**

Interests/Skills:

My Profile

Name: **Jarek**
Age: **23**
From: **Poland**

Interests/Skills:

My Profile

Name: **Silvia**
Age: **26**
From: **Argentina**

Interests/Skills:

SHARE YOUR TASK

Practise discussing the best job for each person until you feel confident.

Film/Record yourself having the discussion.

Share your film/recording with other students.

WORLD CULTURE

AMAZING TRAINS

Shanghai Transrapid

Find out first

1a Work in pairs and discuss. Which towns/cities in your country have an underground railway? How often do you travel on it?

b Discuss. How much do you know about the London Underground? Try to answer the questions below.

1 How old is the London Underground?
2 What do people call it?
3 How many lines/stations does it have?
4 What is 'rush hour'? What time does this happen in the morning/ evening?
5 What is the busiest station on the London Underground?

2 Go online to check your answers or ask your teacher.

Search: London Underground / London rush hour / London Underground busiest station

View

3a You are going to watch a video about night workers on the London Underground. Before you watch, check you understand the meaning of the words/phrases in the glossary below.

GLOSSARY
commuters   people who travel to and from work
Big Ben   a famous clock tower in London
dawn   the time of the day when the sun rises
tunnel   a long passage under the ground
the River Thames   the river that runs through London
automatic gates   electronic barriers

b ▶ Watch the video with the sound off. Number the things in the glossary in the order you see them.

4 Read the text from the video below. Then watch again and complete the gaps with the numbers in the box.

1 a.m.   20,000   300 m   4 million   6:14
Six and a half thousand   7 o'clock   7:15

This is the London Underground. [1]_____ people use the Underground every day and [2]_____ people work on it. It's [3]_____ in the evening – rush hour. A million tired Londoners go home. But when rush hours finishes, [4]_____ Underground workers start their night's work. By [5]_____ everything is quiet. At Waterloo, supervisor Dave closes the Underground station. He's here alone here all night until [6]_____ in the morning. At Blackhorse Road station a team of tunnel cleaners go to work. They clean [7]_____ of tunnel every night. At Regent's Park station, engineers change a broken rail. It's [8]_____ in the morning. The London Underground starts again. No one thinks about the people who work at night on the Underground ... but their work is important.

FIND OUT MORE

6a Look at the famous train lines from different countries in the box below. What do you know about them?

....

Die Bloutrein / The Blue Train   The Glacier Express

The Moscow Metro   The Shanghai Maglev train

....

b Go online to find out more about two of the train lines (or another famous train line you want to know about) and answer the questions.

- Where is it and where does it go?
- How old is it?
- Why is it famous?

....

Search: Die Bloutrein / Glacier Express / Moscow Metro / Shanghai Maglev train

....

World view

5a Look at the statements below. Tick the ones that are true for you.

> I use public transport most days.

> There is a good public transport system in my town/city.

> Most people travel by bus in my town/city.

> There is a rush hour in my town/city.

> I commute to my school/university/work.

> I don't pay for public transport because of my age.

> I think that all public transport should be free ... but not for tourists.

> I prefer travelling on buses to travelling on trains.

b Work in pairs and compare your ideas.

Write up your research

7 Write a paragraph about the train line you chose. Use the prompts below to help you.

Die Bloutrein is a famous train line in _____ (name of country/ies).
It runs from _____ (name of place) to _____ (name of place) – a distance of _____ km.
The line began working in _____ (year).
It is famous because _____ .
I would/wouldn't like to travel on it because _____ .

AFTER UNIT 3 YOU CAN ...

Describe your daily routine.

Give advice and make suggestions.

Take part in a short conversation about suitable jobs.

Express your opinion and agree/disagree with others.

IN THIS UNIT

- Grammar: Present simple and Present continuous; Present continuous for future arrangements
- Vocabulary: Verb phrases for special days; Descriptive adjectives
- Task: Describe your special days
- Language live: Phrases for special days; An invitation

Reading

1 Work in pairs and discuss.
- What is your favourite month of the year? Why?
- What's the most special day of the year for you? Why?

PRONUNCIATION

1  4.1 Listen and mark the stress on the months, like this:

•
January   February   April   July   August   September   October
November   December

2  4.2 Listen and write down the dates. Look at audio script 4.2 on page 168 to check.

3 Listen again and practise saying the dates, paying attention to the pronunciation of *th*.

April the first	July the fifth
/ð/	/θ/

2a Work in pairs and discuss.
- What can you see in the photos?
- What kinds of special days do you think each photo shows?

b Read the text quickly and check your ideas.

Special days around the world

Teachers' Day

People in many countries celebrate World Teachers' Day on 5th October, but in Argentina it is on 11th September – the anniversary of the death of former president, Domingo Faustino Sarmiento in 1888. Sarmiento believed passionately in the importance of education: he wrote 'Schools are the very basis of civilisation'. Children traditionally write poems for their teacher and give them an apple, make a cake or buy flowers. In Vietnam, Educators' Day is in November. Everyone has a day off school, and many students visit their former teachers in their homes to give them presents, or give news about themselves. And at some schools in India, senior students become teachers, and teachers become students for the day!

World Book Day

In many countries, Book Day is on 23rd April every year. It originated in Catalonia in 1923 when booksellers decided to honour the Spanish author Miguel de Cervantes who died on that day in 1616. In 1995, World Book Day became an international event, celebrating books and reading. People exchange presents – usually a book and a rose. There are also events such as writing competitions, and in Madrid there is a public reading of Cervantes's greatest work – *Don Quijote* – which lasts 48 hours! In the UK and Ireland, all schoolchildren receive a £1 book token, and many children now dress up as their favourite character from fiction!

Respect for the Aged Day

Grandparents' Day is popular in many countries, but in Japan – a country where nearly 30 percent of the population are over 60 – people treat older people with special respect. The third Monday of September is 'Respect for the Aged Day' (*Keiro-no-hi*) which became a national holiday in 1966. Everyone has a day off school or work and people organise celebrations for the older people of the village or community where they live. Young people dress up in traditional clothes. They sing and dance and they either prepare a special meal for the older people, or eat out as a family. Nowadays, people also visit relatives and the older people in their families, for a three-day weekend.

3 Read the text again and complete the table.

	Who?	Where?
1 They write a poem for their teacher.	Children	Argentina
2 They become teachers for one day.	senior students	India
3 People prepare a special meal for them.	Older people	Japan
4 They dress up as a character from a book.	children	U.K. and Ireland
5 They have a day off school or work.	Everyone	Vietnam
6 They visit their old teachers.	student	Vietnam
7 They started Book Day in 1923.	Spanish author Miguel de Cervantes	Catalonia

Vocabulary
Verb phrases for special days

1a Match the words in A with the words in B to make verb phrases connected with special occasions.

A	B
1 invite	a presents
2 make	b a cake
3 dress	c up
4 eat	d flowers
5 visit	e cards to people
6 have	f relatives
7 prepare	g out
8 send	h a day off school/work
9 buy	i a special meal
10 exchange	j people into your home

b 🎧 4.3 Listen and check your answers.

2a Complete the paragraph about Friendship Day with the verbs in the box.

buy	dress	eat	exchange	have
invite	make	prepare	send	visit

Friendship Day

Friendship Day began in the United States in 1935, and is becoming more popular around the world. It's on the first Sunday in August – so everyone can ¹ _have_ the day off work. It's a time to ² _visite_ friends in their homes locally, or ³ _send_ cards by post or via the internet to friends who live in other places. Food is often an important part of the day, and many people ⁴ _invite_ friends to their homes, where they ⁵ _prepare_ a special meal for their guests, and some people even ⁶ _make_ a special friendship cake. Others prefer to ⁷ _dress_ up in their best clothes and ⁸ _eat_ out as a group in their favourite restaurant. People often ⁹ _buy_ flowers for each other or ¹⁰ _Exchange_ small presents. So why not show your friends how important they are and organise a Friendship Day celebration this year?

b 🎧 4.4 Listen and check your answers.

3 Work in pairs and discuss. Take turns to choose one of the special days and describe it. Try to use some of the verb phrases in exercise 1.

'DO SOMETHING FUNNY FOR MONEY'

RED NOSE DAY

Comic Relief is an organisation which raises money for charities in the UK and Africa. It started in 1985 and began by raising money for people living in extreme poverty in Ethiopia at that time. After a few years, as it got bigger, it started raising money for many more poor communities. Since it started, Comic Relief has raised over £800 million to help people in over 70 countries around the world.

So, how does Comic Relief raise so much money? The charity works to raise money every day of the year, but their most important day is Red Nose Day. It was first started in 1988, and since then, Red Nose Day has become a unique day in the British calendar. It happens every two years and it's a day when ordinary people and celebrities get together to make money. As the name suggests, everyone wears a plastic red nose as they raise money in schools, at work, at home – anywhere! On television, for several hours during the evening, celebrities and comedians entertain people at the same time as asking them to donate money.

The slogan for Red Nose Day is 'do something funny for money'. Not all the things people do are funny, however. Sometimes they're quite difficult – like running 43 marathons in 51 days. But whatever they do, the British people certainly seem to like raising money in this funny way – Red Nose Day in 2011 raised over £108 million!

Reading and speaking

1a Work in pairs. Look at the photos and discuss.
- What are the people doing?
- Why do you think they are doing this?
- How do you think the word/phrases in the box are connected with the photos?

raise money	donate money	poverty
a unique day	a comedian	a charity

b Read the text and check your answers.

2 Read the text again and answer the questions.
1 Who does the money from Comic Relief help now?
2 Who did Comic Relief help when it first started?
3 How much money has Comic Relief raised so far?
4 When was the first Red Nose Day?
5 How often does Red Nose Day happen?
6 Why is it called Red Nose Day?
7 What is the slogan for Red Nose Day?
8 How much money did they raise in 2011?

3a Read the opinions below. Do you agree or disagree with each opinion? Why?

❝ I think Red Nose Day is great – it's really funny to see famous people doing silly things.

❝ The best thing about Red Nose Day is that so many ordinary people get involved.

❝ It's good that the money from Red Nose Day helps people in other countries – not just Britain.

❝ I think that using humour and comedy is always the best way to raise money.

❝ It's sad that there isn't anything like Red Nose Day in my country.

❝ In my country, there are some better money-raising days than Red Nose Day.

b Work in pairs. Compare and discuss your opinions of each quote.

Grammar focus 1
Present simple and Present continuous

1a Work in pairs. Look at the photos and discuss. What are the people doing?

b Read about the people in the photos and answer the questions.
1 What is Nadia Sawalha's job?
2 What is she doing today?
3 What is James Thornton's job?
4 What is Charlie Baker's job?
5 What are they doing today?

Nadia Sawalha is an actor and TV presenter. She often presents cookery programmes on Breakfast TV in the UK. However, today is Red Nose Day and so she isn't cooking – she's raising money for Red Nose Day. She's walking 100 km across the Kaisut Desert in Kenya. The sun is shining and it's 40°C!

James Thornton is a TV actor – he usually stars in a popular soap opera. Charlie Baker is a comedian – he usually appears in comedy shows, both live and on TV. He is also a talented jazz singer. Right now, they aren't doing their usual jobs. They are taking part in a dance competition on TV for Comic Relief.

GRAMMAR

1 We use the Present simple for things which are generally or always true. Find an example in the texts in exercise 1.

2 We use the Present continuous for things happening at the present moment. Find two examples in the texts in exercise 1.

3 Look at the verbs in bold below. Tick the correct sentences.
1 **I'm not knowing** the answer to this question.
2 **Do you have** a bicycle?
3 **Are you understanding** what he said?
4 **I don't want** any more, thank you.

4 Which of these phrases go with the Present simple? Which go with the Present continuous?

at the moment   every day   never   right now
today   usually

PRACTICE

1 Complete the paragraph with the Present simple or Present continuous form of the verb in brackets.

James Keen is a taxi driver from Windsor, near London. He ¹_____ (work) six days a week, fifty weeks a year. Today – Red Nose Day – he ²_____ (drive) his taxi as usual, but he ³_____ (raise) money for Comic Relief at the same time.
'I usually ⁴_____ (give) something to Comic Relief, but this year I ⁵_____ (want) to do something more. I ⁶_____ (wear) a red wig and a Red Nose Day T-shirt: and my taxi ⁷_____ (have) a Red Nose on the front. But today I ⁸_____ (ask) all my customers to pay £1 extra for Red Nose Day!'

2a Choose the correct answers.
1 *Are you learning / Do you learn* to drive at the moment?
2 How many languages *do you speak / are you speaking*?
3 *Are you liking / Do you like* football?
4 *Do you read / Are you reading* fashion magazines?
5 *Are you playing / Do you play* any sport?
6 *Do you wear / Are you wearing* trainers today?
7 How *are you usually coming / do you usually come* to class?
8 *Do you usually study / Are you usually studying* at the weekend?
9 *Are you looking / Do you look* for a job at the moment?
10 *Are you knowing / Do you know* how to play chess?

b Answer the questions so they are true for you.

c Work in pairs and compare your answers.

Unit 4, Study & Practice 1, page 144

Listening
New Year celebrations

1 Work in pairs and discuss.

- Look at the photos of New Year celebrations around the world. What is happening?
- Do you know any other ways people celebrate New Year?

2a You are going hear Lucas and Freya talking about New Year's Eve in Brazil and Iceland. First, read the sentences below. Do you think they refer to New Year's Eve in Brazil (B), in Iceland (I) or both (B/I)?

1 Everyone goes down to the beach in the evening. *B*
2 The bonfire is huge and that keeps you warm. *I*
3 Everyone wears warm clothes. *I*
4 There is a ceremony broadcast from the cathedral, … so we listen to that on the radio. *I*
5 There's a lot of music and people bring flowers and candles. *B*
6 Everyone wears white. *B*
7 There is a big firework display. *I*
8 We have dinner … usually roast meat, and various tinned vegetables. *I*

b 🎧 **4.5 Listen and check your ideas.**

3 Listen again and complete the information about New Year's Eve in the table below.

	Brazil	Iceland
when it happens	31st December	*31st Dec'*
special clothes	*white*	*warm clothes*
special food	*spice chicken and rice, special dessert*	*Roast dinner and tinned veg.*
other customs	*people go to the beach and play music*	*have dinner together and listen to a ceremony / Broadcast from the cathedral*

4 Work in pairs and discuss.

- Which things are similar about New Year celebrations in Brazil and Iceland?
- Which things are different?

Vocabulary
Descriptive adjectives

1 Look at the descriptive adjectives in the box. Write the words in the correct column below.

~~delicious~~ ~~exciting~~ boiling peaceful tasty
noisy spicy friendly freezing

Food	Atmosphere	Weather
delicious	*exciting*	

2 Choose the correct answers.

1 Everyone is happy and there is a **delicious** / **friendly** / **tasty** atmosphere.
2 She always makes a **boiling** / **delicious** / **noisy** cake for everyone to share.
3 The festival is **exciting** / **friendly** / **spicy** because there is so much to see and do.
4 It's **boiling** / **freezing** / **peaceful** there in July so most people go to the beach to get cool.
5 There is a **freezing** / **noisy** / **peaceful** atmosphere with soft music and low lights.
6 The food is **boiling** / **exciting** / **spicy** so drink a lot of water with it!
7 You can buy **exciting** / **peaceful** / **tasty** cakes and biscuits from people all along the street.
8 The nightclub is always **friendly** / **noisy** / **spicy** and you can't hear anything.
9 You have to wear hats and gloves outside in December because it's always **boiling** / **delicious** / **freezing**.

3 Work in pairs and discuss.

- On what date is New Year's Eve in your country?
- What is the weather usually like?
- What special clothes do people usually wear?
- What special food do they eat?
- Where do you usually spend New Year's Eve? Who do you spend it with? What do you do?

Grammar focus 2
Present continuous for future arrangements

1a Read three people's plans for New Year's Eve and decide which verb in the box goes in each gap.

come   go   have   meet   rent

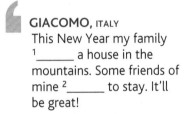

GIACOMO, ITALY
This New Year my family ¹_____ a house in the mountains. Some friends of mine ²_____ to stay. It'll be great!

NICOLA, ENGLAND
I ³_____ a party on New Year's Eve. I've invited loads of people. I hope they all come!

SAM, NEW ZEALAND
I ⁴_____ some friends in town and we ⁵_____ to a restaurant to have a special meal.

b 🎧 4.6 Listen and check your answers. Who has the most interesting plan?

GRAMMAR

1 Look at the three people's plans in exercise 1 and tick the best explanation below (a, b or c).

We use the Present continuous in the future to talk about:
a things we would like to do
b things we will probably do
c things we have arranged to do

PRACTICE

1 Complete the questions below with verbs in the box.

| cooking | doing | going (x3) |
| having (x2) | meeting | taking |

1 Are you _____ out for a meal tonight? Who are you going with?
2 Are you _____ anything interesting this weekend? What?
3 Are you _____ anyone after this lesson? Who?
4 Are you _____ shopping later today? Where? With who?
5 Are you _____ a birthday party soon? When?
6 Are you _____ dinner this evening? Who for? What are you _____?
7 Are you _____ any important exams in the near future? When?
8 Are you _____ abroad soon? Where? Why?

2a Work in pairs. Take turns to interview your partner, using the questions in exercise 1.

> Are you going out for a meal tonight?

> Yes I am.

> Who are you going with?

> I'm going with my girlfriend.

b Make a note of your partner's answers. Which answers were different from yours?

c Tell the class about your partner.

> I'm taking some important exams soon, but José isn't.

Unit 4, Study & Practice 2, page 144

Task

Describe your special days

Preparation Listening

1a Look at the special days in the box. Which days do people celebrate in your country?

New Year	Christmas	Easter
Independence Day	International Women's Day	
Father's Day	Mother's Day	Halloween

b 🎧 4.7 Listen and answer the question. What dates do people in the UK and the USA celebrate each of the special days in the box above?

2 🎧 4.8 You are going to hear some people talking about their special days. Write the dates in the table below and complete the notes about why each day is special.

3 Listen again and tick the phrases you hear in the Useful language box.

Month	Date	Why it's special
JANUARY	26th	1_____ Day. Public holiday, lots of concerts, 2_____, big boat race
FEBRUARY		
MARCH	3_____	Wedding 4_____
APRIL		
MAY		
JUNE	9th	5_____'s birthday ... organising a 6_____
JULY		
AUGUST	7_____ 2012	8_____
SEPTEMBER		
OCTOBER	2nd	starting 9_____
NOVEMBER		
DECEMBER	24th	Flying to Austria ... Spending 10_____ there

a Explaining personal events and special occasions

I wrote ...

It's the day when ...

... is a special day because ...

We always go to ...

We're spending ...

I got married on ...

b Questions

What happens on ... / What happened ... / is happening on ... ?

What are you doing on ... ?

What do you usually do on ... ?

Why is (May 3rd) a special day?

Why is (March 12th) important for you?

Task Speaking

1 Draw a table like the one on page 38. Include as many of the special days in the list below as you can.

- an important birthday or anniversary
- an important day in your country (Independence Day, a national holiday, etc.)
- an important date from your past
- a day in the future when you've arranged to do something
- a day when something interesting happened to you recently

2 You are going to tell other students about one or two of your special days. Ask your teacher for any words/phrases you need.

> Useful language a

3 Work in groups. Take turns to tell each other about your special days. Make notes as you listen and be prepared to ask and answer questions about your special days.

> Useful language a and b

4 Discuss. Which special days sound the most interesting? Why?

SHARE YOUR TASK

Practise talking about your special day until you feel confident.

Film/Record yourself giving your talk.

Share your film/recording with other students.

LANGUAGE LIVE

1 ▶ Watch and listen to the key phrases.

2 Practise saying them. Don't forget that it is important to sound friendly and positive!

21 TODAY!

CONGRATULATIONS!

Speaking
Phrases for special days

1 Work in pairs. Look at the picture and discuss. Which special day can you see in the picture?

2a ▶ Watch the video and answer the questions.

1 What does the groom's father give the couple as a wedding present?
2 Do you think the man likes his birthday present?
3 What do you think the couple want the man to do on New Year's Day?

b Watch again and match the phrases in the box with the special days. You may need to use the phrases more than once.

Happy New Year!	Safe journey!
Thanks for coming	Thank you very much. It's lovely
Happy birthday!	Merry Christmas
Congratulations!	Good luck!
Many happy returns!	I hope you'll be very happy
Cheers!	Thanks for inviting me

• A wedding
• A birthday celebration
• A Christmas party
• A New Year's Eve party

3 Complete the conversations below with a phrase from the box in exercise 2b. More than one phrase may be possible.

1 **A:** I like your **earrings**. Are they new?
B: Yes, they were a present. I'm **21** today!
A: Oh! _____

2 **A: Mum ... Dad ...**
B: Yes?
A: We've got something important to tell you ... **James** and I are **getting married**.
B: _____

3 **A:** Here are your drinks ... that's for you, **Andrew**.
B: Thanks ...
A: Diet cola for you, **Jane**. ... And that's yours, **David** ... so has everybody got a drink?
B: _____

4 **A:** I bought you a present. I hope you like it. I chose it myself.
B: _____

5 **A:** I'd better go now. It's a long drive back to **London**.
B: _____

6 **A:** We've got to go now. Thanks, it was a great party!
B: _____

7 **A:** I'm going. I don't want to be late for my exam!
B: _____

4 Work in pairs. Take turns to practise the conversations in exercise 3. Change the words/names in bold to make them true for you.

I like your shoes. Are they new?

Yes, they were a present. I'm 18 today!

Writing
An invitation

1 Make a list of five reasons why people organise parties (e.g. birthday).

2 Read the email about a party and answer the questions below.

1 Who wrote the email? What is her relationship to Sofie?
2 Where and when is the party? What kind of party is it?

New Message

To: Sofia
Subject:
From: Jenny   Signature:

Hi Sofie,

How are things? … How's life in Bristol? Good I hope. Sorry it took me so long to write. Life is still very busy here in the Marketing Department. We miss you!

Anyway, the main reason I'm writing is to tell you that … Bruce is leaving! (Finally!!) He's got a new job in Australia. So we're having a 'Sorry you're leaving party' for him on the 20th June at his favourite restaurant – Annabel's in Thames Street in central London. Can you come? We'd all love to see you. You're welcome to stay with me if you can't get back to Bristol that night.

By the way, don't tell Bruce … it's all a surprise. We're collecting money to buy a present – everyone's giving around £10 each. Any ideas about what to buy?

Send me an email back if you can come. Be in touch soon!

Love from

Jenny

PS By the way, do you remember Lizzie Hunter? She's coming all the way from Frankfurt to be there. I hope you can make it from Bristol!

3a Read the email again. Number (1–7) the things in column A in the order they appear in the email.

	A	B
	giving/asking for personal news	
	reason for writing	
	invitation	
	details of the event (where? when?)	
1	greeting	*Hi!*
	arrangements for the party	
	signing off	

b Write the phrases in the box in the correct place in column B.

Hi!   How are things?   How's the …   Life is … here in … The big news is that   We're having a (party) on … (day). at … (place)   Can you come?   We'd love to see you Send me an email   Be in touch soon!   Love from All the best   I hope you can make it The reason I'm writing is to tell you …

4 Write an email to a friend inviting him or her to a special occasion. Use the headings in exercise 3 to help you. The special occasion could be real or imaginary. For example:

- a family celebration
- a birthday party
- a leaving party
- another celebration

05

YOUR LOOK

IN THIS UNIT

- Grammar: Comparative and superlative adjectives; Questions with *How, What* and *What ... like?*

- Vocabulary: Physical appearance; Parts of the body

- Task: Do a survey about image

- World culture: City of street style

I t's November again, or should I say: 'Movember'? Yes, it's the month where men stop shaving for four weeks, and grow a moustache for charity (and sometimes a beard too!). I want to say 'Congratulations!' to those men who are taking part this year in order to raise lots of money for men's health charities. And let's face it ... some of them look good. Take Jude Law, for example – there's something about the shape of his face, and the shape of his moustache, which means it actually really suits him.

> "There's something about the shape of his face."

Reading and vocabulary
Physical appearance

1a Look at the photos above. Can you think of any words to describe the appearance of the people?

b Work in pairs and compare your ideas.

> Jude Law has got blue eyes.

> I think he's really good-looking.

2 Read the text and answer the questions.

1 What do many men do for the event called 'Movember'?
2 Which charities does the event raise money for?
3 What does the writer think of Jude Law's moustache?
4 How many tattoos has Lisbeth got?
5 What colour is her hair?
6 Does the writer think she looks good?
7 How did most fans feel about Khan's waxwork model?
8 What did Khan like most about the model?
9 What did his wife think of it?

"She looks exactly as I imagined!"

I loved the book *The Girl with the Dragon Tattoo*, so I was worried that the film would be disappointing. It wasn't! For me, Noomi Rapace, who plays Lisbeth Salander, is one of the main reasons it is so good. She looks exactly as I imagined: she's pale with short hair, which is dyed black and she often wears black lipstick. Her overall look is attractive – even though she has piercings in her nose and eyebrow, and of course, the tattoos: a wasp on her neck and a dragon on her left shoulder. And it's not just her looks, but her amazing performance, that make Noomi Rapace the real star of this film.

Shahrukh Khan is one of the most famous actors and film producers in Bollywood. His look is definitely cool – with his brown eyes, black hair and perfect skin – and he has literally billions of fans. Those fans were excited today, as they saw a new waxwork model of him at Madame Tussaud's for the first time. A reporter asked one fan what she thought of the new model. 'It's amazing!' she said. 'It looks just like the real thing. He's tall and slim, and I can almost believe it is him, here with me!' Khan himself was also impressed – 'What I like most are my eyes,' he told the reporters. And what does his wife think? 'I think she likes it more than me. It looks younger!' he said.

"It looks just like the real thing!"

3a Find words in the texts which mean:

(for eyes) colour <u>*brown*</u>
1. facial hair between the mouth and nose _____
2. facial hair on the chin _____
3. (for skin) light-coloured _____
4. (for hair) opposite of long _____
5. a permanent mark on the skin made with ink ____
6. (for hair) changed from the natural colour _____
7. make-up for the mouth _____
8. (in the ears, nose, etc.) with a hole for jewellery _____
9. good-looking _____
10. (for a person) more than average height _____
11. thin in an attractive way _____

b Work in pairs and answer the questions.

1. Which of these words does <u>not</u> describe skin: pale, fair, blonde, dark?
2. Which of these words does <u>not</u> describe hair: straight, square, wavy, curly?
3. Which of these words does <u>not</u> describe facial hair: beard, moustache, clean-shaven, bald?

4 Work in pairs. Complete the description of American actress Kate Bosworth with the words in the box. You do not need to use two of the words.

~~slim~~ attractive dark blue is
pale wavy got have wearing

She is a very ¹<u>*slim*</u>, young woman, who is probably about 30 years old. She's got ²_____, blonde hair and ³_____ skin. She's ⁴_____ lipstick and a pair of earrings, and I think she is very ⁵_____ . She's ⁶_____ lovely eyes, but there is something unusual about them: one of her eyes ⁷_____ brown and the other is ⁸_____!

5a Choose a photo of any person in the first five units of this book. Write a short description of that person using the description in exercise 4 to help you. Do not write the name of that person or where you found the photo.

b Work in pairs and read out your description. Can your partner find the correct photo in the book?

Grammar focus 1
Comparative and superlative adjectives

1a Look at the photos of Matt at three different times in his life. Read the comments and match them with the photos.

b Work in pairs and discuss. Do you agree with Matt's opinions? Why / Why not?

Profile 👤 | Info ☰ | Comments 💬

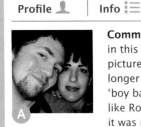

Comment: Hmm ... I look so young in this one, younger than the other pictures, certainly! My hair was longer than it is now ... it was my 'boy band' look. People said I looked like Robbie Williams! I thought it was really cool at the time. But actually, it was probably the worst haircut in the world!!

A

Profile 👤 | Info ☰ | Comments 💬

Comment: I definitely look better in this one – it was about three years ago, on holiday in California. My hair isn't as long as in the other one and I think I look older, maybe because of the sunglasses.

B

Profile 👤 | Info ☰ | Comments 💬

Comment: This is me with Mel a few months ago. It's similar to the last picture, but Mel says I look more serious and more sophisticated with the beard and moustache! I think I look happier in this one – and more relaxed.

....

Comment: You look happier because you're with me! This is definitely the best one because I'm in it! Mel x

---

Comment | Share | Like   👍 5

---

1 Complete the table with the comparative or superlative forms of the adjectives. Look at the texts to help you if necessary.

	Adjective	Comparative	Superlative
1 syllable	young		the youngest
2 syllables ending in - y			the happiest
2/3 syllables		more serious	
irregular forms	good		
	bad	worse	

2 Match the beginnings of the sentences in A with the endings in B to make sentences. Notice the prepositions used.

A
1 She's **older**
2 The **best**
3 It's the **same**
4 It's **similar**
5 They're **different**
6 She **looks**

B
a **from** the others.
b **as** mine.
c **than** me.
d **to** the other one.
e **like** me.
f **in** the world.

PRACTICE

1 Complete the sentences using the comparative or superlative form of the word in brackets.

My hair is _longer_ (long) than it was ten years ago.
1 His style is _____ (modern) than mine.
2 These jeans were _____ (expensive) jeans I've ever bought.
3 This shop is _____ (good) than that one.
4 Could you bring _____ (big) bag you can find?
5 She's _____ (happy) than she was before in her job.
6 That's one of _____ (busy) shops I've been in today.
7 That's _____ (bad) photo I've ever seen of myself!

2a Write the missing word in each sentence.

1 My father is older my mother.
2 I'm very different my sister.
3 His hair is very similar mine.
4 She's nicest person I know.
5 Her nose is the same mine.
6 I look my father.
7 Who's oldest person in your family?
8 My brother isn't tall as me.

b 🎧 5.1 Listen and check your answers.

3a Complete the sentences about you and your family.

Isabel is the youngest person in my family.
1 I look very different from _____.
2 People say I look like _____.
3 My hair is _____ than _____.
4 I'm more _____ than my _____.
5 My mother/father is _____ than _____.
6 My _____ is the oldest person in my family.
7 People say my _____ is similar to mine.

b Work in pairs. Use the sentences in exercise 3a to tell your partner about you and your family.

Unit 5, Study & Practice 1, page 146

Listening and speaking
Special clothes

1 Work in pairs and discuss the questions.

- What sort of clothes do you wear in the week / at the weekend?
- Which of the clothes/shoes in the photos do you like best? Why?
- Which of them do you not like? Why?

2 5.2 Listen to three people talking about special items of clothing. Answer the questions.

1 Which of the items of clothing in the photos is each person talking about?
2 Does he/she wear the item of clothing a lot now?

3 Listen again and complete the table about the three people's special items of clothing.

	1	2	3
What are the most special clothes or shoes you've got?			
When did you get it/them?			
Why is it / are they special?			
Do you wear it/ them a lot now?			

4a Choose an item of clothing which is special to you in some way. Prepare to talk about it by using the questions below.

- What is the item?
- When/Why did you get it?
- What is special about it?
- Do you wear it a lot now? Why / Why not?

b Work in pairs. Take turns to ask and answer questions about your special item of clothing.

> What's your special item of clothing?

> My red jacket.

> What is special about it?

A B C D E

10 STRANGE AND FASCINATING FACTS ABOUT THE HUMAN BODY

1 It is impossible to touch your **mouth** with your **elbow**.

2 Your **eyes** continue growing throughout your life.

3 Your **ears** are the same size from birth onwards.

4 Your **nose** can identify about 50 different smells.

5 You control your **thumb** using nine separate muscles.

6 Your middle **fingernail** grows the fastest

7 An average person has approximately 250 hairs in each **eyebrow**.

8 Each **hair** stays on your head from between two and six months.

9 People's **legs** are usually different lengths.

Pooh!

10 The length from your **wrist** to your **elbow** is the same as the length of your **foot**.

Vocabulary
Parts of the body

1a Work in pairs and read the statements above. Check the meaning of the words in bold.

b Read the statements again and decide if they are true (T) or false (F).

c 🎧 5.3 Listen and check your answers.

2a Work in pairs and write two more statements of your own. You can make them true or false.

b Compare your ideas with other students. Can they decide if they are true or false?

PRONUNCIATION

1 🎧 5.4 Listen to these pairs of words. Are the sounds on the underlined part of each pair of words the same or different?

<u>eye</u> / <u>ear</u>   h<u>ea</u>d / n<u>e</u>ck   sh<u>ou</u>lder / m<u>ou</u>th

elb<u>ow</u> / eyebr<u>ow</u>   n<u>o</u>se / t<u>oe</u>

2 🎧 5.5 Listen to these words. Which letter in each word is silent?

knee   wrist   thumb

3 🎧 5.6 Listen to all the words in 1 and 2 again and practise saying them.

Grammar focus 2
Questions with *How*, *What* and *What ... like?*

1 🎧 5.7 Listen to three mini-conversations and answer the questions for each conversation.

1 What is the relationship between the two people talking?
2 Who are they talking about?

2a Listen again and number the questions in the order you hear them.

a What does he look like?
b What's he like?
c What colour are his eyes?
d What is his hair like?
e How tall is he?
f How old is he?
g Has he got a scar or a tattoo?
h Has he got a beard?

b Match questions a–h in exercise 2a with answers 1–8 below. Listen again and check.

1 Blue.
2 No, he hasn't.
3 No, he's clean-shaven.
4 He's seven now.
5 He seems very nice.
6 It's blond and curly.
7 He's very tall for his age.
8 He's tall, dark and handsome.

GRAMMAR

1 Look at these two questions. Which one asks about appearance and which one asks about personality?
   1 What is he like?
   2 What does he look like?

2 Look again at questions c–h in exercise 2a. Which of the questions is about:
   • height?
   • age?
   • features (eyes, hair, etc.) and things on your face/body (temporary and permanent)?

PRONUNCIATION

1 🎧 5.8 The content words in each question in exercise 2a have the main stress. Listen and underline the main stress. *What does he <u>look</u> like?*

2 Listen again and practise saying the questions.

PRACTICE

1 Put the words in the correct order to make questions.
   1 long / got / Has / hair / he ?
   2 hair / fair / her / or / dark / Is ?
   3 eyes / What / are / her / colour ?
   4 thirties / in / he / Is / his ?
   5 wearing / Is / earrings / she ?
   6 like / What / glasses / his / are ?
   7 me / taller / Is / than / she / or / shorter ?
   8 your / look / What / brother / does / like ?

2 Write appropriate answers for each question in exercise 1.

3a 🎧 5.9 Look at the photo of the characters in a TV soap opera and listen to the descriptions. Which person is the speaker describing in each case.

b Look at audio script 5.9 on page 169. Write the questions the speaker is answering in each case.

4a Choose someone in the photo or someone in the classroom, but don't tell your partner who it is.

b Work in pairs and take turns to guess who it is by asking *Yes/No* questions about this person's appearance.

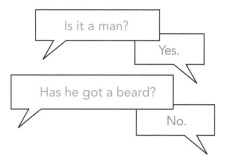

Is it a man? / Yes. / Has he got a beard? / No.

Unit 5, Study & Practice 2, page 146

Task

Do a survey about image

Preparation Reading

1 Work in pairs and discuss.

- What was the last piece of clothing you bought? Where did you buy it? Are you pleased with it? Why / Why not?
- Do you usually buy clothes in the same shop or do you go to different shops? Why?
- Have you got or have you ever had a store card? Why / Why not?

2 Read the introduction to the survey below and answer the questions.

1 What does the shop want you to do?
2 What does the shop promise to give you?

3 Read the questions in the survey below. Work on your own and for each question, circle the option according to your opinion:

👍 = mostly positive

👎 = mostly negative

❓ = neutral.

4 🎧 5.10 Listen to someone doing part of the survey and tick the phrases you hear in the Useful language box.

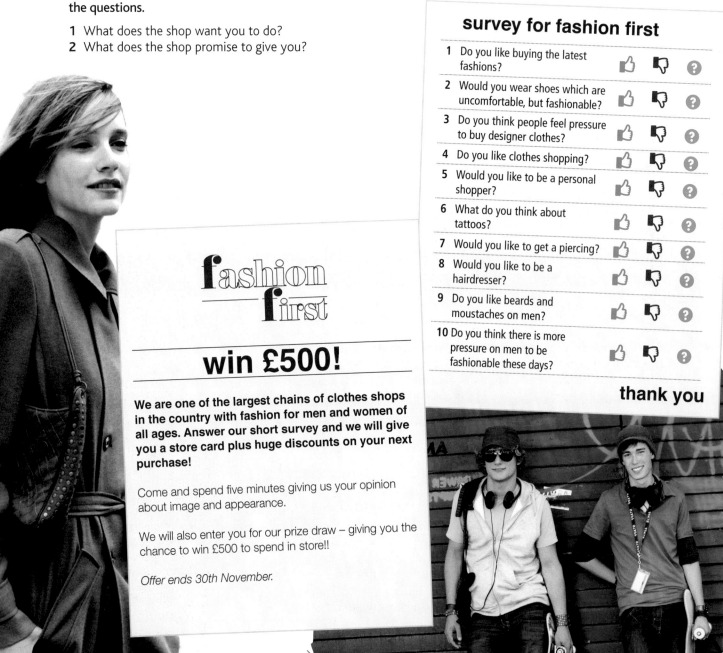

fashion first

win £500!

We are one of the largest chains of clothes shops in the country with fashion for men and women of all ages. Answer our short survey and we will give you a store card plus huge discounts on your next purchase!

Come and spend five minutes giving us your opinion about image and appearance.

We will also enter you for our prize draw – giving you the chance to win £500 to spend in store!!

Offer ends 30th November.

survey for fashion first

1	Do you like buying the latest fashions?	👍 👎	❓
2	Would you wear shoes which are uncomfortable, but fashionable?	👍 👎	❓
3	Do you think people feel pressure to buy designer clothes?	👍 👎	❓
4	Do you like clothes shopping?	👍 👎	❓
5	Would you like to be a personal shopper?	👍 👎	❓
6	What do you think about tattoos?	👍 👎	❓
7	Would you like to get a piercing?	👍 👎	❓
8	Would you like to be a hairdresser?	👍 👎	❓
9	Do you like beards and moustaches on men?	👍 👎	❓
10	Do you think there is more pressure on men to be fashionable these days?	👍 👎	❓

thank you

USEFUL LANGUAGE

a Saying *yes* / Being positive
I love them.
Yes, I'd love to.
Yes, it's my favourite hobby.
I think they're really (cool/attractive/ ...)
Yes, they make (men/people) look (sophisticated/ great/ ...)

b Saying *no* / Being negative
Definitely not.
No, it would be really boring.
I hate them.
No way – never!
No, they always look awful.

c Saying *maybe* / Being neutral
Not really.
Maybe, but I wouldn't be very good at it.
I don't feel strongly either way.
They're OK, I suppose.
It depends on the person.

Task Speaking

1a You are going to do a survey about image and appearance. First, choose five of the questions in the survey on page 48 to ask other students.

b Think about five more questions to add to the survey.

What's your favourite item of clothing?

Do you think €200 is too much to spend on a haircut?

2 Work in pairs and take turns to ask the questions in your survey. Make a note of your partner's answers.

> Useful language a, b and c

3 Work in groups and compare the results of your survey. Which questions did most people agree/disagree about?

SHARE YOUR TASK

Practise asking and answering the questions in your survey until you feel confident.

Film/Record yourself completing the survey.

Share your film/recording with other students.

WORLD CULTURE

CITY OF STREET STYLE

Find out first

1a Work in pairs and discuss. How much do you know about fashion? Try to answer the questions below.

1 Yves Saint Laurent, one of the greatest fashion designers of all time, was born in which country?
  a Algeria
  b France
  c Italy

2 Who is Anna Wintour?
  a a fashion magazine editor
  b a famous fashion designer
  c a famous fashion model

3 The fashion chain Zara now has shops in more than 70 countries: the first was in which Spanish town?
  a A Coruña
  b Barcelona
  c Madrid

4 In which decade did punk fashion first become popular?
  a the 1960s
  b the 1970s
  c the 1990s

b Go online to check your answers or ask your teacher.

....

Search: Yves Saint Laurent / Anna Wintour / Zara history / punk
....

View

2 You are going to watch a video about street style in London. Before you watch, check you understand the meaning of the words/phrases in the glossary below.

....

GLOSSARY

designer fashion	the latest, most expensive fashion
high-street stores	shops which sell clothes at mid-price
street style	a kind of fashion where people invent their own style with cheap clothes
blazer	a kind of jacket
cute	pretty and attractive
rebel	someone who fights against authority
scruffy	untidy
trend	a change or development (e.g. in fashion)
urban	related to a town or city

....

3 ▶ Watch the video and complete the sentences with the colours in the box below.

....

black blue brown light blue red grey white

....

1 In the opening scene, there is a young man wearing a _____ shirt and red trousers.
2 He is talking to a man wearing _____ jeans.
3 Ruth Marshall-Johnson is wearing a _____ shirt.
4 The first street model is wearing a _____ blazer and is carrying a _____ bag.
5 The second street model is wearing _____ jeans and a _____ shirt.

4 Watch again and match phrases 1–6 below to who/what they are about (a–d).

1 ... is able to mix different aspects from different global cultures ...
2 ... has granny chic ...
3 His/Her job is to find the latest trends on the street.
4 ... a bit rock, a bit punk ...
5 ... so anti-establishment, there is a rebel quality ...
6 Very urban, very London, very scruffy, but cool.

a the London street fashion scene
b Ruth Marshall-Johnson
c the first 'street model'
d the second 'street model'

World view

5a Look at the statements below. Tick the ones that are true for you.

❝ I love shopping for clothes – I always try to buy the latest fashions.

❝ I just buy clothes to be comfortable.

❝ I always look for designer labels when I buy clothes.

❝ I never read fashion magazines.

❝ I want to be different from other people – I want people to notice me because of the clothes I wear.

❝ I never waste money on designer labels – you can buy almost the same clothes in a high-street shop.

b Work in pairs and compare your ideas.

FIND OUT MORE

6 Read the text below and answer the questions

1 What is the Creative Cities Network and when did it start?
2 How many cities are on the list?

In 2005, UNESCO (The United Nations Educational, Scientific and Cultural Organisation) began a Creative Cities Network. This is a list of more than 30 cities around the world and each city is famous in a particular creative area.

7a Choose one of the UNESCO Creative Cities in the box below. Can you guess why the city is on UNESCO's list?

Buenos Aires   Chengdu   Dublin   Sevilla   Sydney

b Go online to check your answers and answer the questions below.

1 Where is the city and what is its population?
2 What language do people speak there?
3 When and why did it become a UNESCO Creative City?

Search: UNESCO Creative Cities Network

▶ Write up your research

8 Write a paragraph about the city you chose. Use the example below to help you.

Buenos Aires is the capital city of Argentina. It has a population of around 13 million people and the official language is Spanish. Buenos Aires became a UNESCO Creative City in 2005. One reason for this is the large number of design shops and studios – more than 300 just in one area, Palermo. I would like to visit Buenos Aires because I am interested in fashion and design, and it seems to be a very exciting city.

AFTER UNIT 5 YOU CAN ...

Write a short description of someone's physical appearance.

Use comparatives and superlatives to talk about personal events and opinions.

Ask and answer questions about people's appearance.

Discuss your opinions about image, appearance and fashion.

06

GOING AWAY

IN THIS UNIT

- **Grammar: Plans and intentions;
  Predictions with *will* and *won't***

- **Vocabulary: Going on holiday;
  Describing holidays**

- **Task: Choose a holiday**

- **Language live: Making requests
  and asking for permission;
  A postcard**

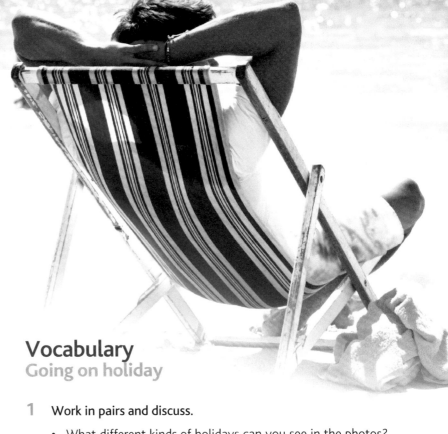

Vocabulary
Going on holiday

1   Work in pairs and discuss.

- What different kinds of holidays can you see in the photos?
- Which do you prefer? Why?
- How often do you go away for the weekend? Where? Who with?

2a Look at the pictures of things you may need to pack for a holiday
and match them with the words in the box.

suncream   sunglasses   guidebook   phrasebook   camera   towel
travel sickness pills   swimsuit   foreign currency   toothbrush
toothpaste   passport   plane tickets   credit cards

b   Work in pairs and discuss. Which of the things do you need:

- on a long journey?
- on a beach holiday?
- in a foreign town/city?

3a You are going on a last-minute holiday and you have 30 minutes to
pack. You can only take five of the things in the box in exercise 2a
and two other things of your choice. Decide on the seven things
you want to take.

b   Work in pairs and decide on the seven things together, giving
reasons for your choices.

Grammar focus 1
Plans and intentions

1a Work in pairs. Read the statements below and decide if they are true (T) or false (F).

1 Most people pack their suitcase in less than an hour. F
2 The majority of people pack their suitcases neatly. T
3 About a quarter of people pack their suitcase at least a week before their holiday. T
4 Men are more organised than women about packing. F
5 About half of all holidaymakers try to pack too much in their suitcase. F

b Read the article below and check your answers.

How do you pack your suitcase?

A survey by MoreSunHolidays found that the average British person takes 1 hour, 16 minutes and 28 seconds to pack their suitcase. And 75 percent of British people pack their suitcases in a neat and tidy way, with 27 percent of people packing at least a week before their holiday. Women are more organised that men: 37 percent of women pack their suitcases at least a week before their holiday, compared with 18 percent of men. 4 percent of holidaymakers pack very few items and leave lots of space in their suitcase, whereas 13 percent try to pack too much and have trouble closing their suitcase.

---

c Work in pairs and discuss. Are you mostly an organised or a disorganised person?

2 Work in pairs and read the sentences about holiday preparations. Which sentences do you associate with an organised person (O) or a disorganised person (D)?

1 I'd like to get to the airport a few minutes before check-in closes.
2 I'd rather not write a list of things I need to pack.
3 I'm planning to get my foreign currency two weeks before my holiday.
4 I'm not going to buy a guidebook or a phrasebook.
5 I'd rather ask local people about places to go than buy a guidebook.
6 I'd like to check in online as soon as I can.
7 I'm going to change my money when I get there.
8 I'm planning to take a camera and a charger for it.

GRAMMAR

1 Choose the alternative with the closest meaning to the sentence.

1 I'**m going to** take a taxi to the airport.
I want to take / *I intend to take* a taxi to the airport.
2 I'**m planning to** take a taxi to the airport.
I want to take / *I've thought carefully about taking* a taxi to the airport.
3 I'**d like to** take a taxi to the airport.
I enjoy taking / *I want to take* a taxi to the airport.
4 I'**d rather** take a taxi to the airport than go by bus.
I prefer to take / *I intend to take* a taxi not a bus to the airport.

2 What form of the verb do we use after:
1 *I'm going*, *I'm planning* and *I'd (would) like*?
2 *I'd (would) rather*?

PRACTICE

1a You're going to do a quick survey about going away. Use the prompts below to make questions using *planning to*, *would like* or *would rather*.

1 (plan / have) any days or weekends away in the near future? Who (plan / go) with?
2 Which places near your home (like / visit) for the day?
3 Which other parts of your country (like / visit) for a few days?
4 For a weekend away, (rather / visit) the mountains, the seaside or a city?
5 Which of these cities (rather / visit) for a long weekend: New York, Paris or London?
6 Which other cities (like / visit) one day?

b Work in groups. Take turns to ask and answer the questions. What interesting 'going away' plans or ideas did you find out?

Unit 6, Study & Practice 1, page 148

Reading and vocabulary
Describing holidays

1a Work in pairs and discuss. What's your favourite way to travel? Why?

b Look at the photos of different methods of transport. Make a list of the good and bad points of each one.

2 Read the online travel brochure from *On The Move Holidays*. Which holiday has the most/least comfortable sleeping accommodation?

3 Match the holidays with statements 1–8.

1 We stayed in really good hotels. *motorbike tour*

Amazon tour 2 It was interesting to see how the local people live.

Moscow-Beijing 3 The whole thing lasted nearly two weeks.

New Zealand 4 We spent some really nice days by the sea.

Amazon 5 There were people selling food.

Amazon 6 It was very noisy in the tent at night! Sometimes we couldn't sleep!

New Zealand 7 We were there for almost three weeks – it was great!

Moscow-Beijing 8 It was good to do some sightseeing in the capital.

4a Match the adjectives in A with the appropriate noun in B.

A	B
1 crowded	4a scenery
2 delayed	5b accommodation
3 long	1c airport lounge 9
4 beautiful	2d flight
5 luxurious	6e excursion
6 interesting	3f queue
7 perfect	g dining car
8 peaceful	8h lake
9 comfortable	7i holiday

b Work in pairs. Think of another word that goes with each of the adjectives in A.

crowded – shop

delayed – train

5 Which of the holiday(s) would/wouldn't you like to go on? Why / Why not?

IT'S A FACT! Russia is 9,000 km wide and has nine time zones. China is 5,000 km wide, but only has one time zone!

Holiday journeys can be a nightmare … sitting in a crowded airport lounge waiting for your delayed flight … stuck in a traffic jam on your way to the coast … or waiting in a long queue with hundreds of others at Immigration. Why not try something a bit different? Try On The Move Holidays, where the journey is the holiday! Here are three of our most popular options:

MOTORBIKE TOUR OF NEW ZEALAND

If you want to see the beauty of New Zealand and love motorbiking, this is the perfect holiday for you: a 19-day motorbike tour of the North and South Islands of New Zealand. Enjoy the peaceful lakes, mountains and forests and relax on the beaches next to the clear water. You can also take part in some sports, such as horse-riding and diving. A fantastic way for any biker to see one of the most beautiful countries in the world! Comfortable accommodation in four-star hotels.

CLICK HERE FOR MORE DETAILS

AMAZON CANOE TOUR

During this six-day canoeing and camping trip, we travel along the River Amazon through the world's biggest rain forest. Our groups have a maximum of 12 people with at least three experienced guides per group. At night we go camping in the jungle, and before you go to sleep you can listen as hundreds of night animals fill the forest with sound. You can also go on interesting excursions to native villages, where you can meet some of the local people, try some of their traditional food and learn more about the native culture.

CLICK HERE FOR MORE DETAILS

MOSCOW TO BEIJING BY THE TRANS-SIBERIAN RAILWAY

A train journey to remember! Moscow to Beijing by train – thirteen days and 6,000 kilometres across Russia, Siberia and Mongolia. 1st, 2nd or 3rd class sleeping cabins – the choice is yours. On the way you can meet the locals, enjoy the beautiful scenery of Siberia, buy your food at the stations or take your meals in the luxurious dining car. You can visit Lake Baikal – the world's largest and cleanest lake – and finally, you can experience the many attractions of Beijing – the world's most exciting capital city!

CLICK HERE FOR MORE DETAILS

Grammar focus 2
Predictions with *will* and *won't*

1a 🎧 **6.1** Luke is planning to go on holiday. Listen to his conversation. What kind of holiday is it?

b Listen again and answer the questions.

  1 When is the best month to go to New Zealand?
  2 What does Donna tell Luke to take with him?
  3 What does Donna tell Luke about getting a visa?

GRAMMAR

1 **Look at these sentences. Which of the following do they describe ?**
  1 You'll need some warm clothes.
  2 It'll be nice to have some sunshine.
  a things you're planning to do
  b things you expect to happen
  c things you would like to happen

2 **What does *'ll* mean?**

PRONUNCIATION

1 🎧 **6.2** Listen to the sentences. What do you hear: *will / 'll* or *would / 'd* ?

2 Look at audio script 6.2 on page 169. Listen again and practise saying the sentences.

PRACTICE

1 Imagine your friend is coming to stay in your town or city in August. Which of the sentences are true for that time? Rewrite the false sentences to make them true for your town/city.

  1 It'll be really hot.
  2 A lot of places will be closed.
  3 There won't be many tourists.
  4 There'll be a lot of insects.
  5 You won't need a warm coat.
  6 It'll be easy to find accommodation.
  7 You won't need a visa.
  8 You'll have a wonderful time.

2a Work in pairs. Student A: You are visiting your friend's city in August. Prepare questions about the things below. Student B: Prepare your answers.

  • weather   • clothes   • accommodation
  • crowded   • visa   • activities

b Take turns to ask and answer your questions.

> Unit 6, Study & Practice 2, page 148

Task

Choose a holiday

Preparation Reading and listening

1 Work in pairs. You are planning a long weekend with some friends. Discuss where you could go and the different things you could do.

> We could go sightseeing in a city.

2 Anabel has won a competition and her prize is a long weekend away with three friends. Read about the competition and answer the questions below.

1 How much do they have to pay for their long weekend away?
2 When do they have to go?
3 How many nights will they stay?
4 In which of the places do they stay in a self-catering apartment?
5 Which of the places do they get to by train?
6 In which of the places will the weather be hot?

3a 🎧 6.3 Anabel and one of her friends, Maria, are choosing where they want to go. Listen to their conversation and answer the questions.

1 Where do they decide to go?
2 Why do they decide on that place?

b Listen again. Number the phrases in parts a and b of the Useful language box in the order you hear them.

Task Speaking

1 You have won the competition and you are going to decide where to go with other students. Before you start, spend some time preparing what you are going to say. Ask your teacher for any words/phrases you need.

> Useful language a

2 Work in groups and agree on a place to go.

> Useful language a and b

3 Take turns to tell other students about the destination you chose and why. Which holiday was the most/least popular? Why do you think this is?

> Useful language c

WIN

RULES OF THE COMPETITION

- The winner can go to one of these amazing places.
- You can go with three friends.
- You will be away for five days.
- You can go anytime in January.
- Your starting point is London.
- All expenses paid including: travel, accommodation and food.

Sights and the city!
Paris, France

From the Eiffel Tower to Disneyland, from cafés to art galleries – there's something for everyone in this historic but modern city!

- Accommodation: self-catering apartment
- Travel from London: 2½ hours by train
- Average January temperature: 3°C

Shopping and shows!
New York, USA

From an unforgettable show with a backstage tour to some world-famous shops and a city that never sleeps – you'll love it!

- Accommodation: self-catering apartment
- Travel from London: 7 hours by plane
- Average January temperature: -3°C

Go and get lazy!
Goa, India

A complete break from the stress of everyday life. Relax with unspoilt beaches, delicious food and perfect sunshine.

- Accommodation: self-catering beach house
- Travel from London: 8 hours by plane
- Average January temperature: 32°C

Spanish spa special!
Seville, Spain

Amazing spa break with unlimited health and beauty treatments, swimming pool, beautiful scenery and delicious food!

- Accommodation: 3* hotel
- Travel from London: 3 hours by plane
- Average January temperature: 8°C

A LONG WEEKEND AWAY!

Paris

New York

Seville

Goa

Dubai

Something for everyone!
Dubai, UAE

You stay in a huge new hotel. You go shopping in a huge new shopping centre. You sunbathe on a huge new beach. What more could you want?

- Accommodation: 5* hotel
- Travel from London: 7 hours by plane
- Average January temperature: 25°C

LANGUAGE LIVE

Speaking
Making requests and asking for permission

1 Work in pairs. Look at the picture and discuss the questions.

- Where are the people? What are they doing?
- What questions or requests do people ask in a hotel? Think about the things below.
  - newspaper
  - wake-up call
  - coffee
  - internet

2a ▶ Watch the video. Choose the best title for the two conversations. You do not need to use one of the titles.

  a Checking in
  b A guided tour
  c Celebrity photo

b Watch again. Put the words in the correct order to make questions.

  1 take a photo / Do you / if / mind / I ?
  2 please / I / Could / take another photo ?
  3 help / Can / I / you ?
  4 your name / tell / Can / you / me / please ?
  5 spelling / mind / that for me / Do you ?
  6 OK / if I / take some personal details? / Is it ?

3a Choose an appropriate answer in the box for each of the questions in exercise 2b.

> No, not at all.   Yes, it's John Smith. Yes, of course.
> Certainly, it's J-O-H-N, S-M-I-T-H.
> Yes, I have a reservation for two nights.   Yes, that's fine

b ▶ Watch and listen to the key phrases and check your answers.

PRONUNCIATION

1 Watch again and listen to the intonation of the key phrases.

2 Practise saying them.

4a Work in pairs. Write short conversations for three of the situations below. Try to use questions and answers from exercises 2 and 3.

- Someone is talking loudly to their friends while you are in the cinema watching a film.
- It's very hot in the bus you are on and you would like to open the window.
- You are waiting at a bus stop and you want to know what time it is.
- You want to ask someone the quickest bus/train route to the town centre.
- Someone's mobile phone is ringing all the time during an English lesson.
- You would like a stranger to take a photo of you and your friend in front of a famous monument.

b Take turns to practise your conversations.

Greetings from Cape Town

1 _Hi Tim !_

2 _____ in Cape Town! 3 _____ in a nice hotel not far from the Waterfront, and many other places to visit. 4 _____ so I'm getting a good suntan!

5 _____ and there's every kind of restaurant you can think of — Indian, Italian, Thai ... ! I'm eating a lot — I think I'll have to go on a diet 6 _____ !

We never get bored in the evenings because 7 _____ .

Give our love to everyone,

8 _____

Paul

CAPE TOWN · SOUTH AFRICA · 20.08.2012 · SOUTH AFRICA · CAPE TOWN ·

Tim Chambers

41 Whitworth Drive

Bournemouth

UK

Writing
A postcard

1 Work in pairs. Look at the postcard and discuss the questions.

- Where is the place on the postcard? Do you know anything about it? What can you see/do there?
- Do you ever send postcards when you go away? Why / Why not?
- Do you like receiving postcards?

2 Read the phrases below and decide which are formal (F) and informal (I). Which phrases are suitable for a postcard to a friend? Why?

1 Hi Tim!
2 Yours faithfully
3 We are pleased to inform you that we have arrived
4 there's loads to do
5 Here we are
6 My postal address is
7 It's warm and sunny
8 We're staying
9 The average temperature is 28°C
10 Dear Mr Buchanan
11 The food is quite cheap
12 when I get home
13 Bye for now
14 The city has more than 50 night clubs
15 The average price for a meal is 150 Rand
16 on 28th January

3 Complete the postcard above with the appropriate informal phrases from exercise 2.

4a Imagine you are on holiday and you are going to write a postcard to a friend. Make some notes about:

- the name and address of the person you are writing to
- how to start the postcard
- where you are now and some information about the place
- other places you have visited
- how to finish the postcard

b Plan where each section above goes on the postcard.

c Write your postcard.

AFTER UNIT 6 YOU CAN ...

Describe your plans and intentions.

Make predictions about the future based on expectations.

Make requests and ask for permission in different situations.

Write a postcard to a friend.

07

SUCCESS

IN THIS UNIT

- **Grammar:** Present perfect and Past simple with *for*; Present perfect and Past simple with other time words

- **Vocabulary:** Verb phrases about ambitions; The internet

- **Task:** Talk about your ambitions

- **World culture:** Success stories

Speaking and vocabulary
Verb phrases about ambitions

1a Think of three ambitions you had when you were a child. Use the photos to help you.

b Work in pairs and compare your ideas. Did you achieve your ambitions? Why / Why not?

> I always wanted to be a ballet dancer.

> Really? My dream was to travel around the world ...

2 Match the verbs in A to the phrases in B to make verb phrases about ambitions.

A	B
1 become	**a** abroad
2 write	**b** children
3 go round	**c** famous
4 earn	**d** a house or flat
5 learn	**e** how to drive
6 start	**f** married
7 go	**g** €1 million
8 get	**h** a book
9 buy	**i** television
10 appear on	**j** the world
11 go to	**k** university
12 have	**l** your own business

TOP FIVE SECRETS OF SUCCESS

Are you ambitious? Follow our five secrets of success and you can succeed!

First: ¹_____ ! That's what popstar Shakira did. She first performed in public aged four, and for nine years, she wrote songs and sang for her friends. By the age of 13, she had a contract with a record company. For the last 15 years, she has been one of the most successful pop singers in the world. If you can't start young, then ²_____ .

When Steven Spielberg didn't get into film school, he pretended he had a job at Universal Studios. He walked confidently past the security guards and worked there for three months. For nearly 40 years, Spielberg has directed many Hollywood films, including

Indiana Jones, Jurassic Park and more recently, *War Horse*.

It isn't just confidence. Our third tip is: ³_____ . The '10,000-hour rule for success' says you need to practise for a minimum of 10,000 hours. That's about six hours a day for five years. Microsoft founder Bill Gates is a good example; for about five years, when he was a teenager, he spent 10,000 hours working on a basic computer. His hard work gave him a big advantage over other people.

Others can also inspire you, so tip number four is: ⁴_____ . At the age of five, Novak Djokovic decided he didn't want to be a good tennis player; he wanted to be the best tennis player in the world. Djokovic got his inspiration from champion Pete Sampras and

he modelled himself on his hero – he tried to be better than Sampras and everyone else. In 2011, Djokovic, aged 24, won three major world championships and became the World Number One.

Finally: ⁵_____ . Luckily for Harry Potter fans, author J K Rowling didn't listen to the negative comments from 12 publishers who rejected her books. For two years, she tried to get them published. Even the publisher who gave her a contract said she had no chance of making money in children's books. He was wrong, and for the last ten years, J K Rowling has been a multi-millionaire. These successful people started at the bottom and got to the top. You can too! Follow our five-point plan and you will succeed!

3a Work in pairs. Put the ambitions in exercise 2 into three categories:

- things that most people do
- things that very few people do
- things that are difficult to do

b Compare your ideas with other students.

Reading and speaking

1 Work in pairs. Read the quotation below and discuss the questions.

- What do you think the quotation means?
- Do you agree with it?
- What do you think is the 'secret' of success?

> **"OUR GREATEST SUCCESS IS NOT IN NEVER FALLING, BUT IN RISING EVERY TIME WE FALL"**
>
> Confucius (Chinese philosopher, about 2,500 years ago)

2 Read the article and write the five secrets of success in the correct place.

- **a** set your goals high
- **b** start young
- **c** work hard – very hard
- **d** be confident
- **e** keep trying

3 Read the article again and answer the questions.

1. What did Shakira do when she was four years old?
2. What did Shakira do when she was 13 years old?
3. How long ago did Spielberg start in the film industry?
4. How long did Bill Gates spend on his computer when he was a teenager?
5. Who did Novak Djokovic want to be like?
6. How many publishers said no to J K Rowling's Harry Potter books?
7. How long did she keep trying to get her books published?

4 Work in pairs and discuss.

- Do you agree with the five secrets of success in the article? Why / Why not?
- Which one do you think is the most important piece of advice?
- Have you or has anyone you know succeeded in doing something by following any of these tips?

Grammar focus 1
Present perfect and Past simple with *for*

1a Work in pairs and discuss. Are these statements true (T) or false (F)?

1 Spielberg worked at Universal Studios for three months when he was 13.
2 Spielberg has directed Hollywood films for nearly 60 years.

b Read the sentences in the Grammar box and check your ideas.

GRAMMAR

1a Look at the sentences. Underline the Past simple verbs and circle the Present perfect verbs.

1 He worked there for three months when he was 18.
2 He's directed films for nearly 40 years.

b Which action is finished? Which action continues up to the present?

2 Match questions 1–2 with the correct answers.

1 How long have you lived here?
2 How long did you live there?

a I lived there for two years.
b I've lived here for six months.

PRACTICE

1 Complete the sentences with the Present perfect or Past simple form of the verb in brackets.

1 I _lived_ (live) in Dublin for two years and then I moved to Cardiff.
2 She _bought_ (buy) a small flat in Paris in 2010.
3 My best friend's name is Millie. I _have known_ (know) her for about eight years.
4 I _had_ (have) a job in a restaurant for a few months last summer.
5 She's a vegetarian. She _hasn't eaten_ (not eat) meat for the last ten years.
6 I love going for walks with my dog – I _have had_ (have) her for five years.
7 He _played_ (play) the guitar for a few months, but stopped last December.
8 I _have been_ (be) in Italy for six years – I live in the capital, Rome.

PRONUNCIATION

1 🎧 7.1 Listen and write down the eight sentences you hear. Notice the pronunciation of *for* and *have*.

2 Practise saying the sentences.

2 Draw six circles. Write the following information in the circles.

- the name of your best friend when you were 11
- the name of someone you know now (a friend/neighbour/colleague)
- the name of a teacher you had in the past
- the town where you live now
- your address when you were ten years old
- your job or the job of someone you know

3 Work in pairs and swap your lists. Take turns to ask and answer questions about each piece of information. Use your own ideas and the questions below to help you.

- Why did you write (Sadie / Mr Jones / Cambridge / architect)?
- How long have you known (him/her)?
- How did you first meet?
- How long have you lived there?
- How long did you live there?
- When did you last go there?
- How long have you been (an architect)?
- What did you do before you were (an architect)?

Why did you write Sadie?

She's a good friend.

How long have you known her?

I've known her for about five years.

Unit 7, Study & Practice 1, page 150

Grammar focus 2

Present perfect and Past simple with other time words

Ameet

Edward

Kate

Me

1 🎧 7.2 Robbie left school in 2003. Listen to him talking about his old school friends and match the photos with phrases 1–6 below.

1 His/Her ambition was to be a millionaire.
2 He/She wanted to become an ecologist.
3 He/She spent most of his time in his bedroom.
4 He/She was very quiet.
5 He/She was interested in business.
6 He/She studied for at least three hours every evening.

2a Work in pairs and discuss. How do you think Robbie's friends' lives have changed in the last ten years?

b Read the posts below and underline one thing each friend has / hasn't done.

⚪⚪⚪

Ameet
Let me see … In the last ten years I've had about ten different jobs. I've worked in import-export, and I've just started a new company selling kitchen equipment, but I haven't made a million yet!

Kate
Since university, I've worked for a number of environmental organisations, mainly as a volunteer. I married Ben a couple of years ago, and we've just had our first baby – Kara.

Edward
I moved to the United States last year and now I work here as a computer game designer. My latest game – Death Trap – has already sold more than ten million copies! But I haven't found a girlfriend yet. And I still spend most of my time playing computer games!

GRAMMAR

1 Look at the time words/phrases in bold with the Present perfect. How does each word/phrase change the meaning?
1 I haven't made a million **yet**.
2 We've **just** had our first baby.
3 My latest game has **already** sold ten million copies.
4 **In the last ten years** I've had about ten different jobs.

2 Look at the time phrases with the Past simple. Are these actions finished or do they continue to the present?
1 I moved to the United States **last year**.
2 I married Ben **a couple of years ago**.

3 Choose the correct tense for these rules.
1 *Present perfect / Past simple* gives the 'news' about someone/something.
2 *Present perfect / Past simple* gives more details about the news.

PRACTICE

1a Choose one sentence in each pair (a or b) which is true for you. Complete the sentences if necessary.

1 a I haven't finished school yet.
  b I finished school _____ (when?).
2 a I've just started learning English.
  b I started learning English _____ (when?).
3 a I've never broken an arm or a leg.
  b I broke my _____ (what?) in _____ (when?).
4 a I haven't been abroad this year.
  b This year I've been to _____ (where?).
5 a I've never met anyone famous.
  b I met _____ (who?) _____ (when?).
6 a I haven't played any sport this week.
  b This week, I've played _____ (what?).

b Work in pairs and compare your sentences.

2 Work in pairs. Take turns to ask and answer questions about things you have done in the last ten years.

1 Which foreign countries have you visited?
2 Have you changed school/jobs?
3 Have you moved house?
4 Have you done any courses?
5 Have you taken up any new sports or interests?
6 What other important things have happened to you?

> Which foreign countries have you visited in the last ten years?

> I've been to Japan and Vietnam.

Unit 7, Study & Practice 2, page 150

Reading and vocabulary
The internet

1 Work in pairs and discuss.

- How often do you use the internet? Where do you use it?
- What do you use the internet for mostly? What are your favourite websites?
- Do you ever use YouTube, Amazon or Google? If so, what do you usually use them for? If not, why not?

2a Work in pairs and discuss. Do you know when YouTube, Google and Amazon first started? Can you match each site to one of these years: 1995, 1998, 2005?

b Read the texts and check your ideas.

3a Read the texts again and answer the questions.

1 How much do you pay to upload videos onto YouTube?
2 How many people used YouTube every day in 2006?
3 Approximately how many people use YouTube every day now?
4 What percentage of people use Google to search the internet?
5 Is it correct grammar to say 'to google something'?
6 Approximately how many searches are there on Google every day?
7 How many people work for Amazon?
8 Approximately how many items do Amazon ship every day at peak times?

b Which of the facts about YouTube, Google and Amazon surprised you most?

AMAZING ACHIEVEMENTS

YOUTUBE

- » YouTube was the first video-sharing website.
- » Three friends from California started the site in 2005.
- » By July 2006, they were getting about 100 million hits a day.
- » You can download films and TV shows from YouTube.
- » Uploading videos onto YouTube is completely free.
- » In November 2006, Google bought the company for $1.65 billion.
- » Now, users upload over 48 hours of videos onto the site, every minute.
- » Every day, YouTube gets more than three billion hits!

GOOGLE

- » Google is the most successful search-engine in the world.
- » 80–90% of people searching the internet use Google.
- » Two students from California, Larry Page and Sergey Brin, started the search engine in 1998.
- » Because of its success, 'google' has now become a verb. Instead of saying 'to search for something on the internet', we say 'to google something'.
- » There are about two billion searches on Google every day.
- » In the first quarter of 2012, Google's profits were nearly $3 billion – this is an increase of 60% on the previous year.

AMAZON

- » Amazon started as an online bookshop.
- » Jeff Bezos, an American computer science graduate, started the site in July 1995.
- » He named the site after the Amazon River. He wanted something starting with the letter A.
- » Amazon now employs about 38,000 people around the world.
- » Amazon stores the things they sell in huge warehouses called 'fulfilment centres' around the world.
- » One of the biggest 'fulfilment centres' in the world is in Swansea, Wales.
- » It covers an area of 800,000 square feet – the size of 13 football pitches.
- » At peak times, Amazon ships over nine million items around the world per day.

4a Complete the sentences with the correct form of the words/phrases in the box.

to upload   to download   to search   to post
a website   a blog   a hit   a video-sharing site
a social-networking site   an online community

I've never _uploaded_ a video onto the internet.
1 I watch short, funny videos on a _____ almost every day.
2 I often _____ music from the internet to listen to.
3 I've never _____ for my name on the internet.
4 I sometimes _____ photos on the internet for my friends to see.
5 One of my videos online got over 1,000 _____.
6 I'd like to write a _____ about my travel experiences.
7 I use a _____ a lot for contacting old friends and chatting.
8 I'm a member of an English-speaking _____.
9 I often use a great _____ to help translate words from my language into English.

b Rewrite the sentences in exercise 4a to make them true for you.

c Work in groups and compare your ideas.

Listening
Finding fame on the internet

1a Work in pairs. You are going to listen to a radio programme. Look at the photos and discuss. What do you think each person did to achieve fame?

b Try to match quotes 1–6 from the programme with the people in the photos.

1 ... lots of different locations throughout the world ...
2 ... uploaded his/her song ...
3 ... went to live in the countryside ...
4 ... some companies sponsored him/her ...
5 ... had some small acting roles ...
6 ... and offered him/her a book deal ...

c  7.3 Listen to the radio programme and check your ideas.

IT'S A FACT!
In 1992, 0.4% of the world's population used the internet. Now its over 30%.

JUDITH O'REILLY

TAY ZONDAY

MATT HARDING

2 Listen again and decide if the statements are true (T) or false (F).

1 Tay Zonday uploaded his first song in 2007.
2 The song has had over 18 million hits.
3 Judith O'Reilly moved to a small village.
4 She earned €8,000 from her first book deal.
5 Matt Harding is a really good dancer.
6 In his third video, he danced in 42 countries.

3 Work in groups and discuss.

• What examples do you know of people who have achieved fame by using the internet?
• What do you think of this way of achieving fame?

Task

Talk about your ambitions

Preparation Reading and listening

1 Match the words in the box to definitions 1–3.

> an ambition   an achievement   a dream

1 something you'd like to do, but probably won't
2 something you want to do one day
3 something you have done which you are proud of

2 Work in pairs. Read the quotations and discuss the questions.

• Which quotation do you most agree with? Why?
• Which quotation do you most disagree with? Why?

> " **To be yourself is the greatest achievement.**

> " *It is more important to know where you are going, than to get there quickly.*

> " **Only people who take great risks can achieve great things.**

> " *When ambition ends, happiness begins.*

> " **I do not try to dance better than anyone else. I only try to dance better than myself.**

> " *Everyone is trying to do big things, not realising that life is made up of little things.*

3a Work in pairs. You are going to listen to five people talking about their ambitions and achievements. Look at the photos and guess what you think each person is going to talk about.

b 🎧 7.4 Listen and complete the table below for each person.

	Ambitions	Achievements
Bill		
Ralph		
Deb		
Pawel		
Swati		

c Listen again and tick the phrases you hear in the Useful language box.

Task Speaking

1   Make a list of your top five ambitions, dreams and achievements. Think about the following:

- job/school
- places you'd like to visit/live
- something you'd like to own (a car, a house, etc.)
- money
- someone you'd like to meet / have met
- something you'd like to discover/invent
- marriage/children
- a sporting dream achievement
- something you'd like to learn / have learnt

2   You are going to talk about your top five achievements and/or ambitions. First, spend some time thinking about what you would like to say. Make notes to help you. Ask your teacher for any words/phrases you need.

> Useful language a and b

3a Work in pairs. Take turns to practise saying what you have prepared.

b   Work with other groups. Take turns to tell each other about your ambitions, dreams and achievements.

- Who has the most interesting or unusual achievement?
- Who has the most interesting or unusual ambition?
- Which people have the same ambition? What is it?

SHARE YOUR TASK

Practise talking about your ambitions and achievements until you feel confident.

Film/Record yourself giving your talk.

Share your film/recording with other students.

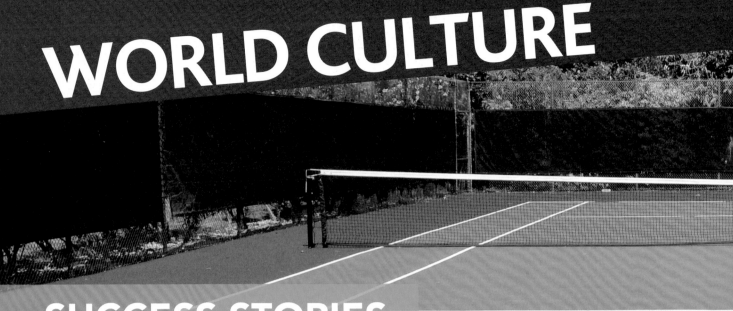

WORLD CULTURE

SUCCESS STORIES

Find out first

1a Work in pairs and discuss. If you want to be a successful sports person, what do you need to do? Make a list of three things.

b How much do you know about tennis? Try to answer the questions below.

   1 What are the names of the four Grand Slam tournaments? When and where do they happen?

   2 Who are the current Number 1 top-ranked male and female tennis players?

c Go online to check your answers or ask your teacher.

....

Search: Grand Slam tennis / men's tennis rankings / women's tennis rankings

....

View

2 You are going to watch a video about Eden Silva, a young tennis player from Essex, England. Before you watch, check you understand the meaning of the words/phrases in the glossary below.

....

GLOSSARY

a career	a job you do for a long time
sponsor	a company who gives money to a sports person
set	a part of a tennis match
a huge gamble	a very big risk
give up your job	to leave your work

....

3a ▶ Watch the video and choose the correct answer to complete the summary.

Eden Silva is from Essex, in England. She is ¹**12 / 20** years old. Her ²**coach / father** believes she will soon be one of the best junior players in the world. Eden also says that her dreams are to be World Number 1 and ³**to play at the Olympics / to win Wimbledon**.

Eden's father has given up his job to help her career, and they spend a lot of their time travelling. Roger's wife and son ⁴**stay at home / travel** with them. One of the people who helps them in California is Robert Landsdorp, who is her ⁵**coach / physio**. In all, Eden's tennis career costs her father ⁶**£8,000 / £80,000** a year.

Finally we see Eden play the most important match of her career, at a World Championship in Florida. Many sponsors and agents come to watch her play against the ⁷**American / Russian** Number 1. In the final set, Eden ⁸**wins / loses** the match, 6–3.

b Complete the phrases from the video with the names in the box below.

....

Eden Silva   Roger   (Robert) Landsdorp   his wife and son

....

1 _____ from Essex is one of the best 12-year-old tennis players in Britain.

2 _____ has taken a huge gamble. He's pulled _____ out of school, given up his job ...

3 ... leaving _____ at home for months at a time.

4 _____ takes his daughter _____ to California for a few months every year ...

5 At £200 an hour, _____ doesn't come cheap.

6 ... _____'s £80,000 a year tennis programme.

World view

4a Read some people's reactions to the video. Which do you agree/disagree with? Write a statement giving your own opinion.

> Poor Eden! She's too young for a life like that.

> It's a good thing that Roger is helping his daughter.

> Eden's brother is probably happier than Eden – he has a normal life!

> Eden is very lucky – she travels around the world and doesn't go to school!

> I think Roger doesn't really love his daughter.

> In my country, it's normal for parents to treat their children like this.

b Work in pairs and compare your ideas.

FIND OUT MORE

5a Look at the names of three people who had success at an early age. Have you heard of them? Do you know why they became famous?

....

Fabiano Luigi Caruana   Lang Lang   Gillian E. Murphy

....

b Go online to find out more about them (or another successful person you are interested in) and answer the questions.

1   What is he/she famous for?
2   Where and when was he/she born?
3   Where does he/she live now?

....

Search: Fabiano Luigi Caruana / Lang Lang / Gillian E. Murphy

....

Write up your research

6 Write a paragraph about one of the people you researched. Use the prompts below to help you.

_____ is a famous _____.
He/She was born in _____ (place) in _____ (year).
He/She started _____ when he/she was _____ years old.
At the age of _____ he/she _____.
He/She is now _____ and at the moment he/she is _____.

AFTER UNIT 7 YOU CAN ...

Describe your hopes, dreams and achievements.

Ask and answer questions about things you've done in the past.

Talk about actions in the past which continue in the present.

Talk about successful people.

08

PLACES TO LIVE

Vocabulary
City life

1   Work in pairs and discuss.

   - Do you live in a city? What other cities have you visited?
   - What are the advantages of living in a city? What are the disadvantages?

2   🎧 8.1 Listen to six people talk about the cities where they live. Who is mostly positive or mostly negative about his/her city?

3   Write the phrases in the box in the correct column in the table.

~~one-way street~~	cycle lane	city centre
pedestrian zone	traffic congestion	public transport
green space	recycling bins	carbon-neutral
residential areas	high-rise apartment blocks	traffic lights
shopping mall		

Transport phrases	Places in a city	Green phrases
one-way street		

4   Work in small groups. Which of the things in exercise 3 do you have in your town or city?

> We have one-way streets in Buenos Aires.

> We don't have any shopping malls in the centre of Venice.

Grammar focus 1
Using articles

1 Read the article about Masdar City and answer the questions.

  1 What is unusual about Masdar City?
  2 Where does the energy for the city come from?
  3 How does the Project Director describe the people who live there?

THE WORLD'S FIRST CARBON-NEUTRAL CITY

Masdar City – a city in the north of Abu Dhabi, in the United Arab Emirates – is special. It plans to be the first carbon-neutral city in the world. Foster & Partners, a company from Britain, is helping to design the city, and the Sultan of Abu Dhabi is providing the money for the project.

There are no traditional cars; instead, people either walk or travel in electric 'podcars'. There are no high-rise buildings; people live in comfortable apartments. And the streets are narrow so that the buildings provide shade for each other.

The biggest solar farm in the Middle East, using power from the sun, will provide the city with its energy. The Project Director says that the people who live there are happy and healthy because the air in Masdar is the best in the world.

GRAMMAR

1a We use the definite article (*the*) for:
  1 something that is unique (there is only one) –
    <u>the sun</u>
  2 a specific person/thing – _____
  3 superlative adjectives – _____
  4 some countries – _____

b Find an example for each in the text.

2a We don't use an article for:
  1 people/things in general – _____
  2 some countries – _____
  3 some cities / place names – _____

b Find an example for each in the text.

3 Check which countries and place names use *the* and which have no article on page 152.

4 We use the indefinite article (*a* or *an*) to mean 'one of many'. Find two examples in the text:
  _____ and _____

PRACTICE

1a Use the words in the boxes to make general statements about the place where you live.

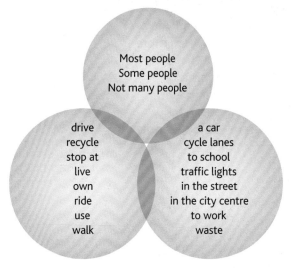

Most people
Some people
Not many people

drive
recycle
stop at
live
own
ride
use
walk

a car
cycle lanes
to school
traffic lights
in the street
in the city centre
to work
waste

b Work in pairs and compare your answers.

2a Write *the* in the correct places in the sentences.

  1 Asia is bigger than Europe.
  2 New York is biggest city in world.
  3 Mount Fuji is in China. It's highest mountain in Asia.
  4 Queen of England lives in Buckingham Palace, London.
  5 Mediterranean Sea is bigger than Pacific Ocean.
  6 Moon is smaller than Sun.
  7 Alps are a mountain range in Scotland.
  8 Mississippi River is in United States.

b Work in pairs. Are the sentences true (T) or false (F)?

c 🎧 8.2 Listen and check your answers.

3a Complete the sentences on a piece of paper and make them true for you. Use the ideas in brackets and include articles where necessary. Write your name on the paper.

  1 I live in _____ (town/city). It's in _____ (middle/north/south/east/west) of _____ (country).
  2 The continent I would most like to visit is _____ .
  3 The country I would most like to visit is _____ .
  4 At 11 a.m., I'm usually at _____ (work/school/university/other).
  5 At 11 p.m. I'm usually (not) at _____ (home / in bed / other).
  6 I have my English lessons in _____ (morning/afternoon/evening).

b Your teacher will give you another student's piece of paper. Read out the sentences, but do not say who wrote them. Can the other students guess who wrote the sentences?

Unit 8, Study & Practice 1, page 152

TOP 5 MOST EXTREME PLACES TO LIVE IN THE WORLD!

Are you bored with your home town ... and thinking of moving somewhere more interesting? Here are a few suggestions of some of the most interesting – and extreme – places in the world where you could go!

1 Fancy a warm climate? The hottest town in the world which is permanently inhabited is Wyndham in Western Australia. All year round the temperature stays between 31–39°C, and this coastal town is close to thousands of miles of unspoilt countryside: mostly desert and hills. There is also spectacular scenery, including the Five Rivers Lookout, where five rivers flow into the sea.

2 What about somewhere a bit colder? The village of Oymyakon in Russia is the coldest place where people live, with temperatures regularly around –40°C. It is between two mountain ranges so the cold air doesn't move and the ground is always frozen. Schools close when the temperature drops to –52°C and locals say that breathing gets difficult at about –60°C.

3 Do you ever complain about the rain...? Then think about the people in Lloró near the west coast of Colombia. They have a lot of rain – more than 1,300 centimetres a year. The people make their money by cutting down trees in the forest nearby, where you can be sure that it will rain every day of the year.

4 From one extreme to another ... Aswan in Egypt is the driest place on Earth where people live, with an average of 0.05 centimetres rainfall a year. The last time it rained in Aswan was on 13th May 2006, and the time before that was in 1994. Luckily, Aswan is in a valley on the banks of the River Nile, which provides water for drinking and farming, as well as transportation.

5 Do you want to get away from everything? Tristan da Cunha is the most remote place in the world, somewhere in the middle of the Atlantic Ocean. These islands consist of mostly mountains and the nearest neighbours are 2,816 kilometres away, in South Africa. There is no airport, but there is a shop, and a swimming pool; which is strange, as there are many beaches along the beautiful coast where you can swim.

A

B

C

Reading and vocabulary
Geographical features

1a Match the photos with the places in the box.

Russia   Western Australia   Colombia

b Work in pairs and discuss. Which place looks most interesting? Why?

2 Read the text above and match the places in the text with the superlatives in the box.

the wettest   the driest   the hottest   the coldest the most remote

3 Read the text again and decide if the statements are true (T) or false (F). Correct the false statements.

1 In Wyndham the temperature gets up to 39°C every day.
2 Wyndham is situated by the sea.
3 The mountains around Oymyakon keep the air cold.
4 Schools in Oymyakon never close.
5 Most people who live in Lloró work in the forest.
6 Every day is a rainy day in Lloró.
7 Recently, Aswan had 12 years of no rain at all.
8 People in Aswan drink the water in the River Nile.
9 Tristan da Cunha is situated east of South Africa.
10 You can swim in the sea and in a swimming pool in Tristan da Cunha.

4 Work in groups and discuss.

• Which place do you think is the nicest / the most difficult place to live? Why?
• What is the hottest / the coldest place you've ever been to?

5 Look at the words in the box and answer the questions.

beach island river mountain forest valley
hill coast sea ocean desert mountain range

1 Which words are connected with the shape of the land?
2 Which is bigger: a mountain or a mountain range?
3 Which words are connected with water?
4 Which is bigger: a sea or an ocean?
5 Which do you lie on when you go sunbathing: a beach or a coast?
6 Which place has a lot of trees?
7 Which place has almost no trees or plants?

PRONUNCIATION

1 🎧 **8.3** Listen to how the letter *i* is pronounced in these words. Is it pronounced / ɪ / or / aɪ / ?

river island hill village climate size
inhabited five centimetre white

2 Listen and check and practise saying the words.

Grammar focus 2
Quantifiers with countable and uncountable nouns

1a Complete the sentences below.

1 There is _____ airport, but there is _____ shop.
2 There are _____ beaches along the beautiful coast ...

b Look again at the text on page 72 and check your answers.

GRAMMAR

1 Read about countable and uncountable nouns and look at the words in the box. Which are countable and which are uncountable?

- A countable noun has a singular and a plural form.
- An uncountable noun has a singular form but no plural form.

beach traffic mountain scenery ocean
water pollution island air forest

2 Look at the quantifiers in bold in the pairs of sentences below. Write S next to the pairs where the meaning is the same and write D next to the pairs where the meaning is different.

1 There's **a** beach.
  There are **some** beaches.
2 There aren't **any** rivers.
  There are **no** rivers.
3 There are **a few** shops.
  There are **a lot of** shops.
4 There aren't **many** mountains.
  There aren't **any** mountains.
5 There's **a lot of** rain.
  There's **too much** rain.

PRACTICE

1 Choose the correct answers.

1 There are *any / much / some* mountains near where I live.
2 There are *no / a few / any* beaches, but they are quite dirty.
3 We're lucky because there is *a lot of / much / many* spectacular scenery around here.
4 There aren't *any / no / much* places to stay on the island.
5 My flat's got a nice view, but there isn't *no / much / many* space.
6 There aren't *many / much / some* people living in the desert now.
7 I'm not going skiing this year because I haven't got *any / no / many* money.
8 There's *many / much / a lot of* traffic on the road to the beach at weekends.

2 Complete the sentences with the most appropriate phrase in the box.

too many   too much (x2)   a lot of (x3)

There is *a lot of* pollution in my city, but it doesn't really affect me.
1 You can't swim in the river because there is _____ pollution.
2 Japan exports _____ cars to Europe every year.
3 I am often late for work because there are _____ cars on the road.
4 This area gets _____ rain so the trees grow well.
5 We didn't enjoy our summer holiday because there was _____ rain.

3 Work in pairs. You are going to try to persuade a visitor to come to an area or a country that you know well. Use some of the ideas in Grammar focus 2 and some ideas of your own.

> You should visit the north east of Brazil. There are a lot of beautiful beaches.

> There are a lot of mountains near my area. And there are a few rivers which you can swim in.

Unit 8, Study & Practice 2, page 152

Task

Give a talk about Canada

CANADA QUIZ!

1 Including all its land and water, Canada is:
- **a** the second largest country in the world
- **b** the third largest country in the world
- **c** the fourth largest country in the world

2 What percentage of the world's population lives in Canada?
- **a** 0.5 percent
- **b** 2.5 percent
- **c** 5.5 percent

3 There are many lakes and rivers in Canada. What percentage of all the fresh water on Earth do they contain?
- **a** 5 percent
- **b** 10 percent
- **c** 20 percent

4 How many of these oceans border Canada?
- **a** the Pacific Ocean
- **b** the Atlantic Ocean
- **c** the Arctic Ocean

5 The country directly south of Canada is:
- **a** the UK
- **b** the USA
- **c** Mexico

6 The capital of Canada is:
- **a** Ottawa
- **b** Montreal
- **c** Toronto

7 How many official languages are there in Canada?
- **a** one
- **b** two
- **c** three

8 What is Canada's national winter sport?
- **a** skiing
- **b** ice hockey
- **c** football

9 What colour is the Canadian flag?
- **a** red
- **b** white
- **c** red and white

10 How many of these singers are Canadian?
- **a** Nelly Furtado
- **b** Avril Lavigne
- **c** Justin Bieber

Preparation Reading and listening

1 Work in pairs and discuss.

- What can you see in each photo?
- Which of the phrases in the box do you think describe Canada?

spectacular scenery   modern cities   hot climate
unspoilt countryside   different types of weather
remote islands   winter sports

2 Read the quiz. How much do you know about Canada? How many questions can you answer?

3a 🎧 8.4 Listen to John talking about Canada. Underline the correct answers in the quiz. How many did you get right?

b Listen again and tick the phrases you hear in the Useful language box.

Task Speaking

1 Work in pairs. You are going to find out more about Canada. Student A: Turn to page 132. Student B: Turn to page 136.

> Useful language a, b and c

2a You are going to give a short talk about visiting Canada. Prepare what you are going to say. Use the photos, the maps and the quiz to help you. Ask your teacher for any words/phrases you need.

b Work in pairs and take turns to practise giving your talks. How many students would/wouldn't like to visit Canada?

> Useful language a, b and c

a Asking about places
Where is ... ?
Why is it important?

b Explaining where a place is
It's in the (west) of Canada / on the (north) coast.
It's west of Ottawa.
It's near ...

c Explaining why a place is important
There is a lot of space ...
There are a lot of mountains ...
It's a really lively and multi-cultural place.
It's most famous for (the beautiful countryside) ...
You can (go skiing) there.
It's the longest/biggest ...
It's a good place for (hiking) ...

IT'S A FACT!
Canada has 52,455 islands and over 200,000 km of coastline.

SHARE YOUR TASK

Practise giving your talk about Canada until you feel confident.

Film/Record yourself giving your talk.

Share your film/recording with other students.

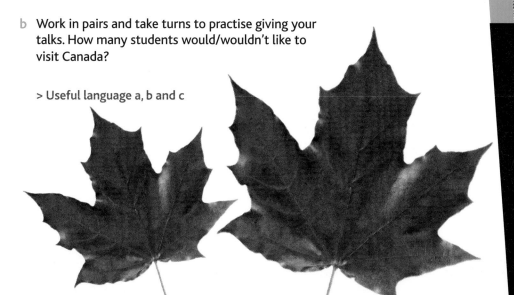

Speaking
Asking for and giving directions

1 Work in pairs and discuss the questions.

- What do you usually do when you arrive in a new town/city/country? Do you do any of the things below?
  - take a taxi to your destination
  - buy a map
  - go to the tourist information office
  - ask people for directions
- Have you ever got lost in a new town/city/country? What happened?

2a ▶ Watch the video and answer the questions.

1 Where are the people going?
2 How many people do they ask for directions?

b Look at these ways of asking for directions. Watch again and complete the gaps.

1 Excuse _____!
2 Can you _____ me?
3 We're _____ for the Grand Hotel.
4 Can you give me some _____, please?

3 Match the phrases in the box to the pictures below.

go to the end of the road	go past the cinema
turn left at the traffic lights	it's on the corner
it's on your left	cross the road
go straight on at the traffic lights	take the next right
on the other side of the road	take the second right

PRONUNCIATION

1 ▶ Watch and listen to the key phrases in exercises 2 and 3.

2 Practise saying them.

4 Work in pairs. You are going to ask for and give directions. First, decide if you are asking someone in the street or phoning someone. Student A: Turn to page 133. Student B: Turn to page 137.

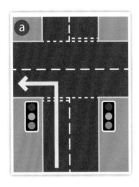 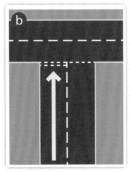 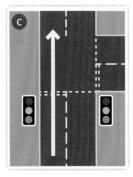 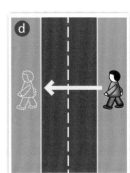 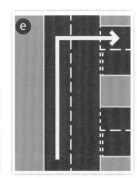

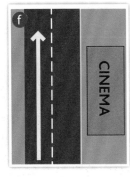 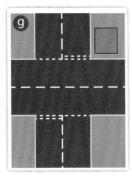 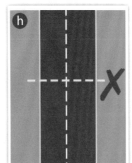 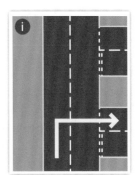 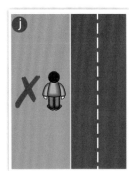

Writing
Directions

1 Hannah has invited her friend Sofia to stay, but she can't meet her at the airport. Complete Hannah's email with the words/phrases in the box.

buy a ticket	catch the number 8 bus
on the right	directions
get off	about 1 hour 40 minutes
leave the station	follow
opposite	take the train

New Message

To: Sofia

From: Hannah   Signature:

Hi Sofia!

Sorry I can't meet you when you arrive next week. I've got a job interview that day! My address is Flat A, 18 Lansdown Road, Bristol and here are the [1]_____ to get there from Heathrow. When you leave Heathrow airport, [2]_____ the signs to the Heathrow Express train to Paddington Station. You don't have to [3]_____ in advance, as there are lots of ticket machines at the station. From Paddington station [4]_____ to Bristol. Make sure you get a fast train – the journey takes [5]_____ and the trains run about every 30 minutes.

When you get to Temple Meads station in Bristol, [6]_____ by the main exit at the front. You'll see lots of bus stops in front of the station. From there, [7]_____ to Clifton (my area). You need to [8]_____ at the stop called 'Queen's Road'. Then, cross the road, and Lansdown Road is the second [9]_____ . I live at number 18, which is just [10]_____ a small supermarket. I'll leave the key with my neighbour, Kim, who lives upstairs in Flat B.

Looking forward to seeing you!

Hannah

2 Match the verbs in A with the appropriate words/ phrases in B.

A	B
1 catch	**a** the road
2 buy	**b** right
3 leave	**c** at the next stop
4 turn	**d** the signs
5 cross	**e** a ticket
6 get off	**f** a bus
7 follow	**g** the airport

3a You are going to write a similar email giving directions from where you are now to one of the places below. Choose a place.

- your house
- the nearest station / bus stop / airport
- another place you know well

b Make some notes about:

- how to begin the journey
- what transport to use (bus, train, walking, etc.)
- the number of any buses/trains you need and where/how to buy a ticket
- how long the journey will take

4 Write your email. Use about 150 words.

09

OLD AND NEW

IN THIS UNIT

- Grammar: *may*, *might*, *will definitely*, etc.; Present tense after *if*, *when* and other time words

- Vocabulary: Modern equipment; Adjectives for describing places

- Task: Plan a café makeover

- World culture: Green cities

Vocabulary
Modern equipment

1 Work in pairs and discuss. Do you prefer old or new styles of buildings/houses/furniture? Why?

> I prefer old buildings because they are more beautiful.

> I don't agree. Modern buildings are more stylish.

2a Make a list of:
- five buildings you can live in (e.g. house).
- five rooms in a house (e.g. kitchen).
- five pieces of furniture (e.g. table).
- five machines you find in a house.

b Compare your lists with your partner.

3 Work in pairs and discuss. Which of the things in the box do you use for:

1 washing/cleaning?
2 keeping warm/cool?
3 entertainment/information?
4 food/cooking?

wi-fi router   central heating   microwave oven   air conditioning
flat screen television   computer   freezer   oven   washing machine
dishwasher   shower   fridge   vacuum cleaner

1 🎧 9.1 Listen to the difference in stress between the compound nouns below.

noun + noun	adjective + noun
•	•
air conditioning	*central heating*

2 🎧 9.2 Mark the stress on the compound words. Listen and check.

washing machine   vacuum cleaner   wi-fi router
microwave oven   dishwasher

3 Practise saying the words, paying attention to the stressed syllable.

4a Look at the items in the box in exercise 3 on page 78 and answer the questions.

1 Which of the items have you used today?
2 Which of the items are in the building you are in now?
3 Which of the items do you often have problems with? Why?
4 How important is each item for you?

b Work in groups. Compare your answers and explain your choices.

Reading

1a Work in pairs and discuss. How has life changed in the last 100 years? Think about washing, keeping cool and entertainment.

b Read the text and check your ideas.

2 Read the text again and answer the questions.

1 In the UK, how did people heat water to wash their clothes?
2 How much water did they use for washing the family's clothes?
3 How often did people wash themselves?
4 Why did people in Spain and Turkey live in 'cave-houses'?
5 In the Middle East, why did houses have 'wind towers'?
6 In Japan, what two kinds of artistic activities did people do?
7 How often did Japanese families get together?
8 What did they do during these family times?

3a Work in groups and discuss. Imagine you could go back to life a hundred years ago. What things would you like about it? What would you miss from your life now? Why?

b Compare your ideas with other groups.

WHAT WAS LIFE LIKE ONE HUNDRED YEARS AGO?

A hundred years ago people all over the world lived very differently from how they live now. Let's look at some ways in which daily life has changed enormously since then.

Washing: A hundred years ago, washing clothes was much more difficult and time-consuming because people didn't have washing machines. In most parts of the UK, for example, there was no running water and people washed their clothes in huge tubs of boiling water. They often collected this water from a public tap in the village and then heated it on a wood fire in the kitchen. To wash all the family's clothes, they used about sixty buckets of water. Keeping clean was not such a priority as it is now, and most people had a bath only once or twice a month, also using the tub in the kitchen.

Keeping cool: Keeping cool was a priority, however – especially for people living in hot countries. Nowadays, we have air conditioning to keep our houses cool but then, no modern air conditioning existed. In some places, like Spain and Turkey, people lived in houses which were partly caves: large holes cut in the rock in the side of a mountain. The air in these 'cave-houses' was always cool and pleasant. Other houses often had high ceilings and large windows. And houses in the Middle East sometimes had 'wind towers' which helped to keep the air moving in the house. It was also common in many places to hang wet washing around the house to cool it down.

Entertainment: The most popular entertainment in the home nowadays involves TVs and computers. In Japan, for example, young people spend an average of two and a half hours watching TV or playing computer games every day. This is a dramatic change from a hundred years ago. Then, Japanese young people often spent time doing origami (a special kind of art with paper) or practising calligraphy (a special kind of artistic handwriting). It was also traditional for the whole family to get together every evening to talk and have tea. Sometimes these sessions included the children doing performances of music or drama for the other family members to enjoy.

Grammar focus 1

may, might, will definitely, etc.

1   Read the comic strip from the 1950s and answer the questions.

   1   What year are the characters talking about?
   2   What rooms do they look at?

2   Work in pairs. Find all the predictions in the comic strip and put them into three groups.

- things that are possible now
- things that are not possible now
- things that may happen in the future

GRAMMAR

1   Number the sentences in the correct order: 1 = most probable, 5 = least probable.
   a   It definitely won't happen.
   b   It'll definitely happen.
   c   It may/might happen.
   d   It'll probably happen.
   e   It probably won't happen.

2a   Do *probably* and *definitely* come before or after *will*?

 b   Do *probably* and *definitely* come before or after *won't*?

CHUCK TAYLOR LOOKS AT...

THE HOUSE OF TOMORROW!

TODAY *CHUCK* IS LEARNING ABOUT *THE HOUSE OF TOMORROW* ... THE YEAR *2025!!*

PRACTICE

1a Use the prompts below to make predictions about 50 years from now.

1 People / live in houses
2 Bathroom mirrors / check your weight
3 People / spend less time / in the kitchen than now
4 Robots / cook meals
5 People / go out / to watch movies
6 People / travel / by train
7 People / buy / books
8 Mobile phones / replace / landline phones

b Work in pairs and compare your answers.

2a Complete the sentences and make them true for you. Add two more sentences with your own ideas.

1 I _____ go to live in another country.
2 I _____ learn to speak English better than my teacher.
3 I _____ live in the countryside when I'm older.
4 I _____ visit the United States.
5 I _____ have a job when I'm 60.
6 I _____ have grey hair when I'm older.
7 I _____ marry a millionaire.
8 I _____ live to be 100 years old.
9 I _____
10 I _____

b Work in groups and compare your ideas.

> Do you think you'll go to live in another country?

> Yes … I might go and live in Spain.

> What about you?

Unit 9, Study & Practice 1, page 154

Listening and speaking
How to clean a house in three minutes

1 Work in pairs and discuss.

• Are you generally a tidy person or a messy person?
• Who is the tidiest/messiest person in your house/family? How do you feel about this?
• Who does the cleaning in your house? How do you feel about this?
• What things do you need to clean your house? Make a list.

2 You are going to listen to a radio programme which tells you how to clean a house in three minutes. Do you think this is possible? Why / Why not?

3a 🎧 9.3 Listen to the radio programme. Which of the things below do they mention?

• wipes
• large rubbish bags
• air freshener
• a vacuum cleaner
• a bottle of bleach

b Listen again and number the instructions in the order you hear them.

a put bleach in the toilet
b close the doors
c spray air freshener around
d clean the TV with wipes
e put things in a rubbish bag   1
f put things in the shower
g put dirty plates in the oven

4 Work in groups and discuss.

• Which of the tips in the radio programme would you use or not use? Why?
• Do you know any other unusual tips about cleaning?
• What tips could you give about how to make your house messy in three minutes?

Vocabulary

Adjectives for describing places

1 Work in groups and discuss.

- Do most people that you know live with their family, live with friends or live alone?
- At what age do people in your country usually move out of their parents' house/ flat? Why do you think this is?

2a Read Georgia's email and answer the questions.

1 Who do you think Georgia is writing to?
2 Why is she writing?
3 Which is her favourite room?

b Read the email again and look at the photos that Georgia attached to her email. Which photo is different from her description in the email?

3 Look at the adjectives in the box and answer the questions.

....
modern sunny light small attractive
shady lively quiet large private
old-fashioned dark comfortable spacious
....

1 Which word means the opposite of:
- modern?
- sunny?
- light?
- small?
2 Which word has a similar meaning to *large*?
3 What is the difference between *quiet* and *private*?
4 Which word describes a place:
- where lots of things are happening?
- which is nice to look at?
- which makes you feel physically relaxed?

4 Cross out one adjective which does *not* go with the noun in bold.

1 **a room**: *old-fashioned / large / dark / lively*
2 **a kitchen**: *light / spacious / shady / attractive*
3 **a street**: *comfortable / quiet / attractive / lively*
4 **a garden**: *sunny / shady / lively / private*
5 **a café**: *modern / shady / spacious / small*

Did I tell you? I'm moving out of my parents' house soon?! I've found a lovely flat to rent and I'm really excited! It's in a nice area and the street is really quiet. But there is a shop just down the road, and a lively café, which is great.

The flat is attractive – it looks quite small from the outside, but it feels spacious inside. The best room is the kitchen – it's mostly white and very modern. Just my style! The living room is nice, too. It's a large, comfortable room and at the moment, it's got old-fashioned furniture in it, but I think my furniture will look really good in there. Also, there's a door to the garden, which is lovely. And the garden is small and quite private … mostly sunny, but with a nice shady area for sitting. There's a small bathroom, and two bedrooms – one's quite dark, but the other is really light and sunny!

I'm attaching some photos of the flat. Of course, it will look different when I move my furniture in, but what do you think? Do you like it?!!

G xx

5 Choose either the house/flat you live in now, or a house/ flat you would like to live in. Work in pairs and take turns to describe it.

> It's a small, modern house in a quiet area of town. There is a small, sunny kitchen – you can see the garden from the window. The garden is very sunny.

Grammar focus 2
Present tense after *if, when* and other time words

1a An old power station near the centre of town isn't used anymore. There are plans to replace it with a cinema, a shopping centre, a hotel or a block of flats. Work in pairs and discuss. Which plan do you like best? Why?

b 🎧 **9.4** Listen to four people talking about the plans and answer the questions.
1 Which plan is each person talking about?
2 Does each person think the plan is a good idea or a bad idea?...

2a 🎧 **9.5** Listen and complete the sentences with the correct form of the verb in brackets.
1 If they _____ (build) new flats, it _____ (help) other businesses in the area.
2 I _____ (be) very pleased when all the work _____ (be) complete.
3 I'm sure they _____ (ask) local people for their ideas before they _____ (make) a decision.
4 After the old power station _____ (go), the area _____ (be) more attractive.
5 As soon as more people _____ (want) to come to the town centre, the traffic _____ (be) terrible.
6 The area _____ (change) completely if they _____ (put) a new shopping centre there.

b Look at audio script 9.5 on page 172 and check your answers.

GRAMMAR

1 Look again at the sentences in exercise 2. Does each sentence refer to the present or the future?

2 Which verb form comes after *if, when, as soon as, after* and *before*?

3 Which verb form comes in the other clause of the sentence?

4 What is the difference between *when* and *as soon as*?

PRACTICE

1 Choose the correct answers.
1 When I **get / will get** a better job, I **buy / will buy** a house in the town centre.
2 Before I **make / will make** a decision, I **ask / will ask** my friends for their opinion.
3 They **start / will start** the new building when everyone **agrees / will agree**.
4 She **travels / will travel** around Australia before she starts her new job.
5 If I **don't pass / won't pass** my exams, I **can't / won't be able** to go to university.
6 After he **finishes / will finish** his course, he **gets / will get** a job in an office.
7 If I **have / will have** time, I **go / will go** to the cinema this weekend.
8 I **start / will start** a business as soon as I **have / will have** enough money in the bank.

2a Work in pairs. Complete the conversations below with your own ideas. Practise reading your conversations aloud.
1 A: Oliver, could you do your homework now?
   B: Oh, Mum, I'll do it when ...
2 A: Are you going anywhere nice this weekend?
   B: We might go for a picnic in the country if ...
3 A: We haven't got any milk!
   B: Oh no! I'll go and buy some as soon as ...
4 A: Are you enjoying your new job more now?
   B: No, I hate it! I want to leave as soon as / when ...
5 A: Are you going to have a holiday this year?
   B: I hope so, if ...
6 A: So when are we going to see each other again?
   B: I don't know. I'm very busy at work at the moment, but I'll phone you when ...

b 🎧 **9.6** Listen and compare your conversations with the ones on the recording.

Unit 9, Study & Practice 2, page 154

Task

Plan a café makeover

BLUE PARROT CAFÉ
HOME | FOOD | DRINKS | GALLERY | EVENTS | CONTACT

WELCOME TO THE BLUE PARROT CAFÉ ...
THE NUMBER ONE PLACE ON SAINT JUDE!

- Lively café – popular with locals and holidaymakers
- Comfortable terrace on the beach
- Beautiful views – sunny 365 days a year
- Clean, modern interior with attractive decor
- Delicious tropical food
- Wide selection of hot and cold drinks
- Polite, attentive staff – waiting to serve you!

Blue Parrot Café, Hopi Beach,
15 km east of Judetown, St Jude

Preparation Reading and listening

1 **Read the information on the website and answer the questions.**

   1 Where is the Blue Parrot Café?
   2 Who owns it?
   3 Do you think it seems to be a good place to go? Find four reasons why.

OWNERS: TINA AND CARLOS DUNNE

HOLIDAYADVICE.COM

Blue Parrot Café   **No. 66 of 66** restaurants on St Jude

★ ★ ★ ★ **Excellent:** 0 reviews; ★ ★ ★ **Good:** 0 reviews;
★ ★ **Poor:** 0 reviews; ★ **Awful:** 24 reviews

NOT a place I will return to! ★
Maggie, TX: When we went to eat at the Blue Parrot we were the only customers in the restaurant. The decor looked old and dirty and some of the chairs were broken.Before our meal arrived, I looked at the bar and there was a mouse eating the peanuts! We didn't stay to find out what the food was like …

Rude service, awful food ★
Davina FL: The 'fish special' came from a microwave oven and was so hot I burnt my mouth. When I complained, the waiter said it was my own fault and walked away! To make things worse, my husband's burger was burnt and his chips were cold!!

No cold drinks ★
Dave, London: My wife and I went in for a coffee one morning. The owner said they didn't sell tea or coffee, only cold drinks. When we asked for two colas, he said he didn't have any cold drinks or ice because the fridge was broken.

USEFUL LANGUAGE

a Making suggestions
How about (changing/painting/putting) … ?
It will look (better / more spacious / cleaner …) if we …
I think we should …
Where shall we put … ?

b Discussing problems
I don't think it's a good idea to …
I don't think we should … because …
If the food is very expensive, people might not …

c Presenting your conclusions
We've decided to …
We'd like to …
If we … people will …

2 Work in pairs. Read the reviews of the Blue Parrot Café. Was each customers' experience good or bad?

3 🎧 9.7 Listen to two customers discussing how to improve the Blue Parrot Café. Tick the phrases you hear in the Useful language box.

Task Speaking

1 Tina and Carlos have asked for your help to improve the Blue Parrot Café. Work in groups and decide what improvements to make, using the questions below. Ask your teacher for any words/phrases you need.

Decor and furniture
- What ideas do you have for improving the look? Think about colours, furniture, paintings, etc.

Food and drink
- What kind of food will you sell?
- Make a list of 10–12 food/drink items for the menu board.

Service
- How will you improve the service?
- Will you get new waiters, cooks, etc., or will you re-train them?

> Useful language a and b

2a Make a list of ideas in your group.

b Work with another group and try to persuade other students that your ideas are the best. Agree on the best plan.

> Useful language c

SHARE YOUR TASK

Practise describing your plan for the café makeover until you feel confident.

Film/Record yourself talking about your plan.

Share your film/recording with other students.

WORLD CULTURE

GREEN CITIES

Find out first

1a Work in pairs and discuss. How much do you know about Abu Dhabi in the United Arab Emirates? Try to answer the questions below.

1 Where are the United Arab Emirates?
   a North Africa
   b Central Europe
   c Middle East, Asia
2 What does Abu Dhabi's wealth come from?
   a banking
   b coal
   c oil and gas
3 What is Abu Dhabi surrounded by?
   a desert
   b lakes
   c mountains
4 What is the climate in Abu Dhabi?
   a very cold
   b very hot and dry
   c very hot and wet

b Go online to check your answers or ask your teacher.

Search: United Arab Emirates / Abu Dhabi wealth / Abu Dhabi geographical features / Abu Dhabi climate

View

2a You are going to watch a video about Masdar City. Before you watch, check you understand the meaning of the words and phrases in the glossary below.

GLOSSARY
from scratch	from the beginning
narrow	not far from one side to the other
on the outskirts	not in the centre (of a city)
wide	far from one side to the other, opposite of narrow

b ▶ Watch the video and decide if the statements are true (T), false (F) or don't know (?).

1 The presenter believes that Masdar City is a true city of the future.
2 The building of Masdar City will cost $18 billion.
3 40,000 people live there at the moment.
4 After you park your car on the outskirts of the city, someone drives you to the centre.
5 The car travels under the city of Masdar City.
6 Masdar City has a lot of tall buildings.
7 The streets of Masdar City are similar to the streets of Abu Dhabi.
8 It is cooler in Masdar than in Abu Dhabi.

3a Look at the phrases from the video. Do they describe Abu Dhabi (AD) or Masdar (M)?

1 ... one of the fastest-growing cities on the planet.
2 ... a new, green city ...
3 ... free for pedestrians to enjoy, with no traffic.
4 ... taller towers and ... wider highways ...
5 ... surprisingly comfortable ...
6 ... the streets are narrow and shady ...

b Watch again to check.

World view

4a Look at the statements about Masdar City. Which do you agree/disagree with? Write a statement giving your own opinion.

> We need to build more cities like Masdar – cities without cars are the future!

> In my city, people like using their cars ... and we don't need air conditioning in the streets. So why change?

> Masdar is an interesting experiment ... but I don't think it will ever happen anywhere else.

> It's important to make our cities greener and more carbon-neutral – not to build new ones.

> I think it would be better to spend $18 billion on other world problems like poverty.

> I'd love to live in Masdar City because it looks like a very good place to live.

b Work in pairs and compare your opinions.

🔊 FIND OUT MORE

5a Look at some other green cities in the box below. Do you know where they are?

....

Växjö   Portland   Curitiba   Reykjavik   Puerto Princesa

....

b Go online to find out more about two of the cities in the box, or another green city you are interested in. Answer the questions.

1 Where is the city?
2 What is the population of the city?
3 Why is it a green city?

....

Search: city name + map / city name + population / city name + green city

....

6 Work in pairs and compare your information.

▶ Write up your research

7 Write a paragraph about some of the places you researched. Use the prompts below to help you.

_____ is a city in _____.
It has a population of _____.
One reason it's a green city is because _____ .
Another reason why it's a green city is _____.
It's similar/different to the place where I live because _____.

AFTER UNIT 9 YOU CAN ...

Talk about living in the past.

Make predictions about the future.

Have short conversations about what you will or might do in the future.

Make suggestions and discuss possible solutions.

10

TAKE CARE!

Vocabulary
Accidents and injuries

1 Work in pairs. Read the information about first aid and answer the questions.

1 When do you give first aid?
2 Who can give first aid?
3 What is the first thing you do when giving first aid?
4 What is the second thing you do?

What is first aid?

First aid is the help you give someone when they are ill or injured before doctors arrive. People who give first aid are ordinary people who are near the person in need. Sometimes they are trained to give first aid. But even if they are not trained, someone who gives first aid could save your life.

There are two basic rules of first aid. Firstly, you need to get the person out of danger. This could mean trying to stop bleeding, or moving the person away from the middle of a busy road. Secondly, you need to get help quickly. In Britain, you need to phone 999 or 112 to get an ambulance.

2 Work in pairs and look at the photos. Which accidents and injuries in the box do you associate with each photo.

break your arm	cut your finger	burn yourself
get a bee sting	get a rash	faint

3a Work in pairs and discuss what you should do if:

1 you cut your finger?
2 you burn yourself on a hot pan?
3 someone faints?
4 someone breaks his/her arm?
5 a bee stings you?
6 you get a rash on your face after eating strawberries?

b Decide which two answers (a–l) could go with each question (1–6).

a Put the burn in cold water.
b Try to stop the bleeding by pressing on it.
c Wait for him/her to come round.
d Phone for an ambulance.
e If possible, don't move the person or his/her arm.
f Stop eating strawberries – you may be allergic to them.
g Don't put a plaster on it.
h If it's a deep cut, see a doctor.
i Don't put cream or anything on your skin.
j Phone a doctor if you feel dizzy or breathless.
k Make sure he/she is comfortable and in a safe place.
l If the area becomes swollen, put some ice on it.

c 10.1 Listen to a nurse giving her answers to the questions. Are they the same as yours?

4 Work in pairs. Think of an accident or injury that you have had or has happened to someone you know. Take turns to explain what happened.

Grammar focus 1
Past continuous

1 10.2 Listen to a conversation between Jason and his friend Rachel. What happened to Jason? Number the injuries in the list in the order you hear them. You do not need to use one of them.

a a broken arm
b a bee sting
c a cut on his head
d an eye injury

2 Listen again and answer the questions.

1 Where was Jason when the bee stung him?
2 What did Marco do after the bee stung Jason? Why?
3 Where was Jason when something flew into his eye?
4 What did he do then?
5 How did he break his arm?

---

1 Look at the verbs in bold in the sentences below. Which ones are the Past simple and which ones are the Past continuous?

1 I **was walking** along when I **felt** something sting my hand.
2 As I **was standing** there, my hand **started** to become swollen and red.
3 While we **were waiting** at the bus stop, something **flew** into my eye.

2 In each sentence, which of the actions in bold started first?

3 Choose the correct tense to complete the rules.

1 We use the *Past simple / Past continuous* to describe the background situation in a story.
2 We use the *Past simple / Past continuous* to describe the main events in a story.

4 Look at the sentences again. What three time words can you find?

PRACTICE

1a Complete the stories with the Past simple or Past continuous form of the verb in brackets.

1 As I ¹___was___ (drive) to a friend's house last week, I ²___heard___ (hear) a fly buzzing around my car. It was really annoying me so I decided to try and kill it. I ³___was trying___ (try) to catch it when I took my eyes off the road and hit a tree. My car was wrecked, but I think the fly ⁴___flew___ (escape) without any injuries!

2 While I ⁵___was___ (drive) home a couple of weeks ago, a man nearly stepped into the road in front of my car. Luckily he didn't, and we avoided an accident. The following week, on my way home, I ⁶___saw___ (see) the man again. As I ⁷___was___ (wave) at him, I lost control of my car and ⁸___crashed___ (crash) into the traffic lights!

b 10.3 Listen to the stories and check your answers.

2a Complete the sentences using the Past continuous and make them true for you.

1 I once had an accident when I …
2 When I left the house today, …
3 I met … when I …
4 One evening a while ago, I …
5 At 8 o'clock this morning, I …
6 I was really surprised when I …

b Work in pairs and compare your answers.

> Unit 10, Study & Practice 1, page 156

Vocabulary

Feeling ill

1a Work in pairs and discuss. Which of the phrases in the box might you say in these situations?

- you've got a cold
- you've eaten something bad
- you fall over

I've got a really bad **cold**.   I've got **toothache**.
I keep **sneezing**!   I've got a **headache**.
My arm/leg/eye **hurts**.   I've got a **sore throat**.
I've got a **fever**!   I feel **sick**!
I'm going to be **sick**!   I've got an **earache**.
I've got a **cough**.   I've got a **stomachache**.
My **temperature** is about 40°C!

b Look at the words in bold in the box and answer the questions.

1 Which ones do we use with the verb *have got*?
2 Which two verbs do we use with the word *sick*?

2 Complete the sentences with the appropriate words from exercise 1.

1 I've got a _____ after listening to that loud music.
2 I think that fish I ate was bad – I feel really _____ now.
3 She feels very hot – I think she's got a _____ .
4 I've got an _____ – it hurts a lot and I can't hear very well.
5 Atishoo!! Oh, I'm sorry! I can't stop _____ today!
6 I can't speak very loudly today because I've got a _____ .
7 My arm _____ a lot – I think it's broken.
8 I need to go to the dentist – I've got terrible _____ .

3 Work in pairs and discuss. Choose three of the symptoms in the box in exercise 1a. What do you usually do when you feel like this?

> When I've got a sore throat, I usually have a hot drink with honey …

> When I feel sick, I usually lie down on the floor …

IT'S A FACT!
A sneeze travels out of your nose at an average of 140 km per hour.

DIRT IS GOOD FOR YOU

Reading

1 Work in pairs and discuss. Some people think that 'dirt is good for you'? Do you agree? Why / Why not?

2 Read the article quickly and put the sentences in the correct place in the text.

a Bacteria and dirt are, in fact, essential for our bodies.
b There is a huge increase in one particular illness in the western world.
c Allergies affect large numbers of the population.

1 _____ There are a variety of different symptoms, like: sneezing, swollen eyes, rashes and feeling breathless. With this illness, people often feel very ill, and sometimes they die. The causes are not deadly bacteria, however, they are everyday things like nuts and flowers. These people are not suffering from terrible diseases, but from allergies. And experts predict this epidemic could become one of the biggest medical challenges of the next century.

2 _____; in some parts of the world, a third of adults and a half of children. So why are our bodies doing this to us? Scientists have used historical evidence: hygiene and medicine were much less advanced a century ago, but allergies didn't exist. People used to drink water from rivers and work on muddy farms. They didn't use to wash much and they used to suffer from many more illnesses. But they didn't use to suffer from allergies. 'Nowadays, everyone thinks hygiene is very, very important,' explains Dr Smythson from a top London hospital. 'We wash our hands, we clean our houses and we make sure our children are clean. We think it is a good thing, but we don't understand that some bacteria are good.'

3 _____ Children who play in mud and get dirty develop strong immune systems in their bodies, which then fight off 'bad' things like diseases. If our immune systems don't develop properly, they become oversensitive to 'good' things, like food, pets and flowers. Scientists in various countries, including England, Germany and Sweden, are finding ways of giving people good bacteria in mud and they have found that this can reduce allergies dramatically. It will take time to find out exactly which bacteria are the best, and how to create a treatment, but they are certainly on the right (muddy) track!

3 Read the article again. Choose the correct answers.

1 The article says that people **can** / **can't** die from allergies.
2 Experts think that allergies **will** / **won't** be a big problem in the future.
3 More **children** / **adults** suffer from allergies.
4 A hundred years ago, people **did** / **didn't** suffer from allergies.
5 A hundred years ago, people got **more** / **fewer** illnesses than now.
6 If you have a **strong** / **weak** immune system, your body fights off bad things.
7 Scientists **have** / **haven't** found exactly which bacteria to use.

4 Read the statements and decide if you agree/disagree with each one.

1 Children should play in mud and get dirty more.
2 We shouldn't wash our hands or clean our houses so much.
3 It's true that 'dirt is good for you' and our clean modern society causes allergies.

Grammar focus 2
used to

1 Look at these examples from the text. In which sentence is _use(d)_ the main verb?

1 People used to drink water from rivers.
2 They didn't use to wash much.
3 Scientists have used historical evidence.

GRAMMAR

1 Look at examples 1 and 2 in exercise 1 again and choose the correct explanation below.

We use _used to_ / _didn't use to_ + verb to talk about:
1 things that happened only once in the past
2 habits (and states) in the past

2 Find two more examples in the text.

PRACTICE

1 Match the prompts in A with the phrases in B to make complete sentences with _used to_ / _didn't use to_.

People didn't use to suffer from allergies.

A	B
1 People / not / suffer	a bottled water.
2 More people / live and work	b as clean as it is now.
3 People / not / wash their hands	c their houses as much as they do now.
4 Food / not / be	d on farms.
5 People / not / drink	e their food in plastic bags from supermarkets.
6 Children / play outside	f as much as they do today.
7 People / not / buy	g from allergies.
8 People / not / clean	h much more than they do now.

PRONUNCIATION

1 🎧 10.4 Listen to four sentences. Notice the different pronunciations of _use(d)_.

2 Listen again and practise saying the sentences.

2a Complete the sentences to make them true for you.

1 I used to think that …
2 I used to be frightened of …
3 I used to like …
4 I didn't use to like …
5 I used to play with …
6 I never used to …

b Work in pairs and compare your answers.

Unit 10, Study & Practice 2, page 156

Task

Choose the funniest story

Preparation Reading

1a Work in pairs. Make a list of different things you can get insurance for, e.g. travel insurance. Compare your ideas with other students.

b Put the things in your list into two groups: essential insurance and non-essential insurance.

c Work in groups and compare your ideas.

2 Read about an insurance company on the right and answer the questions.

   1 What prize is the insurance company offering?
   2 How can you enter the competition?

3a Work in pairs and look at the pictures of Lorraine Carter below. What do you think happened to her?

b Read the text about Lorraine below and number the pictures in the order they happened.

Has anything funny or unusual happened to you?

We are running a competition to find the person who has had the funniest or most unusual accident or mishap. We are offering a £1,000 prize … and free extra insurance for the future! We want to hear from anyone with a story to tell.
Email your story to us now! And remember: funny or unusual - nothing too dramatic or serious please!

Martin Hegarty
Managing Director

Email: comp@accinsurance.com

Lorraine Carter decided to enter the ACC Insurance competition after she broke her arm when she was skiing. A few months later, 35-year-old Lorraine went to a park near her home with her four-year-old daughter, Hannah. She was pushing Hannah on the swings when her phone rang. It was ACC Insurance phoning to say she was one of the three finalists. She was so excited that she forgot her daughter was travelling towards her on the swing. The swing hit her and knocked her to the ground, breaking her arm again!

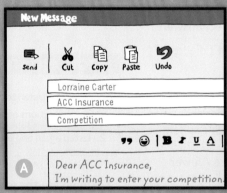

4 Complete the first column of the table below with details about Lorraine.

Name and age	Lorraine Carter, 35	Gareth Barry, 52	Amanda Barratt, 27
Where/When accident/mishap			
What was he/she doing when the accident/mishap happened?			
Other people in the accident/mishap? Who?			
What happened in the end?			

5a Work in two groups, Group A and Group B. Find out what happened to one of the other finalists. Group A: Turn to page 133. Group B: Turn to page 137.

Group A: Turn to page 133. Group B: Turn to page 137.

b Now work with a student from the other group. Ask and answer questions to complete the columns about Gareth and Amanda.

> Useful language a

6 🎧 10.5 Listen to two people discussing who they think should get the prize. Look at part b in the Useful language box and number the phrases in the order you hear them. Do they mostly agree/disagree about who should get the prize?

Task Speaking

1 You are going to decide who gets the prize. First, take some time to prepare what you want to say, including reasons for your decision. Ask your teacher for any words/phrases you need.

> Useful language b

2a Work in groups and decide who should win the prize: Lorraine, Gareth or Amanda.

b Then change groups. Tell your new group what your decision is, giving reasons. Try to persuade the students in your group that your choice is the best one.

> Useful language c

LANGUAGE LIVE

Speaking
Talking about health

1 Work in pairs and discuss.

- Would you like to be a doctor? Why / Why not?
- What kinds of medical problems do people sometimes have on holiday?
- Have you ever been to the doctor when you were on holiday? What happened?

2a ⊙ Watch the video of three scenes in a doctor's surgery. What symptoms does each patient have?

b Read the statements and questions below. Who said each one, the doctor or the patient?

1 How can I help?
2 What can I do for you?
3 A bee stung me.
4 What are your symptoms?
5 I feel very breathless.
6 Are you allergic to anything?
7 What's the problem?
8 I've got an earache.
9 When did these symptoms start?
10 Are you taking any medication at the moment?

c Watch again and check your answers.

3 Work in pairs. Choose one of the medical problems on page 90 or invent your own. Use the diagram below to help you prepare and practise your conversation.

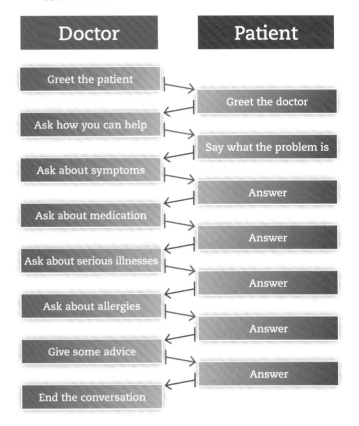

Doctor	Patient
Greet the patient	
	Greet the doctor
Ask how you can help	
	Say what the problem is
Ask about symptoms	
	Answer
Ask about medication	
	Answer
Ask about serious illnesses	
	Answer
Ask about allergies	
	Answer
Give some advice	
	Answer
End the conversation	

4a Work in pairs and practise your conversation.

b Change roles and practise the conversation again.

Writing
Time words in a narrative

1 Work in pairs and discuss.

- Would you like to go on a safari holiday to see wild animals? Why / Why not?
- Would you like to work with wild animals? Why / Why not?

2a Read the story about Paul and answer the questions.

1 What job did Paul do in Zimbabwe?
2 Why is the story called *A bad day 'at the office'*?

A bad day 'at the office'

Paul Templer is probably the luckiest man alive. ¹ _After_ nine years in the British army, he gave up his job and returned to his native country, Zimbabwe, to become a river guide. ² _____ he was leading a group of tourists down the Zambezi River. Everything seemed calm and peaceful ³ _____ they travelled slowly down the quiet river. ⁴ _____ there was a terrifying crash: a bull hippo – one of Africa's most dangerous animals – was attacking one of the canoes from below. ⁵ _____ the hippo turned towards Templer. It took Templer in its enormous mouth and disappeared underwater. ⁶ _____ the hippo opened its mouth for a moment, Templer managed to escape; but ⁷ _____ he could reach the shore, the hippo attacked again. ⁸ _____, a colleague managed to reach Templer and pull him out of the water. ⁹ _____ an eight–hour road trip, they ¹⁰ _____ reached the nearest hospital in the city of Bulawayo. The operation saved Templer's life. A year ¹¹ _____, Paul Templer returned to his job. He ¹² _____ works with people, helping them to be positive about their lives, talking about what he describes as 'A bad day 'at the office''.

b Complete the story with the time phrases in the box.

as   After (x2)   before   Eventually   later   now
One day   Suddenly   Then   When   finally

3 Read what Paul's colleague said about the incident. Choose the correct answers.

1 *Eventually / One day / Suddenly* we were on the Zambezi River with a tour group.
2 *Finally / One day / Suddenly* an enormous hippo appeared from the river. It attacked Paul's boat *after / before / when* I could shout to him.
3 The hippo carried Paul underwater. *After / Then / When* there was a horrible silence. We didn't know what to do. *After / Before / Then* a few minutes, we saw Paul's head coming out of the water. He was alive!
4 *After / As / Before* we were driving to Bulawayo, I told Paul not to worry, everything would be OK. But I was afraid he'd die *after / as / before* we got to the hospital.
5 We got to the hospital about eight hours *finally / later / then*. *After / As / When* we got there, he was in a really bad way.
6 Paul's injuries were really serious, but *eventually / then* he was healthy enough to go back to work. When I look back *later / now / then* at what happened, I see that Paul was a real hero.

4 Work in pairs and discuss. How do you think Paul uses his experience to help other people to be positive about their lives?

5a You are going to write a story about a dramatic accident or rescue. It can be true or imaginary. Decide on a place/situation for your story. Use the time phrases from exercise 2 and some of the phrases below.

- One day, we were ...
- Everything seemed normal ... when suddenly
- Eventually, we were able to ...
- There was a horrible silence ...
- Finally we managed to ...
- As we were going to ... I ...
- A few minutes/hours/years later ...
- When I look back now at what happened ...

b Write your story. Use about 120 words.

11

THE BEST THINGS

IN THIS UNIT

- **Grammar:** *like* and *would like*; Conditional sentences with *would*

- **Vocabulary:** Adjectives with dependent prepositions; Survival items

- **Task:** Take part in a survey

- **World culture:** White gold

Reading

1 **Work in pairs and discuss.**

- Which of the things in the photos make you feel happy and not very happy?
- Which of the things would you choose to make a 'perfect day'?
- What else would you choose? Why?

2a **Work in pairs and discuss what you think the 'best' things in each of the categories below are.**

job   hobby   sport   pet   fruit   age

I think the best job is probably a teacher because it is a really fun, interesting and satisfying job.

b **Read the article. How many of your ideas were the same as the results of the research?**

3 **Read the article again and decide if the statements below are true (T) or false (F).**

1 One of the good things about being a firefighter is working with other people.
2 People like singing in a choir because it is a physical kind of hobby.
3 You can go swimming even if you aren't completely fit.
4 People who have a dog are more hard-working than people who don't.
5 Blackcurrants are healthy, but they don't taste very nice.
6 People over the age of 74 are more irresponsible than younger people.

4 **Work in groups and discuss.**

- Do you agree with the results of the survey? Why / Why not?
- What other ideas do you have for the best things in each category? Explain your choices.

THE BEST THINGS IN LIFE!

Best Magazine has done some research about some of the best things in life ... and you might be surprised about the results! First of all, jobs. Our research showed that the best job you can have is being a firefighter. A job as a firefighter gives plenty of job satisfaction. You're working in a team, you're doing physical work and you're responsible for other people's health and safety.

Secondly, hobbies. Working with other people is also important when it comes to hobbies, and our research showed that the best hobby is belonging to a choir. Singing in a choir is also creative and it is very satisfying to take part in a public performance.

Thirdly, sport and exercise. Our research revealed that the best all round exercise is swimming. People of all ages can enjoy swimming and it provides exercise for all the major muscle groups in the body. It is also suitable for people suffering from injuries. People of all ages can also benefit from owning a pet, and dogs came top of the best pet category. Owning a dog can reduce stress, blood pressure and the risk of heart disease. The research showed that dog owners were generally happier, more sociable and less likely to visit the doctor.

Finally, if you're keen on keeping healthy, you'll be interested in the fact that the best fruit you can eat are blackcurrants. They are really tasty and they contain high levels of vitamin C. They are also full of anti-oxidants which help in fighting diseases like heart disease and cancer.

So if you're a firefighter, who belongs to a choir, goes swimming, owns a dog and eats plenty of blackcurrants, you'll probably be very happy. But it might also depend on how old you are. Our research also looked at when people said they were the happiest. However, the results were unclear. The best age is either 17 – people at this age have finally got the freedom they always wanted as a child. Or, the best age could be 74 – people are free of the responsibilities of adulthood, and ready to enjoy themselves without feeling worried about what other people think of them.

Vocabulary
Adjectives with dependent prepositions

1 Complete the questions with the prepositions in the box.

....

about (x 2)   at   from   for   in   of (x 2)   on   to

....

1 Which results in the research were you **surprised** _____ ?
2 Are you **interested** _____ joining a choir?
3 What form of exercise do you think is **suitable** _____ older people?
4 Are you **keen** _____ healthy eating?
5 At what time of day are you **full** ____ energy?
6 What are you most **worried** _____ when you take an exam?
7 Are you **afraid** _____ animals?
8 What sports are you **good** _____ ?
9 Who are you most **similar** _____ in your family?
10 Is your language very **different** _____ English?

2a Match questions 1–10 in exercise 1 with answers a–j.

a Not really. I love them, especially cats.
b Yes, but I eat biscuits too sometimes.
c Some words are the same, but the grammar is very different.
d I get nervous about running out of time.
e No, not really. I can't sing at all.
f Football. And I also play tennis a bit.
g Swimming is good because it can be gentle.
h My mum. We're both really bossy!
i Definitely in the morning. After lunch I feel really tired.
j I didn't expect the best hobby to be singing in a choir.

b 🎧 11.1 Listen and check your answers.

3 Work in pairs. Take turns to ask and answer the questions in exercise 1. Give details in your answers.

LOVE IT OR HATE IT?

Some things always get a strong reaction – you either love them or hate them. Here are our top ten. What do you think – do you LOVE them or HATE them?

01 Tattoos – Art or not?

02 Poodles – Sweet and pretty or just stupid and ugly?

03 Opera – Some people's idea of a perfect night out; other people's idea of a nightmare ...

04 Fish and chips – Delicious or disgusting?

05 Going to the hairdresser's – A great opportunity to relax or something you try to avoid?

06 Flying – For some people, it's terrifying, for others, it's fun!

07 Sunbathing – Everyone loves sunbathing, don't they? No, some people hate it ...

08 Camping – A relaxing, fun holiday or just uncomfortable, hard work?

09 Blue cheese – Tastes like heaven or tastes like a dirty floor?

10 Football – Quite simply: some people love it and other people hate it ...

Grammar focus 1
like and *would like*

1a Make a list of three things you love and three things you hate.

b Work in pairs and compare your ideas.

2 Read the magazine article. Put a tick by the things you like, and a cross by the things you don't like.

3 Work in groups and compare your opinions.
- What did you agree about?
- Can you think of any other things that people either love or hate?

4 🎧 **11.2** Listen to two friends talking about some of the things from the article in exercise 2 and answer the questions.

1 Which things are they talking about?
2 Which things do they have the same opinion about?

5 🎧 **11.3** Listen to the sentences and underline the verb form (*-ing* or infinitive*)* that you hear.

1 I love *going* / *to go* to the hairdresser's.
2 I like *sitting* / *to sit* there with my magazine.
3 I'd love *visiting* / *to visit* him one day.
4 I hate *sitting* / *to sit* in a small place for all that time.
5 I enjoy *sunbathing* / *to sunbathe* for two reasons.
6 I'd like *living* / *to live* somewhere hot and sunny.

GRAMMAR

1a Look at the examples from the listening in exercise 5.

b Which form of the verb comes after *would like* / *would love*?

c Which verbs are followed by an *-ing* form?
_____ , _____ , _____ and _____

2 Make the sentences below into questions.
1 You like dancing.
2 You would like to dance.

PRACTICE

1a Choose the correct answers.

1 Would you like *living* / *to live* abroad one day? In which country?
2 *Do* / *Would* you like to play a musical instrument? Which one?
3 Would you like *to learn* / *learning* another language apart from English? Which one(s)?
4 *Do* / *Would* you like getting up early? Why / Why not?
5 Which city *do you most like visiting* / *would you most like to visit* one day?
6 *Do* / *Would* you like listening to music? What kind?
7 Do you enjoy *cooking* / *to cook*? What's your speciality?
8 Which famous person *do you most* / *would you most* like to meet? Why?

b Work in pairs and take turns to ask and answer the questions.

> Would you like to live abroad one day?

> Yes, I'd like to live in Hong Kong. What about you?

> I don't think I'd like to live abroad. I like being near my family.

2a Put the conversation into the correct order.

A: That's a good idea. What would you like to see?
A: Would you like to meet up **this weekend**? *1*
A: Yes, I'd like to see **the new Brad Pitt film**. What do you think?
A: Yes, see you then.
A: To be honest, I don't really like **science fiction films**.
B: There's that **new science fiction film** on – what about that?
B: See you on **Saturday**. Bye.
B: Yes, I'd love to. How about going to the cinema? *2*
B: Yes, great. I'd like to see that, too. Shall we go on **Saturday night**?
B: Well, is there something else you'd like to see?

b 🎧 **11.4** Listen and check your answers.

PRONUNCIATION

1 🎧 **11.5** When we make an invitation it's important to sound friendly. Listen and notice the intonation.

2 Look at audio script 11.5 on page 173. Listen again and practise saying the sentences.

3a Work in pairs and write a similar conversation to the one in exercise 2 by changing the words in bold.

b Compare your conversations with other students. Don't forget to use friendly intonation.

> Unit 11, Study & Practice 1, page 158

Speaking and vocabulary
Survival items

1 Work in pairs and discuss. What do you think is the best and the worst thing about camping? Why?

2 Match the words in the box with the photos.

tent knife torch batteries bottled water
blanket compass insect repellent matches
magnifying glass mirror rope sunglasses
suncream toilet paper water purification tablets

3 Work in pairs and discuss the questions. Which of the things in the box:

- have you got at home?
- do most people have at home?
- do you usually take on a camping holiday?
- do you usually take on a holiday to a hotel?

4 Work in pairs. Take turns to think of one of the items in the box in exercise 2, but don't tell your partner what it is. Your partner should ask questions (maximum 10) to guess the item. You can only answer *Yes* or *No*.

Grammar focus 2
Conditional sentences with *would*

1a 🎧 11.6 You are going to listen to two people talking about surviving on a desert island. Listen and tick which of the items in the box in exercise 2 they mention.

b Work in pairs and compare your answers.

GRAMMAR

1 Look at the sentences and answer the questions. Do the sentences refer to a real possibility or an imaginary situation?

If clause	main clause

If you **were** on a desert island, you **would have** to find your own food.

If you **didn't have** a tent, you **wouldn't sleep** properly.

A tent **would keep** you dry if it **rained**.

If you **went** to live on a desert island, what **would** you **take**?

2 What is the verb form in the *if* clause?

3 What is the verb form in the main clause?

4 Can you change the order of the *if* clause and the main clause?

5 Do the sentences refer to the past, the future or no specific time?

Do you take it on a camping holiday?

Yes.

Can you sleep in it?

No.

IMAGINE AN ISLAND
Saturday 10:30 a.m., Radio 6 FM.

Imagine an Island is a new radio show, starting this week. Interviewer, Jamie Plummer, asks his guests to imagine they are going to live on a deserted tropical island for a long time – maybe forever, if nobody rescues them. There is nothing and no-body on the island – apart from plants and animals. The guests have nothing with them – apart from the few things they are allowed to take. On the show, they talk about how they would feel living on this island and what they would take. Jamie's first guest is film star Anna Loveday. Find out what she imagines.

IT'S A FACT! An average person can survive for between three and five days without water.

PRACTICE

1a Choose the correct answers.

1 If I **won / would win** a million pounds, I **spent / would spend** it on holidays and cars.
2 I **went / would go** to the moon if I **had / would have** the chance.
3 If I **could travel / would travel** back in time, I **visited / would visit** the time of my grandparents' childhood.
4 If I **had / would have** a superpower for a day, I **chose / would choose** to be invisible.
5 If I **found / would find** €500 on the street, I **kept / would keep** it.
6 If I **could have / would have** dinner with a famous person, I **chose / would choose** Barack Obama.
7 I **provided / would provide** free health care for all if I **was / would be** president of my country.
8 If I **was / would be** rich and famous, I **lived / would live** in Hollywood.

b Rewrite the sentences where necessary to make them true for you. Compare your sentences with other students.

2a Imagine you were going to live on a desert island. Choose five items from the box in exercise 2 on page 100 that you would take.

b Work in pairs and compare the items you chose. Try to decide together on the five items you would take, giving reasons for each one.

c Read the text written by a survival expert on page 134 and check your ideas. Were your choices similar or not?

3 Read the paragraph above. What kind of show is *Imagine an Island* and what do the guests do?

4a Complete the questions with the correct form of the verb in brackets.

1 How would you feel if you _____ (live) alone on a desert island?
2 If you were on a desert island, _____ (you / be) good at surviving?
3 If you took one song or piece of music, what _____ (you / take)?
4 If you _____ (have to) choose one book to take, what would it be?
5 If you had to choose either the book or the song, which one _____ (you / choose)?
6 If you _____ (decide) to take one useful item, what would you take?
7 What _____ (you / take) if you could take one luxury item?
8 If you had to choose either the useful item or the luxury item, which one _____ (you / choose)?

b Imagine you are taking part in the radio show *Imagine an Island*. Work in pairs and take turns to interview each other. Use the questions above and your own ideas. Who do you think made the best choices?

Unit 11, Study & Practice 2, page 158

Task

Take part in a survey

Preparation Reading

1a Look at the photos and think about the important things in life. Using the photos and your own ideas, make a list of:

- three things that were important to you as a child
- three things that are important to you now
- three things that will be important when you are over 60

b Work in pairs and compare your lists. Were your ideas similar or different?

2 Read the questions in the survey. Answer them for yourself. Try to remember your answers.

3a 🎧 11.7 Listen to two people asking and answering questions in the survey. Which three questions in the survey does the man ask? What answers does the woman give?

b Listen again and tick the questions and answers you hear in the Useful language box (part a).

SURVEY

WHAT ARE THE MOST IMPORTANT THINGS IN LIFE?

1 What is the most important thing in life for you?
- ○ **a.** having a lot of money
- ○ **b.** being in love
- ○ **c.** becoming famous
- ○ **d.** making a difference to other people's lives
- ○ **e.** other (Please state: _____)

2 If you could choose the perfect number of children, what would it be?

○ 0   ○ 1   ○ 2   ○ 3   ○ 4   ○ 5+

3 If you could choose any pet, what would it be?
- ○ **a.** a cat
- ○ **b.** a dog
- ○ **c.** a fish
- ○ **d.** none
- ○ **e.** other (Please state: _____)

4 If you could choose your perfect place to live, where would it be?
- ○ **a.** in a city
- ○ **b.** in the suburbs
- ○ **c.** in a small town
- ○ **e.** in the country
- ○ **d.** it doesn't matter

5 Would you ever marry for money?
- ○ **a.** Yes, possibly.
- ○ **b.** Not sure.
- ○ **c.** No, definitely not.

6 What advice would you give to your great-great-grandchild? Tick the advice you most agree with and cross the advice you least agree with?
- ○ **a.** Take time to be with your family. They're your most important possession.
- ○ **b.** Money isn't everything. Enjoy your job if you can, because you will have to do it every day of your life.
- ○ **c.** The most important thing in life is to be happy. But to be happy, you need to give as well as receive.
- ○ **d.** Money! A big car! A big house! A family! You can have it all!
- ○ **e.** Love learning and education. Being well-educated makes you a better and happier person.

a Asking and answering
Which of these is the most important ... ?
If you could choose ... , what/where would ... ?
Which one do you (dis)agree with ... ?
I like making a difference ...
I'd like to have one or two children / live in a city /
have a dog ...
I hate having animals in the house ...

b Presenting the results
Most / Some / Not many people think that ...
Both of us would choose ...
We didn't agree about ...
I was the only one who thought that ...

Task Speaking

1 Work in pairs. Take turns to ask and answer the survey questions.
Make a note of your partner's answers.

> Useful language a

2a 🎧 11.8 We asked a hundred people the questions in the survey.
Listen and write the most popular answers in the table below.

Question	Survey results: Most popular answers
1	50% said:
2	40% said:
3	45% said:
4	40% said:
5	45% said:
6: most agree	30% said:
6: least agree	8% said:

b Look again at all the results. Prepare a short summary about the
most interesting similarities and differences. Ask your teacher for
any words/phrases you need.

> Useful language b

SHARE YOUR TASK

**Practise your talk about
the survey results until
you feel confident.**

**Film/Record yourself
giving your summary.**

**Share your film/recording
with other students.**

WORLD CULTURE

WHITE GOLD

Find out first

1a Work in pairs and find the places below on a map. Which is nearest to where you are now? Which is the furthest away?

- Papua New Guinea
- The Caribbean
- The Middle East
- The Mediterranean

b Discuss. Which products do you associate with the places below? Which of them do you think are important sugar exporters?

- Australia
- Brazil
- EU countries
- Japan
- Sweden
- Thailand

2 Go online to check your answers or ask your teacher.

Search: name of country + map / main exports / world sugar producers

View

3a You are going to watch a video about sugar. Before you watch, check you understand the meaning of the words/ phrases in the glossary.

GLOSSARY
colony   a country that another country controls
plantation   a large farm
slave   a person who works for other people without pay
sugar beet   a vegetable that grows below ground and produces sugar
sugar cane   a small tree that grows above ground and produces sugar

b ▶ Watch the video and number the things below in the order you see them. All of the things contain or use sugar.

- cakes
- chocolate
- sugar cane
- sugar beet
- sugar cubes
- bags of sugar

c Watch again and choose the correct answer.

1 In the 1970s, how much sugar did people in Britain eat?
   a They ate 4 million tons of sugar every year.
   b They ate more sugar than now.
   c They didn't eat as much sugar as now.

2 Where did the first people grow sugar 8,000 years ago?
   a in India
   b in the Mediterranean
   c in Papua New Guinea

3 Why did people call sugar 'white gold' 500 years ago?
   a because it was difficult to find
   b because it was so expensive
   c because of its colour

4 Why did sugar become cheaper?
   a because transport became cheaper
   b because it was easy to grow in the Caribbean
   c because people started to produce sugar in Europe

World view

4a Look at the statements and tick the ones that you think are true for your country.

> ❝ Most people in my country put sugar in tea/coffee.

> ❝ It's normal to have something sweet (e.g. cereal, cake) for breakfast.

> ❝ Health experts say we should eat less sugar.

> ❝ People usually have a dessert at the end of a meal.

> ❝ My country is famous for its desserts.

b Work in pairs and compare your answers.

🛜 FIND OUT MORE

5a What do you know about food/desserts from different countries/regions? Look at the desserts in the box below. Do you know what they are or where they come from?

....

arroz con leche   baklava   gulab jamun
quindim   sticky toffee pudding

....

b Go online to find out more about three of the desserts above (or another dessert you like) and answer the questions.

1 What's the dessert's country of origin?
2 Where is it popular?
3 What are the main ingredients?

....

Search: name of dessert + origin / name of dessert + recipe / name of dessert + ingredients

....

▶ Write up your research

6 Write a paragraph about some of the desserts you researched. Use the prompts below to help you.

_____ is a popular dessert in _____. The main ingredients are _____ , _____ and _____.
People usually serve it with _____.
I'd like / wouldn't like to try it because _____.

AFTER UNIT 11 YOU CAN ...

Talk about what you like doing and what you would like to do.

....

Ask and answer questions about imaginary situations.

....

Take part in a survey and discuss the results.

....

Talk about food from different countries.

IT'S A FACT!
The word logo originally comes from a Greek word meaning *word* or *thought*.

WHAT MAKES A GOOD BRAND GREAT?

Nowadays, clothes aren't just clothes, and drinks aren't just drinks: they're brands. But what – apart from a good product – makes a good brand great?

A good name is the first thing. Ideally, it should be memorable and it should be easy to say in any language (think Zara, or Coca-Cola). When Steve Jobs and Steve Wozniak started their computer company in the 1970s they considered names like Matrix Electronics. But Jobs once worked on an apple farm in California and that gave him the idea for Apple Computers.

Spelling isn't important either. Google was originally 'Googol' (which refers to a number 1 followed by 100 zeros – indicating the amount of knowledge it would make available on the internet). Some popular brand names have surprising origins. Starbucks is named after a character in the American novel *Moby Dick*, and the founders of Yahoo! got the name from the English classic book *Gulliver's Travels*.

You also need a good logo. Millions of dollars are spent every year by companies looking for ways to give the consumer a clear, simple image of the product. Although the person who created the Nike 'swoosh' received just $35 for it! But money doesn't guarantee popularity:

the logo for the London Olympic Games of 2012 cost £400,000 and took a year to design ... and proved to be unpopular with almost everyone.

Colours are also important. Red represents passion and excitement, white represents purity and simplicity (although in some countries white is the colour of death). Blue is the 'male' colour, yellow is good for eye-catching messages, while green signifies nature, quietness and calm. And of course you need a slogan. Slogans have to be simple and easy to remember – but not necessarily grammatical: McDonald's *'I'm lovin' it'* and French Connection's *'You are man?'* are both not quite correct English!

It also helps if your product is supported by the right celebrity. When Barack Obama drank from a bottle of Buxton mineral water during a visit to the UK, sales of the water increased immediately. Product placement like this has become big business since the 1980s. *Transformers: Revenge of the Fallen* currently holds the record for the movie with most product placement. If you watch carefully, you will see that 47 different products are shown!

Reading and vocabulary

Types of product

1a Match the products/services in the box with the logos. (Some companies produce more than one type of product.)

clothes	electronic goods	soft drinks
internet search engine	sportswear	fast food
chocolate bars	coffee and pastries	trainers
accessories	electronic mail	

  COSTA

b Look at the logos again and read the article. Which of the companies are mentioned?

2 Read the text again and answer the questions.

1 Where did Steve Jobs have a job on a fruit farm?
2 Who was the original Mr Starbuck?
3 How much did the designer of the Nike 'swoosh' receive?
4 How long did it take to design the London Olympics logo?
5 Which colour has different meanings in some cultures?
6 Why did sales of Buxton mineral water suddenly increase?
7 How many different products can you see in *Transformers: Revenge of the Fallen*?

3 Work in groups and discuss.

- Which brand mentioned in the text has the best name? Why?
- Which do you think is more important for a brand: the name or the logo? Why?
- Are there any brands from your country that are famous internationally? Which ones?

Grammar focus 1

Present simple passive

1 Look at the verbs in bold in the sentences below. Which are passive forms and which are active forms?

1 Some popular brand names **have** surprising origins.
2 Green **signifies** nature, quietness and calm.
3 Millions of dollars **are spent** every year by companies.
4 It helps if your product **is supported** by the right celebrity.

GRAMMAR

1 Look again at the verbs in bold in the sentences 3 and 4 in exercise 1. How do we form the Present simple passive?

2a Who or what is the subject of sentences 3 and 4?

b In sentence 3, who spends millions of dollars?

c In sentence 4, who advertises the product?

d In sentences 3 and 4, are we more interested in the action or the person/people who do the action?

PRACTICE

1 Complete the sentences with the Present simple passive of the verbs in brackets.

1 KFC fast food restaurants _____ (find) in more than 100 countries worldwide.
2 The sportswear company Nike _____ (name) after the Greek goddess of victory.
3 The logo of the soft drinks company Coca-Cola _____ (recognise) all over the world.
4 Hershey's _____ (describe) as 'the greatest American chocolate bar'.
5 Four colours (blue, red, yellow and green) _____ (use) in the logos for both Google and Windows.
6 Free wi-fi _____ (provide) in most Costa Coffee shops.
7 The company Monsoon _____ (divide) into two parts: Monsoon for clothes and Accessorize for accessories.
8 Millions of iPods and iPads _____ (sell) every year around the world.

2a Match questions 1–6 with possible answers a–f.

1 Which brand of sportswear is supported by David Beckham?
2 What colours are used on the Burger King logo?
3 How many different brands of mineral water are sold around the world?
4 What is provided free with every McDonald's happy meal in some countries?
5 What animal is used on the logo for Ferrari?
6 Which chocolate bar is described as something to enjoy during a break at work or school?

a a Mars bar or a KitKat bar
b a toy or a piece of fruit
c Adidas or Nike
d a black panther or a black horse
e about 300 or about 3,000
f brown, yellow and blue or red, yellow and blue

b Work in pairs and decide what you think the correct answers are for all the questions.

Unit 12, Study & Practice 1, page 160

Vocabulary
Personal items

1a Work in pairs and discuss. Which of these things can you see in the advertisements?

- jewellery
- cosmetics
- toiletries
- hair products
- products for men

b Put the words in the box into the five groups above.

perfume   aftershave   lipstick   comb   earrings
nail varnish   shaving foam   deodorant   hairbrush
necklace   eyeliner   hair gel   moisturiser
razor   bracelet

c Can you add one more item to each list? Compare your ideas with other students.

2 Work in pairs and discuss. Which of the items in the box in exercise 1:

1 is advertised a lot on TV?
2 is usually very expensive?
3 have you given to someone as a present?
4 would you like to receive as a present?
5 have you bought in the last month?
6 have you never bought?
7 have you used today?
8 do you take with you when you go out / go on holiday?

3a Look at the pictures on page 135 and try to remember as many details about them as you can.

b 12.1 Cover the pictures and listen to ten questions about the items. Write short answers for each one.

1 It was pink.

Grammar focus 2

Past simple passive

1a Read the information below. Work in pairs and choose the correct answers.

ADVERTISING: FACTS AND FIGURES

1 The first TV advert in the world was shown in the USA in 1941. It was a 20-second advert for **Gibbs toothpaste / Bulova watches**.

2 The world's most expensive advert was made in 2004. It was a two-minute advert for Chanel Nº5 perfume, starring Nicole Kidman. She was paid **$1 million / $5 million** for four days' work.

3 Actor and sportsman Isaiah Mustafa was not well-known before he starred in his first advert. In February 2010, he immediately became famous when he was chosen for the hugely successful **Old Spice aftershave / Gillette razors** campaign.

4 The famous Marlboro man cigarette adverts were first seen in 1955. TV adverts for cigarettes were later banned in **1971 / 1991**.

5 In **2003 / 2007**, McDonald's first global advertising campaign was launched. The 'I'm lovin' it' campaign, featuring Justin Timberlake, was different because the same slogan was used in over 100 countries at the same time.

6 In 2011, during the TV showing of the Superbowl in the USA, around $3 million was spent on each **30-second / two-minute** advertising spot.

b 🎧 **12.2** Listen and check your answers. Which of the facts surprised you?

GRAMMAR

1 Underline the passive forms in the sentences below.
1 The world's most expensive advert was made in 2004.
2 TV adverts for cigarettes were banned in 1971.

2 How do we form the Past simple passive?

3 Why would you choose the passive sentences above instead of these active sentences?
1 They made the world's most expensive advert in 2004.
2 They banned TV adverts for cigarettes in 1971.

4 Look again at the advertising facts and figures. Underline all the Past simple passive forms you can find.

PRONUNCIATION

1 Notice that the pronunciation of regular past participles can be:

a /ɪd/ e.g. started   b /d/ e.g. named   c /t/ e.g. watched

2 Look at the list of regular past participles. Are they pronounced like a, b or c?

considered	needed	looked	created
received	proved	represented	loved
helped	supported	increased	appeared

3 🎧 **12.3** Listen and check. Practise saying the past participles.

PRACTICE

1 Choose the correct form (active or passive) to complete the sentences.

1 The disposable razor **invented / was invented** by King Camp Gillette about 100 years ago.
2 The most expensive earrings ever **created / were created** by the House of Winston jewellery designers in 2006. They are worth $8.5 million.
3 The first kind of lipstick **worn / was worn** by the Ancient Egyptians. In 1884, a perfume company in Paris **sold / was sold** the first modern lipstick.
4 Nail varnish **invented / was invented** in the 1920s. At first, the colours were only reds and purples. Other colours like blue, gold and black **introduced / were introduced** in the 1990s.
5 Hungarian László Biro **invented / was invented** the world's first ballpoint pen in the 1930s.
6 The most expensive item ever sold on eBay was a yacht. It **bought / was bought** by Russian billionaire Roman Abramovich in 2006 for $168 million.
7 The first DVD players **manufactured / were manufactured** in 1997 in Japan. In 2007, 7.3 million DVD players **sold / were sold** in the UK, but the number has dropped since then with the rise of the internet.
8 Ingvar Kamrad **started / was started** the Swedish furniture company IKEA more than 50 years ago. He **named / was named** the company after his own initials (IK), his parents' home (Elmtaryd = E) and his home village (Agunnaryd = A).

> Unit 12, Study & Practice 2, page 160

Task

Present a new product

Preparation Reading and listening

1 Look at the photo and read the paragraph about the *Dragons' Den* TV programme. Work in pairs and discuss the questions.

- What is the aim of the programme?
- What is one of the most successful products from the show?
- Do you have any similar programmes in your country?

Dragons' Den is a TV series in the UK. In each programme, several people present their new products and business ideas to five rich and successful businesspeople, called the 'dragons'. Each person talks about their new product or idea and then asks the dragons for money to invest in their new companies. A man called Levi Roots presented one of the most successful ideas on the programme. He developed a sauce from a traditional Jamaican recipe and called it Reggae Reggae Sauce. He made it in his own kitchen and desperately needed investment, as he only had $20 left. The 'dragons' invested in his product and now his business is worth over $30 million.

2a 🎧 12.4 Listen to someone presenting a new product and complete the table.

	Your notes
Type of product	
Name	
Slogan	
Important points	
Target market	
Money needed	

b Listen again and tick the phrases you hear in the Useful language box.

3 Work in groups and discuss.

- What do you think about this new product?
- Would you change anything about it, e.g. the name, the slogan, important points?
- Do you think this product could be successful? Why / Why not?

Task Speaking

1 Imagine you are going to take part in a programme similar to *Dragons' Den*. Work in pairs and choose one of the products in the list below.

- a personal item (e.g. cosmetics, jewellery, toiletries)
- something to eat or drink (e.g. fizzy drink, chocolate bar, biscuit, breakfast cereal)
- a gadget, new technology or a new feature for a phone

2a Work in pairs. Prepare for your presentation by making notes in the table. Use some of the ideas in the pictures below to help you or invent your own.

	Your notes
Type of product	
Name	
Slogan	
Special features	
How/Why you first thought about the idea	
Target market	
How much you need to produce your idea	

All you need is your phone

If you don't have it, get it

Smaller but bigger

Good morning! Very good morning!

Go on, have one!

Energy all day

You're amazing! *Just for you*

All right – all white

b Divide your presentation into three parts using the Useful language box to help you. Remember to include appropriate phrases in your presentation.

> Useful language a, b and c

3a Present your product to other students.

b Work in groups. Decide which product you think is the best and why.

SHARE YOUR TASK

Practise presenting your product until you feel confident.

Film/Record yourself presenting your product.

Share your film/recording with other students.

LANGUAGE LIVE

Speaking
Making and responding to suggestions

1 Work in pairs and discuss.

- Have you bought any expensive items in the last few months/years?
- What decisions did you make before you bought them, e.g. brand, price, colour, etc.?
- What suggestions or advice did you get from friends, family or shop assistants?

2 ▶ Watch the video and answer the questions.

1 What does the woman want to buy?
2 How many people give her suggestions?

3 Watch again and complete the gaps in the sentences below.

1 _____ don't you buy a new one?
2 I _____ so.
3 How _____ a smartphone?
4 Good _____ .
5 We _____ go there now.
6 All right. _____ go!
7 _____ we look at some over here?
8 You _____ get one of these.
9 Well, _____ but ...

1 ▶ Watch and listen to the key phrases for making and responding to suggestions.

2 Practise saying them. Add the phrases to the groups below.

Making suggestions	Agreeing	Disagreeing
What about ... ?	All right.	I don't think so. No, I'd prefer to ...

4a Work in pairs and choose one of the situations below. Prepare a conversation of 8–10 lines.

- Your partner is going to stay with an English-speaking family for a month and wants to buy a present to give them. He/She only has a small space in his/her suitcase. Make suggestions about what to buy.
- You are trying to decide what to buy to wear for a special occasion (e.g. a wedding or a party). You don't want to spend too much money. Your partner will make some suggestions.
- You and your partner are going to cook dinner for some friends. One of the friends is a vegetarian. Make suggestions together about what to cook.

b Practise your conversations and take turns to make suggestions and respond to them.

★ ★ ★ ★ ☆

1 PERFECT FOR YOUR HOLIDAY
By <u>Andrew Morton</u>
(Liverpool, England)

I bought these to wear on my holiday in Spain and they are really **well-designed** and **fashionable**. **They're made of** canvas, so they're very **comfortable** – perfect for when you're at the swimming pool. **The price was very reasonable** too … in fact, I think they **were** definitely **worth the money**. They arrived in the post only two days after I ordered them too. **Highly recommended**!

★ ★ ★ ☆ ☆

2 AN IDEAL PRESENT
By <u>Anne Piper (Mrs)</u>
(Watford)

I bought this as a birthday present for my teenage son and now he's playing on it 16 hours a day! There is a great choice of games. **The only problem was** it was quite difficult to connect it to my TV. I phoned technical support a couple of times and they were very helpful, so we solved the problem quickly. Now we enjoy playing games together. **Good for the whole family!**

★ ☆ ☆ ☆ ☆

3 BELOW AVERAGE!
By <u>Shona</u>
(West Midlands)

My old hairdryer was broken, so I decided to buy a new one on the internet. This one **looked nice** in the box, and **I like the colour** (blue), but **I was disappointed with it**. When I was drying my hair, the dryer was very noisy. Also, it was not as powerful as I expected it to be and it took me a long time to dry my hair. **I don't recommend this** as it was **not good value for money**.

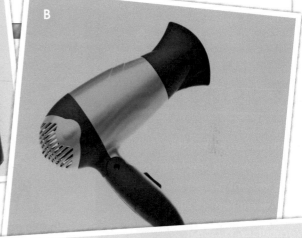

Writing
A customer review

1 Look at the three products in the photos. Read the consumer reviews from an online shopping website and answer the questions.

   1 Which product is each person reviewing?
   2 Is each review generally positive or negative?

2 Read the reviews again and look at the words/ phrases in bold. Which show:

   1 positive points about the product?
   2 negative points about the product?

3a Choose one of the products below (or a product you have bought recently).

   • an item of clothing (e.g. swimwear, sunglasses, T-shirt, trainers)
   • a gadget (e.g. a personal computer, a pair of headphones, a camera)
   • a DVD, CD or video game
   • a personal item (jewellery, cosmetics, hair products)

b Write a review of the product. Use about 80–100 words and include information about:

   • why you bought it
   • good points about the product
   • bad points about the product
   • if you would recommend it to other people and why / why not

AFTER UNIT 12 YOU CAN …

Take part in a discussion on brands and products.

Present a new product.

Make and respond to suggestions in different situations.

Write a consumer review about a product.

13

THE RIGHT PERSON

FINDING MR RIGHT

In this age of uncertainty, perhaps we can learn something from arranged marriages? Laura Simpson finds out.

They are seen by many people as business deals that have little to do with love. But experts claim that you are more likely to find happiness in an 'arranged' marriage than in a 'love' marriage. According to research by American academic Robert Epstein, people who have arranged marriages or people who have chosen a partner in a business like way, over time usually feel more in love, whereas those in regular 'love' marriages feel less in love. He reveals that after ten years of marriage, there is twice as much affection in arranged marriages than in other marriages.

Other research, by Reva Seth in her book, *First Comes Marriage*, supports this. She talked to more than 300 women whose marriages were arranged or chosen deliberately. According to Reva, the divorce rate for such marriages is around 6 percent. This compares with a 40 percent divorce rate in the UK, where 'love' marriages are normal. Reva found her own husband by 'arranging' it for herself in a thoughtful way. She wrote down the characteristics and interests that she wanted in a husband and then went to as many social engagements as she could. She got engaged to her husband after meeting him seven times. 'As we started talking,' she says, 'I could tell he was involved in lots of things that interested me, and I got a sense that he could be a person I could fall in love with. I wasn't in love with him when we got engaged. But I had a strong sense that this was what I was looking for.'

Five years later, Reva is happily married with a two-year-old son. Her research and her own experience have led her to strongly support the principles of arranged marriage. Her findings are clear: you are more likely to have a happy marriage if you think about common backgrounds, shared values and personal characteristics, than if you rely on falling in love by chance, as many Hollywood films would like us to believe.

Reading

1 Work in groups and discuss.

- Do you think it is easy or difficult to find (a) the right partner/husband/wife, (b) the right flatmate and (c) the right person for a job? Why?
- What different ways do you know of finding each one? Give details.

2 Read the article about arranged marriages. According to the article, is the research generally positive, generally negative or mixed?

3 Read the article again and decide if the statements are true (T) or false (F). Correct the false statements.

1 Robert Epstein's research says that people in 'love' marriages are usually happier than people in 'arranged' marriages.
2 In Britain, 40 percent of people in arranged marriages get divorced.
3 Before Reva Seth met her husband, she thought about the type of person she was interested in.
4 When she decided to get married, Reva Seth was already in love with her future husband.
5 Reva Seth believes her arranged marriage has been successful.
6 It's more important to think about common backgrounds than personal characteristics.

4 Work in pairs. Read the comments below and discuss the questions.

- Which comments do you agree/disagree with? Why?
- Would you ever try to meet someone on an internet dating site? Why / Why not?
- In your country, at what age do people usually get married?

> 'There is a big difference between this type of 'arranged' marriage and the 'forced' type of arranged marriages. I think arranged marriages like this are really good. It doesn't matter that you're not in love with each other.'

> 'Internet dating sites are the modern-day arranged marriage. You can find out about a new partner in a clear and business-like way. It's better than meeting someone at a party.'

> 'I totally disagree with any kind of arranged marriage. I really think that marriage is about love and that people should marry someone who they are really in love with.'

IT'S A FACT! The average age for marriage in the UK was 22 years old in 1966, 25 in 1999 and 30 in 2011.

Vocabulary
Personal characteristics

1 Work in pairs. Write three adjectives which describe your personality. Compare your adjectives and try to explain why you chose them.

2a Complete the sentences below with the words in the box.

....
~~sympathetic~~ affectionate ambitious easy-going
hard-working honest open organised patient
reliable sensitive sociable
....

He's very _sympathetic_ to other people – he listens when they have problems.
1 She's always _____ – she always tells the truth.
2 He's a very _____ person – he arranges things well and plans things properly.
3 She's very _____ – she's friendly and enjoys being with other people.
4 He's a _____ person – he always works a lot.
5 She's very _____ – she's very good at understanding other people feelings.
6 He's _____ – you always know that he will do what he says.
7 She's _____ – she really wants to do well in her career.
8 He's _____ – he doesn't get upset or annoyed very easily.
9 She's a very _____ person – she finds it easy to talk about her feelings.
10 He's a very _____ person – he is good at waiting calmly without getting angry.
11 She's very _____ – she shows in a gentle way that she cares about people.

b Work in pairs and compare your answers.

3a Work in pairs and discuss.

- Which three adjectives from exercise 2a do you think:
  - most apply to you?
  - definitely don't apply to you?
- Which three personal characteristics do you think are most important in:
  - a partner/husband/wife?
  - a teacher?
  - a student?
  - a colleague?

b Compare your ideas with other students.

Grammar focus 1

Present perfect continuous with *how long*, *for* and *since*

1 Work in pairs and discuss.
- What do you think is difficult about sharing a flat with other people? Why?
- What are the three most important personal characteristics of a flatmate? Why?

2 Two friends, Maddie and Tom, are looking for another flatmate. Read the emails they received. Work in pairs. Which person do you think sounds like the best new flatmate? Why?

3 🎧 13.1 Listen to Maddie and Tom discussing which flatmate to choose. Did they choose the same one as you? Do you think they have made the right decision? Why / Why not?

findaflatmate.com

Fabio

'I'm easy-going and sociable.'

My name's Fabio. I'm Brazilian and I'm 25. I've never shared a flat before – I've been living with my aunt since I came to London three years ago. My aunt does everything for me! She cooks for me and does my washing, but now I'll do these things for myself. I'm easy-going and sociable – and I like talking to people. I earn a good salary as I've been working as an accountant for two years.

Anicka

'I'm very reliable, and I can cook.'

I'm Anicka. I'm 22 and I'm from the Czech Republic. I've been renting my own flat in London for two years, but now I'd like to pay less rent. I work in a restaurant in the evenings to earn money. I'm very reliable, and I can cook! I also play the piano – I've been playing the piano since I was three. I'm ambitious, so I need to practise between four and eight hours a day. Will there be space for my piano?

Liam

'I'm very hard-working and I like being alone.'

My name is Liam and I'm 28. I'm from Ireland, but I've been living in England since 2005. I've been working in computers for ten years and I run my own business – repairing and selling computers. I earn good money, I'm very hard-working and I like being alone. I will share the housework, but I need some space to keep a few computers. Also, I can fix any problems with your computer free of charge!

GRAMMAR

1 Look at the examples of the Present perfect continuous below. How do we form the Present perfect continuous?
  1 I**'ve been living** with my aunt since I came to London.
  2 I**'ve been working** as an accountant for two years.

2a In sentence 1, is he living with his aunt now?

 b In sentence 2, is he working as an accountant now? When did he start doing this?

3 Which of these phrases do we use with *for*? Which do we use with *since*?

two years   1965   last year   2004   Tuesday
five hours   six o'clock   six months   October
I came to London   I was a child

PRONUNCIATION

1 With the Present perfect continuous, we often use contracted forms when we speak, for example:

He has been working = He's been working
You have been living = You've been living

2 🎧 **13.2** Look at audio script 13.2 on page 174. Listen to the full and contracted forms.

3 Listen again and practise saying the contracted forms.

PRACTICE

1a Write questions about Fabio, Anicka and Liam using *How long* ... and the prompts.

Fabio / live with his aunt?
How long has Fabio been living with his aunt?

1 Fabio / work as an accountant?
2 Anicka / rent her own flat?
3 Anicka / play the piano?
4 Liam / live in the UK?
5 Liam / work in computers?

 b Answer the questions in exercise 1a, using the words in brackets below and the information in the emails in exercise 2 on page 116.

  (since) *He's been living with his aunt since he came to London.*
1 (for) _____
2 (for) _____
3 (since) _____
4 (since) _____
5 (for) _____

2a Read the information about Sumiko. Where does she live? What is her job?

Sumiko Tanaka came to New York to study graphic design six years ago. Two years later, she got a job in a top graphic design company, designing magazines and brochures. While she was working for the company, she met her partner, Michael. They got married and bought a flat together three years ago. She stayed in the job for two years and then decided to start her own business with her husband. 'I enjoyed working for the company,' she said, 'but it's great to run my own business, especially as I work with Michael.'

 b 🎧 **13.3** Listen to four questions about Sumiko. Write answers to the questions using *for* and *since*.

3a Complete the sentences below about you. You can use true information or you can invent different facts about yourself.

1 I live in a ... (flat/house/ ...) in ... (London/Quito/Barcelona/ ...)
2 I work as ... (a designer / an accountant / ...)
3 I study ... (English / jewellery design / ...)
4 I play ... (tennis / the piano / ...)
5 I am a member of ... (a football team / a choir / ...)
6 I can ... (drive a car / speak Russian / ...)

 b Work in pairs. Ask and answer questions about your partner's information. Ask extra questions to find out more details.

How long have you been living in Kuala Lumpur?

I've been living here for about three months.

Do you enjoy it here?

Yes, I love living here because ...

Unit 13, Study & Practice 1, page 162

Grammar focus 2
Present perfect continuous and Present perfect simple

1 Work in pairs. Look at the list of different ways to look for a job. Which do you think are the most/least effective? Why?

- look online
- look in a newspaper
- ask family and friends
- go to the company with your CV
- phone and ask for an interview
- queue up for an audition

2 Read the newspaper article and decide if the statements are true (T) or false (F).

1 People were queuing up because they wanted a job.
2 Marco Pierre White is the manager of the Hotel Indigo.
3 Sam Jones already has a job.
4 Catherine Emberson doesn't like this way of interviewing people.
5 Marco Pierre White was one of the interview panel.

Two-minute audition for job at celebrity restaurant

Hundreds of people queued patiently today to try for one of 50 jobs at celebrity chef Marco Pierre White's new Liverpool restaurant. The X-Factor-style auditions were an opportunity to work in Marco Pierre White's Steakhouse Bar and Grill, part of the new £15m Hotel Indigo, which opens in June. Applicants had only two minutes to make a good impression on a panel of hotel and restaurant managers. First in the queue was 20-year-old Sam Jones, from Liverpool. 'I've wanted to work in a restaurant all my life. I've applied for hundreds of jobs, but I haven't been lucky so far,' she told us. 18-year-old Lucy Withall told us, 'I've been taking cookery lessons for three months and I've learnt how to make many top dishes. This is my big chance to work for a top chef.' Catherine Emberson and her friend Rebecca Chan were not so impressed. 'We've been waiting for more than two hours. Why can't we apply for jobs in the normal way?' A statement from chef Marco said: 'We're looking for enthusiastic people who have a passion for food.' Mr White, who is filming a new cookery series in Italy, was not at the auditions.

3 Work in pairs and discuss.

- What do you think of auditions as a way of applying for a job?
- Would you like to work as a chef in a top restaurant? Why / Why not?

1 How do we form the Present perfect continuous and the Present perfect simple?

2 Look again at the sentences in exercise 4. Which sentence (1 or 2) describes the time spent doing the action, and which sentence (1 or 2) describes the number of things done?

3 Why don't we use the continuous form with the verb *wanted* in sentence 3?

4 Look at the sentences below and answer the questions. Which two verbs in bold are the Present perfect simple? Which verb in bold is the Present perfect continuous?

1 We**'ve been waiting** for more than two hours.
2 I**'ve applied** for hundreds of jobs.
3 I**'ve wanted** to work in a restaurant all my life.

5 Look again at the text in exercise 2 and find one more example of:

1 a Present perfect continuous verb (focussing on the action/time)
2 a Present perfect simple verb (focussing on the number of things done)
3 a Present perfect simple verb (using a state verb)

PRACTICE

1a Work in pairs and take turns to ask and answer the questions. If your partner answers *Yes*, you can ask the 'follow-up' questions. Make a note of your partner's answers.

1 Are you learning another language?
   Follow-up questions: What language are you learning? / How long have you been learning it?
2 Do you own a car?
   Follow-up questions: How long have you owned your car? / How long have you been driving?
3 Do you have a pet?
   Follow-up questions: What's it called? / How long have you had your pet?
4 Do you play a sport?
   Follow-up questions: Which sport do you play? / How long have you been playing it?

b Tell other students two interesting things you found out about your partner.

> Unit 13, Study & Practice 2, page 162

Vocabulary
Getting a job

1a Work in pairs and discuss.

- Is finding a job a problem in your country?
- What would be your ideal job?

b Read the questions from a website giving advice about jobs. Match the questions to the answers below.

GOV.WEB   Home   Help   Feedback

Getting a job: your questions answered

Q

A: I've just left school. I'm unemployed and I need to **look for a job** … but I don't know where to start!! Can you help?

B: I want to get a **part-time job** over the summer at a fast food restaurant. Is it better to **apply online** or in person?

C: What information should I include when I **write a CV**?

D: I'm **going for an interview** in a local fashion store. What tips can you give me about how to dress?

E: I am worried about making mistakes with my English when I **fill in an application form**.

A

1 Wear clothes that are appropriate for the job you want. You don't need to wear a suit and tie when you apply for a job in a coffee shop, but don't go for an interview at a fashion store wearing an old T-shirt and a pair of dirty jeans. Good luck!

2 Include your **personal details** (full name, address, etc.), information about your **education and qualifications** and your skills (e.g. languages, **computing skills**, driving licence). Remember that the interviewer probably has a lot of CVs to read, so keep it short and easy to read.

3 Get an English-speaking friend to check it for you, or you can find some useful phrases from different job websites.

4 Look for **job vacancies** in the local newspaper and **log on to** some **job websites**. You can also register with **recruitment agencies** and ask friends and family if they know about any jobs.

5 Generally, it's better to go in person and ask to see the manager. Choose a time when the restaurant isn't too busy: mid-morning is best. Take your CV with you and if you don't hear anything, phone back a few days later.

2a Match words in A with words in B to make phrases connected with applying for a job. Then do the same with the words in C and D.

A		B	
1	log on to	a	online
2	go for	b	a job
3	apply	c	job websites
4	fill in	d	an interview
5	look for	e	an application form
6	write	f	a CV (= Curriculum Vitae)

C		D	
1	education	a	agency
2	computing	b	details
3	job	c	job
4	a part-time	d	and qualifications
5	personal	e	skills
6	a recruitment	f	vacancies

b Work in pairs and check your answers in the text.

3a Work in groups and write five pieces of advice for an English-speaking person looking for a job in your country.

b Compare your advice with other students. What were the best two pieces of advice?

Task

Choose an ambassador

Preparation Reading

1 Work in pairs. Read the text below and discuss the questions.

- What kinds of issues do Goodwill Ambassadors want to make people aware of?
- What kinds of people usually become Goodwill Ambassadors?
- Which of the Goodwill Ambassadors in the text do you know about?

WHAT IS A GOODWILL AMBASSADOR?

A Goodwill Ambassador is a representative of his/her country who, as well as his/her usual job, works for a charity or organisation. He/She travels to other countries, creating friendly links between countries and raising awareness of problems (including poverty, environmental issues and disease). The people who are chosen are usually well-known, such as celebrities, scientists, authors and businesspeople. They try to use their fame and their knowledge to influence people and create change. Famous Goodwill Ambassadors recently include Angelina Jolie (for the United Nations), Lionel Messi (for UNICEF) and Veronica Varekova (for the African Wildlife Foundation).

THE CANDIDATES

A

Don Barris is a hero to millions of young sports fans around the world. He now lives in Florida, where he plays for the local basketball team. As a child, his ambition was to be a doctor and he still has a strong interest in medicine. He frequently visits hospitals in the United States and in his native Fredonia. He has taught himself French, Spanish and Chinese. He describes himself as 'a good family man, but a little shy'.

B

Millionaire businesswoman Deborah Curtin made a fortune selling Fredonian fashion to the world. She is now best-known as a judge on the popular TV show *Mean Business*. She owns a chain of fashion shops around the world and is the author of the best-selling book *How to make £1 into £1 million*. Still living in Fredonia, she supports a local scheme to help Fredonians start their own, environmentally-friendly businesses.

2a The island of Fredonia is going to choose its first Goodwill Ambassador. There are four candidates. Read about each candidate above and match quotations 1–4 with candidates A–D.

1 When I talk business, people listen.
2 I will not rest until poverty is abolished.
3 We can unite the world through sport.
4 I am the most famous Fredonian in the world. I want to use my fame to raise awareness of the world's issues.

b Read the texts again and answer the questions.

1 Which two candidates don't live in Fredonia?
2 Which two candidates have worked in television?
3 Which two candidates work on projects to help people?
4 Which candidate speaks other languages?
5 Which candidate isn't known around the world?

3a 🎧 13.4 Listen to two people discussing the candidates. Which three candidates do they talk about? Do they agree?

b Listen again and tick the phrases you hear in the Useful language box.

C

D

Unknown outside Fredonia, lawyer Tracey Valentine grew up in poverty in the Fredonian capital, St Paul's. An orphan at the age of 12, she looked after her five brothers and sisters while studying at night school to become a lawyer. She still lives in Fredonia and now specialises in environmental issues. Two years ago, she began the Valentine Foundation, which helps the poorest children in St Paul's to receive an education.

Singer and actor Pete Power is one of the world's hottest celebrities. After winning a talent show, his first single was Number One in more than 20 countries. And his latest song *Let's Help the World* is another huge international success. He has appeared on American TV in the popular soap opera *Hearts and Flowers*, and he now lives in Hollywood where he wants to start a career in movies.

Task Speaking

1a Work in pairs and make notes for each candidate under the following headings.

- Personal characteristics
- Useful experience
- Interest in important issues
- Ability to talk to media/politicians
- Worldwide fame

b Who do you think is the best candidate? Number the candidates from 1–4. 1 = best, 4 = worst.

2a You are going to try to decide who should be the Goodwill Ambassador. Prepare what you are going to say by using your notes to give reasons for your choice. Ask your teacher for any words/phrases you need.

> Useful language a and b

b Work in pairs. Take turns to say who you think should be the Goodwill Ambassador and why. Use your notes to persuade your partner to agree with you.

> Useful language a, b and c

3 Work in larger groups and compare your ideas. Agree on the best candidate.

WORLD CULTURE

THE SEARCH FOR COOL

Find out first

1a Work in pairs and discuss. One of the ways people define 'cool' is by the clothes they wear. Do you know what these 'cool' items of clothing are? In which decade(s) were these items fashionable?

- trainers
- flared jeans
- fedora
- bandana

b Go online to check your answers or ask your teacher.

Search: trainers / flared jeans / fedora / bandana + image

View

2a You are going to watch a video about 'the search for cool'. Before you watch, check you understand the meaning of the words/phrases in the glossary.

GLOSSARY

go mad for something	to really love something
launch	when a company puts a new product on the market
check out	find out
to be obsessed with something	to think about something all the time
to get out of hand	to become too important

b ▶ Watch the video and decide if the statements about each person are true (T) or false (F).

1 Martin Cole works only in the UK.
2 Martin helps companies to make adverts.
3 The man isn't happy with his new trainers.
4 He probably buys trainers quite often.
5 Neil Boorman never buys cool designer brands.
6 Neil is going to burn some of his clothes.

3a Complete phrases 1–6 with the words in the box.

clothes   trainer   dream   cool   free   products

1 This is Martin Cole. For some people, he has a _____ job.
2 More and more, he finds they're looking for one thing – they want their _____ to be cool.
3 And everyone thinks they know what _____ is.
4 An easy way to show how cool you are is through your _____ .
5 These people are at the launch of a new, limited edition _____.
6 Martin is going to meet someone who wants his life to be completely 'brand-_____' .

b Watch again and check your answers.

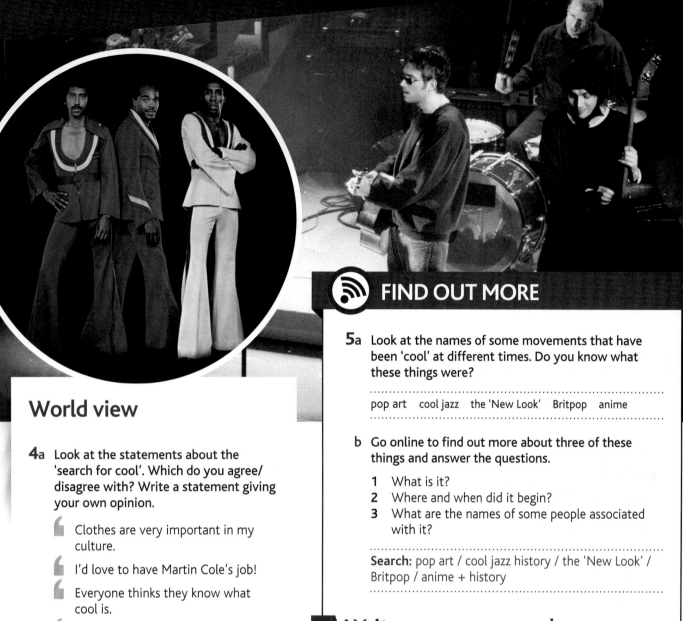

World view

4a Look at the statements about the 'search for cool'. Which do you agree/ disagree with? Write a statement giving your own opinion.

> Clothes are very important in my culture.

> I'd love to have Martin Cole's job!

> Everyone thinks they know what cool is.

> Being cool isn't at all important to me.

> I always notice if people are wearing designer brands.

> Neil Boorman has had a very good idea.

> Being kind is more important than being cool.

> I would rather be rich than cool.

b Work in pairs and compare your ideas.

5a Look at the names of some movements that have been 'cool' at different times. Do you know what these things were?

pop art   cool jazz   the 'New Look'   Britpop   anime

b Go online to find out more about three of these things and answer the questions.

1 What is it?
2 Where and when did it begin?
3 What are the names of some people associated with it?

Search: pop art / cool jazz history / the 'New Look' / Britpop / anime + history

▶ Write up your research

6 Write a paragraph about one of the movements you researched. Use the prompts below to help you.

_____ was a (fashion / music / art) movement in the _____.
It began in _____ (where?) in the _____ (when?).
Some of the people associated with it were in _____ (where?).
I am / am not interested in this movement because _____ (why?).

AFTER UNIT 13 YOU CAN ...

Describe your own personal characteristics and discuss those of others.

Talk about your views on different ways of meeting a husband/wife.

Discuss candidates for a job/flatshare and choose the best one.

MONEY FACTS

1 Over _____ countries use the dollar as their currency, including the USA, Canada, New Zealand, Australia, Ecuador and Singapore.

2 The Euro was first used on 1st January 2002. Over _____ people in more than 20 countries now use the Euro as their currency.

3 At the beginning of 2002, the euro-dollar exchange rate was €1 = $0.88. At the beginning of 2012, it was €1 = $_____.

4 The first cashpoint machine was used in 1967 in the UK. By 2019, it is expected that we will get approximately _____ percent of our money from cashpoints.

5 In 2010 in the UK, women carried an average of £ _____ cash in their purse or wallet.

6 In 2010, _____ credit cards were owned by people in the USA. 14 percent of Americans own more than ten credit cards.

7 On average, coins stay in use for approximately 30 years, whereas bank notes last about _____ year.

8 The smallest bank note in the world was made in Romania in 1917. It was a _____ 'bani' note and measured 2.75 x 3.8 cm.

9 In 2011, there were over _____ dollar billionaires in the world. Four of the top ten richest people in 2011 were from the USA. The rest were from Mexico, Brazil, France, Spain, the UK and India.

Vocabulary
Money

1 Look at the words in the box and answer the questions.

> coins bank notes change credit card receipt bill cashpoint
> foreign currency exchange rate purse wallet

Which of these things do you usually:
1 find in a handbag?
2 find in the street?
3 find in a bank?
4 get in a shop?
5 get in a café?
6 need when you travel abroad?

2a Work in pairs. Complete each statement in the Money facts above with the numbers in the box.

> 1   1.33   10   28   30   90   1,200   332 million   8 million

b 🎧 14.1 Listen and check your answers. Which fact(s) do you find most surprising? Did you know any of them already?

PRONUNCIATION

1 🎧 **14.2 Listen and write down the numbers you hear.**

2 Look at audio script 14.2 on page 174 to check your answers.

Notice that we say:
two thousand pounds (not: two <u>thousands</u> pounds)
four hundred and fifty (not: four hundred fifty)
nineteen point seven (not: nineteen <u>comma</u> seven)

3 Practise saying the numbers in the 'Money facts' in exercise 2a.

3 Work in groups and discuss.

- What currency is used in your country?
- What famous people (or places or things) are on your country's bank notes? Why?
- Do you know what the exchange rate of your currency to the US dollar is at the moment?
- Do you think it's better to pay with a credit card or with cash? Why?
- Have you ever complained about the bill in a café or restaurant? Why?
- Have you ever taken something back to a shop without a receipt? What happened?

Grammar focus 1
Past perfect

1 🎧 **14.3 Listen to three jokes. Which two people are in each joke? You do not need to use one of the options.**

a a comedian and a robber
b a car salesman and a bank manager
c a man and his millionaire friend
d a company boss and an employee

2 Listen again and write the last line of each joke. Which joke do you think is the funniest?

Joke 1: '_____,' said the young man.
Joke 2: '_____,' said the old man.
Joke 3: '_____,' said the millionaire.

GRAMMAR

1a Look at this sentence. Which verb is in the Past simple? Which is in the Past perfect?
He **had been** to the bank and he **was** on his way home.

b Which action was happening first: 'going to the bank' or 'on his way home'?

2 Look at audio script 14.3 on page 174. How many other examples of the Past perfect can you find?

PRACTICE

1a Complete the text with the verbs in the box.

~~sent~~   sold   discovered   had   was   wasn't   tried
had arrested   had arrived   had made   had bought
had sold

When, in 1926, a US court ¹ <u>sent</u> a man called Arthur Ferguson to prison for five years, it ² _____ the end of an amazing criminal career. The police ³ _____ him several months earlier as he ⁴ _____ to sell the Statue of Liberty to an Australian tourist. After the arrest, the police soon ⁵ _____ that Ferguson ⁶ _____ money by selling famous buildings several times before.
Ferguson ⁷ _____ in the United States from Scotland the previous year. Soon after his arrival, he ⁸ _____ a luxurious house in Washington to a rich Texas farmer. But for the farmer, this ⁹ _____ an ordinary house: he quickly realised that he ¹⁰ _____ the White House – the home of the US president for 150 years. Before coming to America, Ferguson ¹¹ _____ Buckingham Palace, home of the English royal family, for £2,000, Big Ben for £1,000 and Nelson's Column for £6,000 – all to rich Americans who perhaps ¹² _____ more money than intelligence.

b 🎧 **14.4 Listen and check your answers.**

2a Work in pairs and complete each sentence with a verb in the Past perfect and your own ideas.

1 Before I entered the shop, I ...
2 Several months before that day, I ...
3 When I looked in my wallet, I realised I ...

b Choose one of the sentences. With your partner, write a short story using your sentence as the first line. Write about 100 words.

c Work in groups and tell each other your stories.

Unit 14, Study & Practice 1, page 164

Vocabulary
Verbs and phrases about money

1 Work in pairs. Look at the verbs in bold in the questions and decide which ones increase the amount of money you have and which ones decrease the amount of money you have.

Have you ever:
1 **won** any money?
2 **lost** a large amount of money?
3 **earned** a lot of money?
4 **inherited** a lot money?
5 **spent** a lot of money on a present for someone?
6 **saved up** a lot of money to buy something?
7 **paid a fine** for something?
8 **lent** money **to** someone?
9 **borrowed** money **from** someone?
10 forgotten to **pay back** money you have borrowed?

2 Work in pairs and take turns to ask and answer the questions in exercise 1. Find out as much information as you can about each one.

How often do you borrow money from people?

Occasionally …

Grammar focus 2
Narrative tenses review

1 Read the story below and decide which of the headlines fits best.

a **What a waste of money!**

b **Never borrow money from your friends …**

c **Greedy George can't stop spending**

One day, Englishman George Jenkins was looking at his bank account online when he noticed there was an extra £100,000 in it. He started spending the money immediately. He organised expensive parties for his friends and bought things he hadn't been able to afford before. The money actually belonged to a much richer man with the same name, but when the bank realised their mistake, George had spent £85,000. A court ruled that the money wasn't his, and ordered him to pay back the full amount.

1 Look at the verbs in bold in the sentences below. Which verb(s) is/are:
  • Past simple?
  • Past continuous?
  • Past perfect?
  1 George **was looking** at his bank account when he **noticed** an extra £100,000 in it.
  2 When the bank **realised** their mistake, George **had spent** £85,000.

2 Look at the uses below of the three different narrative tenses and match them with the correct tense.
  1 to talk about the main events and actions in a story
  2 to talk about actions which happened before the main events in a story
  3 to talk about actions which describe the background to a story, or actions in progress at a certain time in the past

PRACTICE

1a Choose the correct answers.

A man in Germany ¹*had / was having* a horrible surprise when he ²*had checked / was checking* his email one morning. Thomas Vogel, aged 22, found he ³*had bought / was buying* items worth nearly €1 million from an internet auction company. Thomas said he ⁴*didn't hear / hadn't heard* of the company before and ⁵*didn't know / wasn't knowing* anything about the €800,000 house, the €100,000 car or the €25,000 small plane he ⁶*was buying / had bought*. The internet company ⁷*insisted / was insisting* he paid for the items, however, as it seemed that he ⁸*bought / had bought* the items in his name.

b 🎧 14.5 Listen and check your answers.

2 You are going to tell a story using narrative tenses and verbs/phrases in exercise 1 of the Vocabulary section. Work in groups and take turns to say one sentence of the story each.

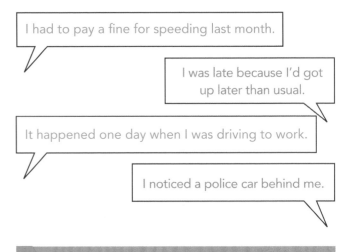

I had to pay a fine for speeding last month.

I was late because I'd got up later than usual.

It happened one day when I was driving to work.

I noticed a police car behind me.

Unit 14, Study & Practice 2, page 164

Reading

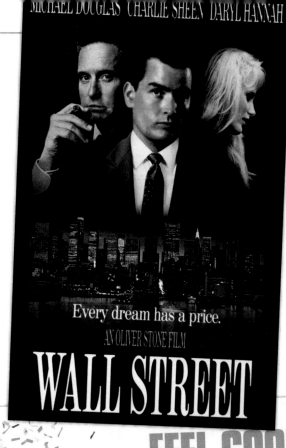

1 Work in pairs and discuss.

- Have you seen/heard about the films in the posters?
- What do you think the films are about?

2 Read the blog entry below and answer the questions.

1 When was each film made?
2 Which country does each film take place in?

3 Read the blog again. Which film is about:

1 someone who succeeds in money and love?
2 two men working in finance in the USA?
3 inheriting and spending money?
4 discovering that people are more important than money?
5 someone with a secret they can't tell?
6 what happens when you want money too much?
7 someone who doesn't have a job at the end of the film?
8 the life of a young boy?

4 Work in groups and discuss.

- Which of the films would you most/least like to see? Why?
- What other films can you think of which are about money?

💰 💰 💰 MONEY MOVIES

Money is a part of everyday life and can motivate people to be very good and sometimes also very bad. That's why money makes a great movie subject. Here are four of my favourites from the last three decades.

💰 *Brewster's Millions* (1985)

This classic comedy features Richard Pryor as a baseball player in the United States who is given an offer he can't refuse. He will inherit $300 million … but only if he spends $30 million in 30 days. But he mustn't spend it on himself and he can't tell anyone about the deal. Everyone thinks he's crazy as he starts spending the money. But, he soon discovers spending money is not as easy, or as fun, as he thinks.

💰 *Wall Street* (1987)

This classic movie, set in New York in the late eighties, comes with the slogan, 'greed is good'. And its money-hungry characters reflect that. Gordon Gekko is a stockbroker who worships money and the power that it gives him. Bud Fox is a young broker desperate to work with him, and the promise of financial success leads Fox into all kinds of trouble. This is a great film that takes a long, hard look at greed.

💰 *Jerry Maguire* (1996)

Jerry Maguire, played by Tom Cruise, is a typical sports agent in the USA, who values money and huge contracts above people and their feelings. Then, one day, he changes his mind and realises that people and their feelings are more important than money. He then loses his job, and his career is ruined, but that's when he discovers what and who is most important in life.

💰 *Slumdog Millionaire* (2008)

Dev Patel stars as Jamal, a poor Indian teenager living in Mumbai, who takes part in *Who Wants to Be a Millionaire*. The film follows him finally winning the big prize, and also falling in love. It looks back at Jamal's life and the events that helped him win the prize. The gap between rich and poor is clearly shown. However, it is not the rich, powerful people who win in the end.

Task

Tell a story from pictures

The Million Pound Bank Note

Preparation Reading

1a This is a story called 'The Million Pound Bank Note'. It is about a young man, Henry Adams, a young woman, Portia Langham and another man. Work in pairs and say which character(s) you can see in each picture.

b Match sentences 1–6 with pictures A–F.

1 I saw that the envelope contained a letter and something amazing.
2 'Can you change this for me, please? I don't have anything smaller.'
3 Soon I became famous. People invited me to all the best parties. And I met Portia Langham ... the most beautiful woman I had ever seen.
4 Without money, food or accommodation, I was in total despair.
5 Portia and I are now married.
6 'My darling daughter!'

Task Speaking

1a Work in pairs. Spend some time preparing how to tell the story, using the pictures and the phrases in exercise 1b. Ask your teacher for any words/phrases you need.

> Useful language a

b Practise telling your story to your partner.

2 🎧 14.6 Listen to the version of the story told by the young man and answer the questions.

1 Where was Henry Adams from?
2 What was the old man doing when Henry went in?
3 What two things were in the envelope?
4 Did Henry pay for his meal at the restaurant?
5 Where did Henry go to live?
6 How did he meet Portia Langham?
7 How much money did Henry actually spend during the month?
8 What bet had the man made?
9 What was the relationship between the old man and Portia?

3 Make a list of differences between your story and
   the one on the recording. Compare your list in pairs.

   > Useful language b

4 Listen to the story again and number the phrases in
   the Useful language box (part a) in the order that
   you hear them.

LANGUAGE LIVE

Speaking
Dealing with money

1 Work in pairs and discuss.

- How often do you use a cashpoint?
- Do you ever check your change in a shop?
- How much money do you usually leave as a tip in a restaurant?

2 ▶ Watch the video of three conversations. In which conversation (1, 2 or 3) does:

1 someone borrow money from someone else?
2 someone say he doesn't have any change?
3 a machine refuse a credit card?
4 someone ask a shop assistant for help?
5 someone ask for the bill in a restaurant?
6 someone think about giving a tip?
7 someone use a cashpoint machine?

3a Complete the phrases with the words in the box.

....
assistance bill change keep lend owe tip
PIN number receipt smaller
....

1 Can we have the _____ please?
2 Could you _____ me £40?
3 Do you think we should leave a _____ ?
4 How much do I _____ you?
5 Have you got _____ for a £50 note?
6 Have you got anything _____ ?
7 _____ the change.
8 Please enter your _____.
9 Please ask for _____.
10 Please take your change and _____.

b Watch again and check your answers.

4 Put the phrases from exercise 3a into two groups.

- phrases a customer might say
- phrases a customer might hear.

PRONUNCIATION

1 ▶ Watch and listen to the key phrases. Notice the polite intonation that people use when making requests like these.

2 Practise saying the phrases.

5a Work in pairs and write a short conversation (8–10 lines) that could take place in a restaurant/shop/school/work. Use the prompts to help you prepare your conversation.

Who speaks?
• a customer
• a taxi/bus driver
• a shop assistant
• colleagues

What happens?
• ask the price of something
• ask for change / a bill / a receipt
• leaving a tip
• using a machine
• borrowing money

b Compare your conversation with other students.

Writing
An essay expressing your opinion

1 Work in pairs and read the statements. Do you agree with them or not? Why?

1 Money can't buy happiness.
2 You only stop worrying about money when you have a lot of it.
3 Spending money on museums and art galleries is a waste of money.

2 Read the notes that a student made about one of the statements above. Which statement do they apply to? Tick the points that support the statement and cross the points that are against it.

- *Best things in life are free (love, good health, friends)*

- *Many millionaires seem to be unhappy*

- *Difficult to be happy if you have no money*

- *Life is stressful if you can't afford clothes/food, etc.*

- *Ideal = happy with enough money (not too much and not too little)*

'Money can't buy happiness.' Do you agree?

Is it true to say that money can't buy happiness? **On one hand**, **people often say that** the best things in life are free, and I think that's true, but **there are arguments on both sides**.

For some people, money is much too important. They spend all their life working and have no time to enjoy life. There are many examples of millionaires who are unhappy. **In my view**, this isn't a good way to live and you will never be happy that way.

On the other hand, people who have little or no money have a very stressful life. Life is very difficult if you haven't got a job, or can't afford to buy food or clothes. **For me**, the ideal thing is to have enough money, and to be happy with that.

In my opinion, it's difficult to be happy if you have no money at all. But the most important things in life, like love and good health, can't be bought with money.

3a Read the final version of the essay. Does the student mostly agree with the statement or not?

b Look at the phrases in bold in the essay. Put them in the correct column in the table.

Introducing the question	Introducing arguments	Giving your opinion

4a Work in pairs and choose one of the other statements in exercise 1. Make some notes with your partner about whether you agree or not. Organise your essay like this:

- Introduce/Summarise the question
- Make two or three points which are in favour of the statement
- Make two or three points which are against the statement
- Give your own opinion

b Write your essay using your notes to help you. Write about 120 words.

Communication Activities

Unit 8: Task, Speaking
Exercise 1, page 75
Student A

1a Look at the map and information about the west part of Canada. Student B has a map with information about the east part of Canada. Ask questions to Student B and find out where the following places are and why they are important. Mark them on your map.

- Ottawa
- Niagara Falls
- Hudson Bay
- Alert
- Quebec

b Now answer Student B's questions.

- Yukon Territory – 80% of the land here is completely unspoilt
- Mackenzie River – 4241 km long; the longest river in Canada,
- Vancouver – beautiful harbour city; views of ocean and mountains; centre for the 2010 Winter Olympics
- Rocky Mountains – millions of visitors a year; huge, spectacular mountain range; walking, biking, fishing and skiing
- Dinosaur Provincial Park – incredible scenery; dinosaur bones from 75 million years ago

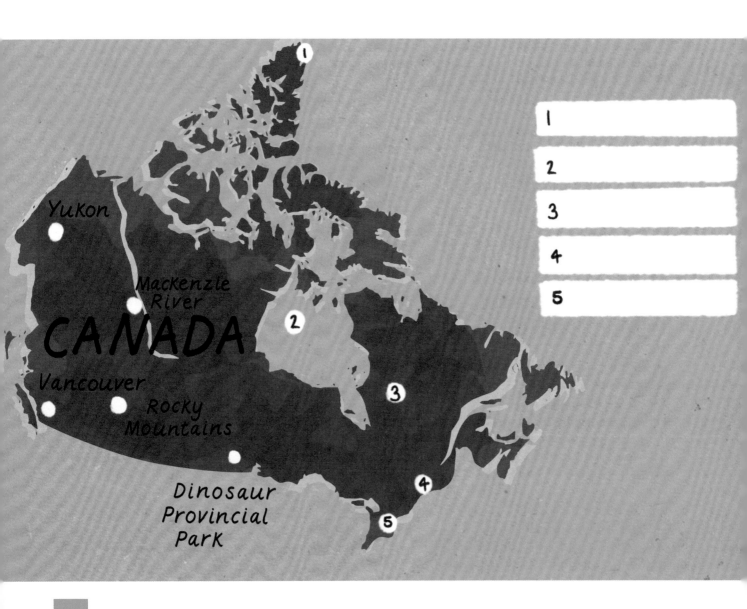

Unit 10: Task, Preparation
Exercise 5a, page 93
Group A: Gareth Barry

Look at the pictures and text about Gareth Barry. Try to remember the situation as well as you can.

Gareth Barry, aged 52, from Cardiff, was walking home when his mobile phone fell out of his jacket pocket.

Unfortunately, the phone fell down a drain and Gareth couldn't reach it.

Gareth lay down on the pavement and tried to reach the mobile phone, but unfortunately he got stuck in the drain and was unable to escape.

Some people were walking by and phoned the Fire Brigade. It took them two hours to free him!

Unit 8: Language live, Speaking
Exercise 4, page 76
Student A

4a Look at the map. Find the station. Ask for directions to:

- a bank
- a book shop
- a car park
- a cinema
- Rosehill Park
- Fast Save supermarket

b Then give Student B directions to the places he/she asks for.

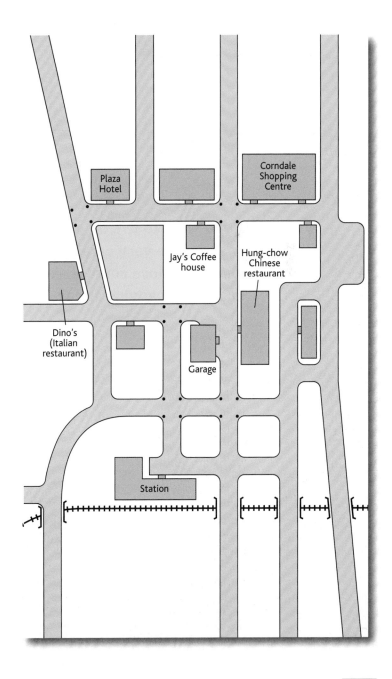

Communication Activities

Choose carefully

If you went to live on a desert island, you would need to choose what to take very carefully. If you could only take five things, then what you chose could mean the difference between life and death. So, read my advice and travel safely!

1. Water purification tablets: Your number one priority for survival is water. If you drank dirty water from rivers, you would get very ill so water purification tablets are essential.

2. Knife: There are hundreds of reasons why a knife would be useful, for example: cutting plants to eat, killing fish and animals to eat, cutting plants to make a shelter, etc. ...

3. Matches: Fire is essential for warmth and cooking. You could make fire without matches if you were an expert, but matches make the job much, much easier.

4. Insect repellant: You might think this is a luxury but mosquitoes can be deadly so you would need to make sure you had protection.

5. Blanket: Again, you might think this is a luxury. But the temperature on a desert island is often very hot during the day, but it can get extremely cold at night.

Unit 12: Vocabulary
Exercise 3a, page 108

Communication Activities

Unit 8: Task, Speaking
Exercise 1, page 75
Student B

1a Look at the map and information about the east part of Canada. Student A has a map with information about the west part of Canada. Answer Student A's questions.

 b Ask questions to Student A and find out where the following places are and why they are important. Mark them on your map.

- Rocky Mountains
- Vancouver
- Dinosaur Provincial Park
- Mackenzie River
- Yukon Territory

- Alert – furthest north inhabited place in Canada; temperatures above freezing only in July and August
- Hudson Bay – home of many polar bears, seals, whales and other important wildlife; freezes from November to June
- Quebec – the only officially French-speaking province in Canada
- Ottawa – capital city; population about 900,000
- Niagara Falls – one of the largest and most famous waterfalls in the world; over 28 million visitors a year

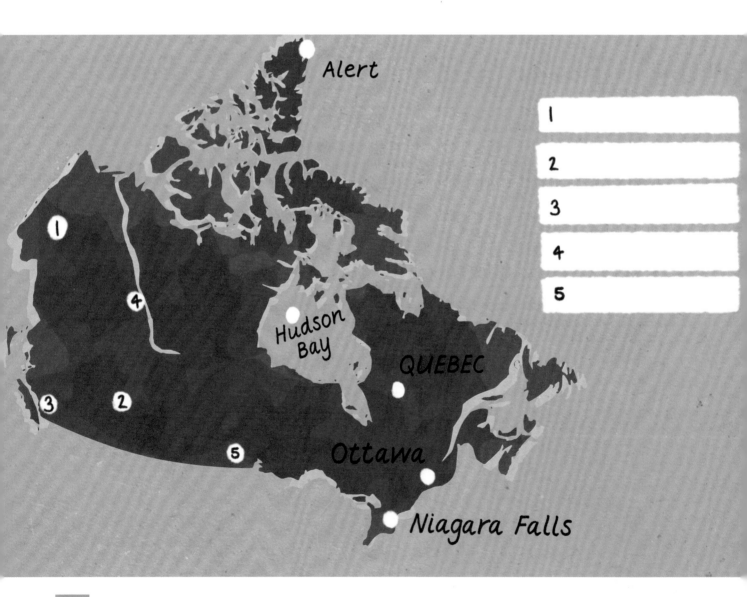

Unit 10: Task, Preparation
Exercise 5a, page 93
Group B: Amanda Barratt

Look at the pictures and text about Amanda Barratt.
Try to remember the situation as well as you can.

Amanda Barratt, aged 27, was on holiday in the
Seychelles with her boyfriend, Josh. They were sitting on
the beach when they decided to go for a swim.

Amanda was worried that someone might steal her
camera while they were in the sea. So she hid the
camera by burying it in the sand.

They spend about 20 minutes swimming
in the beautiful sea.

When they got out of the sea and walked back to get
Amanda's camera, they couldn't remember where it
was. They searched for an hour, but never found it!

Unit 8: Language live, Speaking
Exercise 4, page 76
Student B

4a Look at the map. Find the station. Give Student A
directions to the places he/she asks for.

b Then ask for directions to:

- a garage
- an Italian restaurant
- The Corndale Shopping Centre
- a good Chinese restaurant
- Jay's Coffee House
- The Plaza Hotel

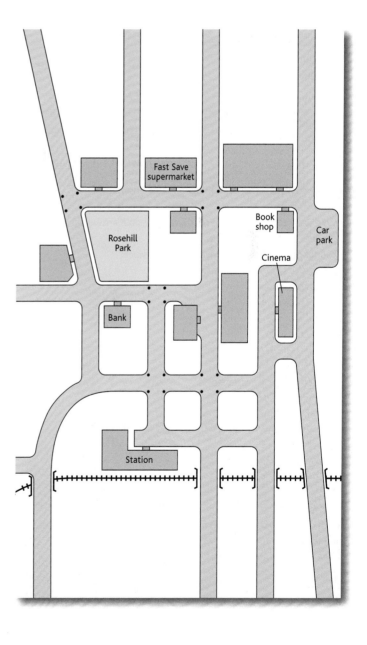

STUDY 1

Revision of questions

1 Question words

To ask about:	We use:
a person	**Who**'s your favourite film star?
a place	**Where** do you live?
a thing	**What**'s that under the table? **Which** is your coat?
a time	**When**'s your next holiday?
the reason for doing something	**Why** do you always wear black?
the way you do something	**How** do you open this?
a period of time	**How long** does this film last?
the number of times you do something	**How often** do you go to the gym?
the type of thing	**What kind** of car have you got?
the number of people or things	**How many** cousins have you got?
the cost of something	**How much** does the ticket cost?

- We use *what* if there are many possible answers.
  What's your name?
- We use *which* if there are only a few possible answers.
  Which do you prefer: tea or coffee?
- Some other expressions with *what* and *which*:
  What sort of films do you like?
  What time does the restaurant open?
  What colour are her eyes?
  What size are your shoes?
  Which places do you want to visit?
  Which part of Madrid do you live in?

2 Word order in questions

THE VERB *BE*

With the verb *be* we 'invert' the subject and the verb to form the question.

They are in the kitchen.	*Are they in the kitchen?*
You were late for class.	*Were you late for class?*

MODAL VERBS

With modal verbs (*can, will, might* ...), we also invert the subject and the verb.

Erika can ride a motorbike.	*Can Erika ride a motorbike?*
Tomás will be here tomorrow.	*Will Tomás be here tomorrow?*

- With other verbs, we put the auxiliary verb *do* or *does* before the subject.

  They play football.   **Do** *they play football?*
  Jamie lives near the school.   **Does** *Jamie live near the school?*
- The question word comes before the auxiliary verb.
  Where do you play chess?
  How often do you go to the cinema?

PRACTICE 1

1 Complete the questions with question words or phrases.

1 '_____ were you born?' 'In 1990.'
2 '_____ did the journey take?' 'About two hours.'
3 '_____ colour do you prefer: red or pink?' 'Red.'
4 '_____ is that young woman?' 'That's my sister.'
5 '_____ do you get to school?' 'I walk.'
6 '_____ of music do you like?' 'R&B and soul.'
7 '_____ do you have for breakfast?' 'Coffee and toast.'
8 '_____ do you live?' 'In Beijing.'
9 '_____ colour are his eyes?' 'Blue.'
10 '_____ did you phone me?' 'Because I wanted to ask you something.'
11 '_____ do you go to the gym?' 'Three times a week.'
12 '_____ children has he got?' 'Three.'

2 Put the words in the correct order to make questions.

1 Cristina / Does / play / computer games ?
2 at home / Is / today / your brother ?
3 football / Can / play / tomorrow / you ?
4 late / the train / this morning / was / Why ?
5 come shopping / Will / with me / tomorrow / you ?
6 did / have lunch / today / Where / you ?

STUDY 2

Present simple

+	I/You/We/They **work**.	
	He/She/It **works**.	
−	I/You/We/They **don't** (= does not) **work**.	
	He/She/It **doesn't** (= does not) **work**.	
?	**Do** I/you/we/they **work**?	
	Does he/she/it **work**?	

- We use the Present simple for:
  – habits or things we do regularly.
    *I **play** tennis every Saturday.*
  – things that are generally or always true.
    *They **live** in a small village.*

- These are the spelling rules for *he/she/it*.

Verb	Rule	Example
ends in: -s (e.g. *miss*) -x (e.g. *fix*) -ch (e.g. *catch*) -sh (e.g. *wash*)	add -es	She **misses** him. Mike **fixes** old cars. He **catches** the train on Mondays. She **washes** her hair every day.
ends in a consonant + -y (e.g. *fly*)	change -y to -ies	This airline **flies** to Mexico.
do and *go*	add -es	He **does** all the shopping. She **goes** swimming every day.
all other verbs	add -s	My sister **speaks** French.

Frequency phrases

1 Adverbs

never   sometimes   often   usually/generally   always

0% _____ 100%

- With most verbs, we put the adverb before the main verb.
  *I **never** get up before 9 a.m. on Sundays.*
- With the verb *be*, we put the adverb after the verb.
  *He is **always** late for class.*

2 Other phrases

every	day
once / twice / [x] times a	week month

- We usually put these phrases at the end of the sentence.
  *We go swimming **every week**.*
- We can also put them at the beginning of the sentence.
  ***Every day** I go for a walk in the park.*

PRACTICE 2

1 Rewrite the sentences in the negative form.

1. I like rainy days.
2. My brother lives in the town centre.
3. They have dinner very late.
4. She is a good singer.

2 Rewrite the sentences in the question form.

1. You know my cousin.
2. Your friend plays the guitar.
3. He is a maths teacher.
4. They like tea with milk.

3 Rewrite the sentences starting with *She ...*

1. I speak fluent Spanish.
2. I fly home once a year.
3. I have lunch at home.
4. I catch the early train to work.

4 Put the words in brackets in the correct place in the sentences.

1. We go to our holiday home a month. (once)
2. I watch the news on TV. (always)
3. I am tired when I get home from work. (usually)
4. We go to the beach day in summer. (every)
5. Joana is late for class. (never)
6. We go to the gym before breakfast. (often)

REMEMBER THESE WORDS

LEISURE ACTIVITIES

to go out with friends	to play a musical instrument
to go to evening classes	to play computer games
to go to the cinema	to play sport
to go to the gym	to use the internet
to listen to music	to watch live music
to listen to the radio	to watch TV

SPORTS AND GAMES

a ball	a player
a champion	a racket
equipment	to score a goal
a games console	a team
to hit a ball	to throw a ball
to kick a ball	a winner

OTHER

an ambition	a music channel
to be scared of	a nickname
a board game	a number game
to do yoga	a professional musician
favourite	a puzzle
free time	a survey
a hobby	to train
an injury	a word game

PRACTICE

1 Match the verbs in A with the phrases in B.

A		B	
1	use	a	live music
2	listen	b	computer games
3	go	c	the internet
4	watch	d	with friends
5	go out	e	to the gym
6	play	f	to the radio

2 Complete the sentences with the words in the box.

throw   team   racket   score   champion   equipment

1. When you put the ball in the basket, you _____ one point.
2. The _____ received a silver cup and $10,000.
3. Do you have to stand still when you _____ the ball in basketball?
4. I'd like to play tennis with you, but I haven't got a _____ .
5. There are seven players on each _____ .
6. You don't need special _____ to play football.

STUDY 1

Past simple – positive and negative

Regular Past simple forms end in -ed in the positive form. But many verbs have an irregular past form (see the list on page 175).
In the negative form, we use *did* + the base form of the verb.

+	I/You/He/She/It/We/They **started**.
	I/You/He/She/It/We/They **won**.
−	I/You/He/She/It/We/They **didn't** (= did not) **start**.
	I/You/He/She/It/We/They **didn't** (= did not) **win**.

- We use the Past simple to talk about a finished action or state in the past. It can be something that happened once or many times. We often say **when** it happened.
  *He **died** in 1980.* (= once)
  *My father always **took** me to school when I was young.* (= many times)
  *We **lived** in a very small house in those days.* (= state)
- For regular verbs, we add -ed (*watched*, *started*). But there are some exceptions.

Verb	Rule	Example
ends in -e (e.g. *like*)	add -d	I **liked** the film.
has one syllable and ends in vowel + one consonant (e.g. *stop*)	double the final consonant	They **stopped** for lunch.
ends in consonant + -y (e.g. *carry*)	change -y to -ied	He **carried** the bags all the way home.
has two syllables and ends in one vowel + -l (e.g. *travel*)	double the final consonant	They **travelled** at night.

- The past of *be* is *was/were*.
  We don't use *did* in the negative form of *was/were*.

+	I/He/She/It **was** late.
	We/You/They **were** late.
−	I/He/She/It **wasn't** (= was not) late.
	We/You/They **weren't** (= were not) late.

PRACTICE 1

1 Rewrite the sentences in the Past simple.

1. We watch a DVD with some friends.
2. He is a very popular actor.
3. I don't get home until midnight.
4. The match begins at 8:30 p.m.
5. They worry about their exams.
6. My brother and I stop eating meat.
7. They are very tired.
8. He doesn't travel very much.
9. My sister travels a lot for work.
10. The shops aren't open.

2 Complete the sentences with the Past simple form of the verb in brackets.

1. In 1900 the USA _____ (win) the first Davis Cup tennis competition.
2. In 1911 Roald Amundsen from Norway _____ (become) the first person to reach the South Pole.
3. In 1920 the British writer Agatha Christie _____ (write) her first detective novel.
4. In 1930 a New York businessman, Clarence Birdseye _____ (make) the first frozen vegetables.
5. In 1940 American soldiers _____ (drive) the first Jeeps®.
6. In 1950 people _____ (use) the first 'Diner's Club' credit card to pay for dinner or drinks.
7. In 1960 the USA _____ (put) the first weather satellite in space.
8. In 1970 Pan American World Airways _____ (start) the first Boeing 747 'jumbo jet' service.
9. In 1979 Sony _____ (invent) the first 'Walkman®' personal cassette player.
10. In 1990 Nelson Mandela _____ (walk) as a free man for the first time after 27 years in a South African prison.
11. In 2000 10,651 athletes _____ (participate) in the Summer Olympic Games in Sydney, Australia.
12. In 2010 a volcano in Iceland _____ (stop) flights in northwest Europe for several days.

STUDY 2

Past simple – questions

When we make questions using regular verbs and irregular verbs (not *be*) in the Past simple, when use *did* + the base form.

Question form	Short answers
Did I/you/he/she/it/we/they **start**?	Yes, I/you/he/she/it/we/they **did**.
Did I/you/he/she/it/we/they **win**?	No, I/you/he/she/it/we/they **didn't**.

We don't use *did* in the question form of *was/were*.

Question form	Short answers
Was I/he/she/it late?	Yes, I/he/she/it **was**. No, I/he/she/it **wasn't**.
Were we/you/they late?	Yes, we/you/they **were**. No, we/you/they **weren't**.

1 Object questions

Scott Fahlman invented the first <u>emoticon</u>.
<u>What</u> *did Scott Fahlman invent?*

'Emoticon' is the object of the question. When the question word refers to the object in the question, we use:
Question word + *did* + subject + base form of verb

2 Subject questions

<u>*John Logie Baird*</u> *invented the first television.*
<u>Who</u> *invented the first television?*

'John Logie Baird' is the subject of the question. When the question word refers to the subject in the question, we do not use *did*. The word order is the same as in a positive sentence:
Question word + past form of the verb + object

PRACTICE 2

1 Write questions for these answers. Use the words in bold.

1 I went to Italy on holiday last year.   **Where** ... ?
2 Anya phoned her very late last night.   **Who** ... ?
3 He was at home all day.   **Where** ... ?
4 Your ticket fell out of your bag.   **What** ... ?
5 He went to bed early because he was ill.   **Why** ... ?
6 His brother taught him to play the guitar. **Who** ... ?
7 When they finished their exams, they
   had a party.   **What** ... ?
8 They were in New York on a business trip. **Why** ... ?
9 Natasha made a birthday cake.   **What** ... ?
10 Brian used all the milk in the fridge.   **Who** ... ?

2 Choose the correct answers.

1 Where *were* / *did* you buy your shirt?
2 What *was* / *did* Eddie say when you told him?
3 Who *did teach* / *taught* you to speak Spanish?
4 *Why* / *Where* did you go home at 10 p.m.?
5 Who *were* / *did* those people?
6 What kind of food *was* / *did* there at the party?
7 How much *was* / *did* your watch cost?
8 What *happened* / *did happen* to Suzannah in Mexico?
9 Who *did buy* / *bought* the red car?
10 When *were* / *did* your parents in Ecuador?
11 *How often* / *What* did Amita phone you yesterday?
12 *Why* / *Who* was Pat so angry?

PRACTICE

1 Put the time phrases in the box in the correct place in the table.

a~~ year ago~~	2002		a minute ago
the 1850s	last week		18th June
last year	the winter		11 o'clock
Friday afternoon	the 21st century		November
Independence Day	yesterday afternoon		

at	on	in	Ø
			a year ago

2 Choose the correct answers.

1 I felt very *excited* / *worried* about my exam because I didn't study very much.
2 She was *bored* / *stressed* because there was nothing to do.
3 We were *disappointed* / *scared* because when we got to the museum it was closed.
4 The workers were *embarrassed* / *angry* that the boss didn't pay them for over two weeks.
5 I was really *surprised* / *relaxed* to see her because I thought she was on holiday.
6 His team won the match so he was *excited* / *in a good mood*.
7 She was *bored* / *in a bad mood* because her manager shouted at her.
8 When I last did an exam, I was *stressed* / *disappointed* for weeks before it.

STUDY 1

should, shouldn't

+	I/You/He/She/We/They **should** start now.
-	I/You/He/She/We/They **shouldn't** (= should not) start now.
?	**Should** I/you/he/she/we/they start now?

- We use *should* to say that something is a good idea or the right thing to do. We use *shouldn't* to say that something is not a good idea or not the right thing to do.
  *You **should** buy a new alarm clock.*
  *You **shouldn't** leave your bag open on a bus.*
- *Should* is not as strong as *have to*.
  *We **have to** go now or we'll be late.* (= it is necessary to go)
  *We **should** go now or we'll be tired tomorrow.* (= this is a good idea)
- The forms below are often used for giving advice:
  Why don't you check the price on the internet?
  Try drinking hot milk before going to bed.

PRACTICE 1

1 Complete the sentences with one word only.

1 *Why* don't you ask that man for directions?
2 *Try* putting a little salt in the water; it'll taste much better.
3 You *don't* worry so much. I'm sure everything will be OK.
4 *Should* I go to the hairdresser's or not? What do you think?
5 You *should* go to bed early before an exam.
6 *Why* don't you tell him how you feel?
7 You *shouldn't* shout at the children. It frightens them.
8 *Try* joining a gym. It's a good way to get exercise.

2 Complete the tips for runners with *should* or *shouldn't* and a verb in the box.

go for a run   start   see   try   eat   take   buy   do

Running: Top Tips for Beginners
1 First of all, if you are over 45 you _____ your doctor to check that running is OK for you.
2 Then you _____ a good pair of trainers, check that they're comfortable and give you good support.
3 You _____ to do too much at the beginning. Start with ten minutes' running, then walk a little and then run again.
4 You _____ running without doing some warm-up exercises to stretch your legs.
5 When you finish, you _____ some cool-down exercises.
6 At the beginning, you _____ every day. Have a break every second or third day to give your legs time to relax.
7 You _____ immediately before you go for a run. Wait at least one hour.
8 You _____ some water with you especially if it's hot.

STUDY 2

can, can't, have to, don't have to

1 *can, can't*

+	I/You/He/She/We/They **can** speak English.
-	I/You/He/She/We/They **can't** (= cannot) speak English.
?	**Can** I/you/he/she/we/they speak English?

We use *can* and *can't* to talk about different kinds of possibility.
- ability
  *Sue **can** dance quite well, but she **can't** sing.*
- permission
  *You **can't** come in!*
  ***Can** we go home now?*

2 *have to, don't have to*

+	I/You/We/They **have to** go now.
	He/She/It **has to** go now.
-	I/You/We/They **don't have to** go now.
	He/She/It **doesn't have to** go now.
?	**Do** I/you/we/they **have to** go now?
	Does he/she/it **have to** go now?

- We use *have to* if something is necessary.
  *We **have to** be at the airport by 6 o'clock.*
- *Have to* is very similar to *must*.
  *We **must** go now.* (= it's necessary)
  *We **have to** go now.* (= it's necessary)
- We use *don't have to* if it is not necessary to do something.
  *We **don't have to** wear a uniform at my new school.* (= it isn't necessary)

REMEMBER!

Have to and *must* are similar, but *don't have to* is not the same as *mustn't*.
*You **mustn't** take any photographs.* (= you can't, it's prohibited)
*You **don't have to** take any photographs.* (= you can, but it's not necessary)

---

1 Rewrite the phrases in bold using *can, can't, have to* or *don't have to*.

1 **You are able to** leave early if you want to.
2 **It's necessary for you to** get a visa for the USA. It's the law.
3 **It's not necessary for you to** pay me back today.
4 **Is it possible for my friend to** come, too?
5 **Is it necessary to** carry my student card with me?
6 **It's not possible for you to** see him at the moment.
7 **It's not necessary to** wear a tie, but you can if you want to.
8 **It is necessary for you to** pay for the tickets now.
9 **It's not possible for you to** bring dogs in here.
10 **You are able to** work in the library all evening. It's open until 10 p.m.

2 Complete the conversation with *have to / don't have to* or *can/can't* and the verb in brackets.

A: Congratulations – you've got the job!
B: Thanks. What time ¹_____ (I / start)?
A: The shop opens at 9 a.m., but you ²_____ (be) here at 8:45 a.m. every day.
B: And ³_____ (I / wear) a uniform?
A: No, you don't, but you ⁴_____ (wear) smart clothes.
B: Where ⁵_____ (I / have) lunch?
A: You ⁶_____ (eat) in our cafeteria or you ⁷_____ (bring) your own food and eat in the staff room. Remember, you ⁸_____ (eat) anything when you are working.
B: I'm worried because I don't know the names of all the perfumes.
A: You ⁹_____ (know) everything about the perfumes when you start. You ¹⁰_____ (ask) me for help.
B: ¹¹_____ (we / get) any free perfume?
A: We ¹²_____ (get) free perfume, but we ¹³_____ (pay) the full price. Only 75 percent of the price.

REMEMBER THESE WORDS

DAILY ROUTINES

to fall asleep	to have a bath/shower
to feel energetic	to have a cup of tea/coffee and
to feel tired	something to eat
to finish school/work	to have a nap
to get up	to relax at home
to go off (alarm clock)	to wake up
to go to bed	

JOBS

an accountant	a nanny
a cook	a plumber
a doctor	a taxi driver
a judge	a translator

OTHER

a barman	a reward
to concentrate	a routine
a dentist	a short sleeper
an exam	special qualifications
a ghost	a story-teller
to have a break	a study buddy
haunted	a subject
personal qualities	a tour guide
to revise	to wear a uniform
a revision timetable	to work long hours

PRACTICE

1 Match the beginnings in A with the endings in B.

A		B	
1	fall	a	asleep
2	feel	b	at home
3	finish	c	tired
4	get	d	to bed
5	go	e	work/school
6	have	f	a nap
7	relax	g	up
8	wake	h	up

2 Choose the correct answers.

I had a bad night last night. First of all I ¹*finished / came* work late and got home at nine. My husband Henry was away on business. I ²*felt / came* very tired and so I decided to go to bed early. I ³*had / made* a shower and then ⁴*got / went to* bed. I set my alarm clock for 7 o'clock in the morning, turned off the light and I soon ⁵*went / fell* asleep. In the middle of the night I woke ⁶*out / up* suddenly. It was only 12 o'clock, but I heard a noise downstairs. I ⁷*went / got* up and went downstairs and opened the kitchen door. It was Henry!

3 Read the definitions and add the letters to complete the jobs.

1 someone who works with languages:
t _ _ _ _ _ _ _ r
2 someone who makes food in a restaurant:
c _ _ k
3 someone who looks after your teeth:
d _ _ _ _ t
4 someone who tells you about tourist sites:
t _ _ r g _ _ _ e
5 someone who looks after children:
n _ _ _ y
6 someone who helps you when you are ill:
d _ _ _ _ r
7 someone who repairs water pipes and toilets:
p _ _ _ _ _ r
8 someone who keeps and checks financial accounts:
a _ _ _ _ _ _ _ t
9 someone who makes and serves you drinks:
b _ _ _ _ n
10 someone who drives you where you want to go:
t _ _ i d _ _ _ _ r

STUDY 1

Present continuous

+	I**'m** (= I am) **working.**	
	You/We/They**'re** (= are) **working.**	
	He/She/It**'s working.**	
–	I**'m not** (= I am not) **working.**	
	You/We/They **aren't** (= are not) **working.**	
	He/She/It **isn't** (= is not) **working.**	
?	**Am** I **working?**	
	Are you/we/they **working?**	
	Is he/she/it **working?**	

- We use the Present continuous for something happening at this moment or something happening in the present period, but perhaps not exactly at this moment.
  She's talking to someone on the phone.
  We're studying French this term.
- For *-ing* forms with most verbs, we add *-ing* (*starting, going, buying*). But there are some exceptions.

Verb	Rule	Example
ends with one *-e* (e.g. *make*)	take away *-e*	making leaving
has one syllable and ends in vowel + one consonant (e.g. *stop*)	double the final consonant	stopping getting
ends in *-ie* (e.g. *lie*)	change *-ie* to *-y*	lying dying
has two syllables, ends in vowel + one consonant, stress on the last syllable (e.g. *begin*)	double the final consonant	beginning forgetting
has two syllables and ends in *-l* (e.g. *travel*)	double the *-l*	travelling

Present continuous or Present simple?

- We use the Present simple for actions which are generally or usually true.
  I speak four languages.
- We use the Present continuous for actions which are in progress now or around now.
  Who is she speaking to?
- We usually use the Present simple with phrases like *always, never, every day, usually, normally.*

- We usually use the Present continuous with phrases like *now, at the moment, today, right now.*
- We do not usually use some verbs in the continuous form. These are:
  – describing mental states
    believe   know   understand
  – verbs connected with likes and dislikes
    like   love   want
  – verbs connected with possession
    have   own   possess

PRACTICE 1

1 Rewrite the sentences in the Present continuous. Be careful with the spelling of the verb.

1 We travel first class.
2 It begins to rain.
3 My brother lies on the sofa!
4 This train stops at every station.
5 They make a lot of noise.
6 I study architecture.
7 She gets the bus to school.
8 He has a shower.
9 She works in Berlin.
10 You talk very loudly.

2 Choose the correct answers.

1 Who **cooks** / **is cooking** the dinner? It smells great!
2 **Do you know** / **Are you knowing** what that sign means?
3 I **speak** / **am speaking** Italian, Spanish and Russian.
4 I **don't like** / **'m not liking** tea.
5 Julio **is living** / **lives** in Moscow at the moment.
6 He **has** / **is having** three mobile phones.
7 **Do you want** / **Are you wanting** any more bread?
8 Normally, I **take** / **'m taking** the train to work, but this week I **walk** / **'m walking**.
9 He always **goes** / **is going** to the gym at 7 a.m.
10 I **don't take** / **'m not taking** any evening classes right now.

STUDY 2

Present continuous for future arrangements

- We use the Present continuous to talk about what we have arranged to do in the future.
  A: What are you doing next weekend? (= what have you arranged?)
  B: I'm taking my son to the zoo on Saturday, then I'm cooking lunch for some friends on Sunday. (= I've arranged to do this)
- When we use the Present continuous like this, either we give a future time (e.g. this weekend) or we know from the situation that we are talking about the future.

PRACTICE 2

1 Put the words in the correct order.

A: [1]anything / Are / you / special / at / weekend / the / doing ?

B: [2]Yes, / I'm / a meal / Saturday evening / out / for / some friends / going / with / on

A: That sounds nice.

B: What about you? [3]are / What / doing / you ?

A: [4]doing / We / aren't / Saturday morning / anything / on

B: How about Saturday afternoon?

A: [5]I'm / Sara / swimming / going / with

B: [6]are / doing / you / What / on Sunday ?

A: [7]Simon's / going / to / afternoon / We're / barbecue / in / the

B: Me, too! See you there.

2 Complete the sentences with the correct form of the verb in brackets.

1 We _____ (have) a party for my daughter's birthday next Saturday.

2 Where _____ (you / meet) Rita for lunch tomorrow?

3 How often _____ (you / go) for a long walk?

4 Alan _____ (look) for a new job at the moment.

5 Maria _____ (not come) to the party tonight.

6 What _____ (your brother / want) to do after university?

7 I _____ (come) from Ukraine, from Kiev.

8 Oh no! It _____ (rain).

9 This weekend Greg and I _____ (visit) some old friends.

10 _____ (you / like) cats?

11 Susan and Tim _____ (get married) in the summer.

12 James _____ (hate) going to the dentist.

REMEMBER THESE WORDS

VERB PHRASES FOR SPECIAL DAYS

to buy flowers	to invite people into your home
to dress up	to make a cake
to eat out	to prepare a special meal
to exchange presents	to send cards to people
to have a day off school/work	to visit relatives

DESCRIPTIVE ADJECTIVES

boiling	noisy
delicious	peaceful
exciting	spicy
freezing	tasty
friendly	

OTHER

an anniversary	to pass your driving test
a boat race	to raise money
a bonfire	a real treat
candles	to respect
to celebrate	a special occasion
a celebration	a telethon
a ceremony	a three-day weekend
a festival	tinned vegetables
a firework display	traditional
a former president	a wedding
a nightclub	

PRACTICE

1 Complete the sentences with the correct form of the verbs in the box.

buy   prepare   dress   eat   exchange   have   invite
make   send   visit

1 We usually _____ out every Saturday night at an Italian restaurant near us.

2 On Thanksgiving Day, we travel to the south of the country to _____ relatives.

3 Everyone _____ a day off work on Independence Day.

4 I _____ a special meal tonight because I'm celebrating my new job.

5 I forgot to _____ Caroline a card for her birthday!

6 He always _____ me flowers when he wants to say sorry.

7 It's traditional for people to _____ presents at Christmas.

8 My neighbours always _____ people into their home on New Year's Eve.

9 I _____ a cake for you, but I'm afraid I burnt it!

10 They _____ up in traditional costume for a big parade through the town.

2 Add letters to complete the adjectives.

1 She invited us round for a d _ _ _ _ _ _ s meal.

2 The sun was shining and it was b _ _ _ _ g, so I sat under a tree all day.

3 Everyone in the class is very f _ _ _ _ _ y – you'll really enjoy it.

4 She doesn't like s _ _ _ y food, so we can't have Indian.

5 Don't forget to bring warm clothes. It will be f _ _ _ _ _ g later this evening.

6 I had a very p _ _ _ _ _ l weekend away from all the stress of work.

7 That dessert is very t _ _ _ y, but I can't eat any more!

8 I can't do my homework in the living room because it's always very n _ _ _ y.

9 I love going to see a football match. There is always an e_ _ _ _ _ _ g atmosphere!

05 STUDY, PRACTICE & REMEMBER

STUDY 1

Comparative and superlative adjectives

1 One-syllable adjectives and two-syllable adjectives ending in -y

Adjective	Comparative	Superlative	Spelling rule
young tall	younger taller	the youngest the tallest	most adjectives: + -er, the -est
nice large	nicer larger	the nicest the largest	adjective ends in -e: + -r, the -st
thin big	thinner bigger	the thinnest the biggest	one vowel + one consonant: double the final consonant
pretty dirty	prettier dirtier	the prettiest the dirtiest	change -y to -i

2 Other two-syllable adjectives and longer adjectives

serious	more serious	the most serious
sophisticated	more sophisticated	the most sophisticated

But we usually use -er and the -est with two-syllable adjectives: *clever, quiet, simple, gentle.*

3 Irregular forms

good	better	the best
bad	worse	the worst
far	further	the furthest

4 Negative comparisons

She's **not as** tall **as** her sister.

5 Prepositions in comparative phrases

*I think she's more attractive **than** her sister.*
*Your eyes are similar **to** your mother's.*
*Are these glasses different **from** your old ones?*
*She looks **like** a businesswoman.*
*Her earrings are the same **as** mine.*
*He's the tallest **in** the family!*
NOT *He's the tallest of the family.*

PRACTICE 1

1 Complete the sentences with the correct form of the adjective in brackets.

1 People are now ten centimetres _____ (tall) than 150 years ago.
2 In the UK _____ (popular) boys' baby names are Jack and Oliver.
3 In Britain in the 14th century sugar was nine times _____ (expensive) than milk.
4 Roger Federer is _____ (high) paid tennis player in the world.
5 Egyptians made _____ (early) ship in the world in 2600 BC.
6 Football is _____ (popular) sport in the world.
7 Scientists say that green tea is _____ (good) for you than black tea.
8 Wellington is _____ (far) from Sydney than Auckland.
9 Tourism is the world's _____ (big) industry with 240 million jobs.
10 London Waterloo is _____ (busy) station in London with 82 million passengers a year.

2 Choose the correct answers.

1 This jacket is *cheaper / cheapest* than that one.
2 My sister looks very different *than / from* me.
3 That's one of the *worse / worst* films I've ever seen!
4 I like your bag! It's the same *as / like* mine!
5 This book is *more / most* interesting than the one I read before.
6 He doesn't look *than / like* his brother at all.
7 She's one of the *most happy / happiest* children I know.
8 My daughter is about three centimetres taller *from / than* me.
9 My dress is very similar *to / from* yours.
10 They are the most famous pop group *of / in* the world.

STUDY 2

Questions with *how, what* and *what ... like?*

- To ask about someone's physical appearance, we use the question: *What does he/she look like?*
  What does your friend look like? He's tall, dark and handsome.
- To ask about someone's personality (not their appearance), we use the question: *What's he/she like?*
  What are your neighbours like? They seem very friendly.
- To ask about someone's health, we use the question *How is he/she?*
  How's your mother? Oh, she's much better thanks!
- We also use *How is/was ... ?* to ask about someone's work, or their day at school, or their journey.
  How is school? It's OK ... a bit boring!
  How was your journey? Fine. No problems.

REMEMBER!

We do not use *like* in the answer.
A: What's the new teacher like?
B: She seems very nice.
NOT *She seems like very nice.*

- We use the verb *be* to ask about age, height and colour.
  (Age) *How old **is** she? She's about 35.*
  (Height) *How tall **is** he? He's about average height.*
  __Is__ he tall or short? He's very tall.
  *What colour **is** her hair / **are** her eyes? Brown.*
- We use *have got* to ask about features such as hair, eyes, glasses or beard.
  *__Has__ he **got** a beard? No, he hasn't.*
  *__Has__ she **got** nice eyes? Yes, they're beautiful!*
- If we use more than one adjective, the order of the adjectives is important:
  – *long/short*, etc., before 'colour' adjectives (*dark, fair, brown*)
  *He's got **short, brown** hair.*
  – 'opinion' adjectives (*nice, lovely, horrible*) before other adjectives
  *She's got **lovely, blue** eyes.*
  – We do **not** put *and* between the two adjectives.
  He's got long, blonde hair.
  NOT *He's got long and blonde hair.*

PRACTICE 2

1 Choose the correct answers.

1 A: ¹*How / What* does Ana look like?
  B: She ²*'s got / 's* long dark hair.
  A: And what colour ³*are / have got* her eyes?
  B: They ⁴*'re / have got* brown.
  A: ⁵*What's / How's* she like?
  B: She ⁶*likes dogs / 's very friendly*.

2 A: ⁷*How / How much* tall is Luke?
  B: He ⁸*has / 's* 1.80 metres.
  A: ⁹*Has he got / Has he* a beard?
  B: No, he hasn't. He's clean-shaven.

3 A: How is Morgan?
  B: Very well, thanks. It's her birthday on Friday.
  A: Oh, how old ¹⁰*has / is* she?
  B: 29.

2 Complete the questions with one word.

1 'What _____ your brother look like?' 'He's tall and he's got brown hair.'
2 'What _____ are his eyes?' 'They're green.'
3 'How _____ is your sister?' 'About the same height as me.'
4 '_____ is her hair like?' 'She's got long black hair.'
5 'What _____ your holiday like?' 'It was great – really relaxing.'
6 '_____ is your mother?' 'She's fine, thanks.'
7 'What's your brother _____ ?' 'He's really kind.'
8 'How _____ is your dog?' 'About four years old.'

PRACTICE

1 Choose the correct answers. In two sentences both of the alternatives are correct.

1 She is very tall and she's got beautiful, dark *skin / hair*.
2 Those glasses you're *wearing / carrying* really suit you.
3 She has to be careful in the sun because her skin is very *pale / blonde*.
4 When he was young, his hair was long, but now he's completely *bald / clean-shaven*.
5 He didn't get the job because the company didn't like the *piercings / tattoos* on his face.
6 She always has *straight / dyed* hair now – I don't know what her natural hair colour is.
7 At the moment he's got a strange *beard / moustache* under his chin.
8 She is naturally very beautiful and doesn't need to wear so much *lipstick / tattoo*.

2 Read the clues and add the letters to complete the words.

1 At the top of your arm: s _ _ _ _ _ _ r
2 One on each hand: t _ _ _ b
3 Between your arm and your hand: w _ _ _ t
4 Half way up your arm: e _ _ _ w
5 At the end of your finger: f _ _ _ _ _ _ _ _ l
6 Half way up your leg: k _ _ e
7 Between your body and your head: n _ _ k
8 Around your mouth: l _ _ s

STUDY 1

Plans and intentions

1 *going to*, *planning to*

+	I'm going to / planning to buy a car.
	You/We/They're going to / planning to buy a car.
	He/She's going to / planning to buy a car.
–	I'm not going to / planning to buy a car.
	You/We/They're not going to / planning to buy a car.
	He/She's not going to / planning to buy a car.
?	Am I going to / planning to buy a car?
	Are you/we/they going to / planning to buy a car?
	Is he/she going to / planning to buy a car?

- We use *going to* to talk about what we intend to do in the future. It can be the near future or the more distant future.
  I'm going to be a famous actor.
  Are you going to see him again?
- We normally use *planning to* when we have thought carefully about the plan and decided how to do it.
  What are you planning to say at the meeting?
  I'm planning to leave this company next year.

2 *would like to*, *would rather*

+	I/You/He/She/We/They'd (= would) like to / rather stay at home.
–	I/You/He/She/We/They wouldn't (= would not) like to stay at home.
	I/You/He/She/We/They'd (= would) rather not stay at home.
?	Would I/you/he/she/we/they like to / rather stay at home?

- We use *would like to* to say what we want to do.
  I'd like to travel round the world one day.
  It is less direct than *want to* and we often use it to be polite, especially in questions.
  Would you like to see the menu?
- We use *would rather* to say we prefer one thing to another thing. We don't have to state the other preference; it can just be implied. After this form, we always use the infinitive without *to*.
  I'd rather go on a walking holiday. Beach holidays are boring.
  Would you rather sit inside (or outside)?

REMEMBER!

We do **not** usually use *would rather* in the negative form.
I would rather go on a walking holiday.
I would rather not go on a beach holiday.
NOT *I wouldn't rather go on a beach holiday.*

PRACTICE 1

1 Put the words in bold into the correct form in these sentences.

1 I would like to **visiting** India one day.
2 Actually, we'd rather **to take** the early train.
3 I'm not **go** to take a holiday this year.
4 Are you **plan** to stay at home this evening?
5 **Did** you rather go to a different restaurant?
6 We are planning **invite** about 50 people.
7 Are you going **come** out with us this evening?
8 I **had** like to say something, please.

2 Complete the conversations with the correct form of the words in brackets.

1 A: What ¹_____ (you / plan / do) after university?
  B: I ²_____ (like / go) to the UK to study English. My sister, Sharon, wants to come, too.
  A: Where ³_____ (you / like / go)?
  B: Sharon wants to go to London, but I ⁴_____ (rather / go) to Cambridge. What about you?
  A: I ⁵_____ (go / have) a long holiday and just relax!

2 A: I've got some news. We ⁶_____ (plan / move) to New Zealand.
  B: No! Really? Why?
  A: Well, Susan's got a new job. She ⁷_____ (go / work) in the National Museum.
  B: And what about you?
  A: Well, I ⁸_____ (like / start) my own online company.
  B: Wow! And when ⁹_____ (you / plan / leave)?
  A: Probably in the summer but we ¹⁰_____ (rather / leave) earlier, next month if possible.
  B: Well, the best of luck for your future!
  A: Thanks.

STUDY 2

Predictions with *will* and *won't*

+	I/You/He/She/We/They 'll (= will) be there at six.
–	I/You/He/She/We/They won't (= will not) see him next week.
?	Will I/you/he/she/we/they have time to phone them?

- We use *will* to say what we expect to happen. We use it when there is no particular plan or intention.
  The weather will be very hot in July. (= this is what I expect)
  Will there be a lot of people? (= what do you expect?)
- Notice the difference between *will* and *going to* here.
  We're going to visit the London Eye today. (= this is what we intend/plan)
  It'll be busy and we'll have to queue. (= this is what I expect)
- We use *will/won't* in short answers.
  Will it be very hot? Yes, it will. / No, it won't.
  Will you need an umbrella? Yes, you will. / No, you won't.
- Notice that there are no *will* forms of *can* and *must*. We use *will be able to* and *will have to*.
  We'll be able to go swimming every day.
  You'll have to take warm clothes.

PRACTICE 2

1 Make the sentences refer to the future by using the correct form of *will* or *won't*.

1 It's difficult to find a parking place.
2 She isn't at home on Tuesday.
3 Is your cousin at home?
4 Can you find your way without a map?
5 The last bus has gone so we must walk.

2 Put the words in the correct order to make questions.

1 will / long / the / take / How / bus ?
2 I / be / able / online / Will / to / book ?
3 will / flight / How / the / cost / much ?
4 expensive / accommodation / be / Will / Tokyo / in ?
5 need / Will / I / bring / to / suncream ?
6 Will / busy / beaches / be / the / in / March ?
7 flight / be / Will / it / a / direct ?
8 the / be / Will / exam / difficult ?
9 the / be / the / open / in / museums / Will / summer / holidays ?
10 Madrid / the / like / food / in / Will / I ?

3 Match questions 1–10 from exercise 2 with answers a–j below.

a I think it'll be about $2,400.
b Yes, it'll be very sunny.
c Yes – it won't be cheap in the city centre.
d I think the journey will be about four hours.
e Yes, you will. You can also book by phone.
f No, they won't. Everyone will be at school or work.
g Yes, you'll love it – it's delicious.
h Yes, they will, but some might be closed on Mondays.
i No, it won't – you have studied very hard.
j No, you'll probably stop in Bangkok on the way.

REMEMBER THESE WORDS

GOING ON HOLIDAY

a camera
credit cards
foreign currency
a guidebook
a passport
a phrasebook
plane tickets

suncream
sunglasses
a swimsuit
a toothbrush
toothpaste
a towel
travel sickness pills

DESCRIBING HOLIDAYS

beautiful scenery
comfortable accommodation
a crowded airport lounge
a delayed flight
an interesting excursion

a long queue
a luxurious dining car
a peaceful lake
a perfect holiday

OTHER

average temperature
to check in online
first class
to get a visa
to get foreign currency
to go camping
to go canoeing
a holidaymaker
a last-minute person

to order a taxi
an organised person
a reservation
a self-catering apartment
a suitcase
to sunbathe
a time zone
a train journey

PRACTICE

1 Add letters to the words to complete the sentences.

1 It'll be really sunny and hot, so don't forget your s _ _ _ _ _ m.
2 I'm taking a p _ _ _ _ _ _ _ k because I want to try and speak to the locals.
3 It's expensive there, so I'm taking plenty of foreign c _ _ _ _ _ _ y.
4 If you go swimming, don't forget your t _ _ _ l.
5 I don't need a c _ _ _ _ a because I'll take photos on my mobile phone.
6 The g _ _ _ _ _ _ _ k says there are lots of interesting places to visit.
7 I felt awful on the flight because I forgot to take my travel s _ _ _ _ _ _ s pills.
8 The sun is very bright and I can't see properly without my s _ _ _ _ _ _ _ s.
9 We couldn't find my p _ _ _ _ _ _ t, so we nearly missed the ferry to France.
10 I went to the chemist because I left my t _ _ _ _ _ _ _ h at home.

2 Complete the sentences with the adjectives in the box.

beautiful   peaceful   comfortable   delayed   long
interesting   perfect   luxurious

1 We waited for six hours in the airport because of a _____ flight.
2 The hotel provided _____ accommodation, but it was very expensive.
3 The company has many _____ excursions to choose from in their brochure.
4 We spent the day beside a _____ lake with only a few other visitors.
5 There was _____ scenery and the weather was amazing!
6 When we arrived at the airport, I couldn't believe the _____ queues at check-in.
7 We had a lovely dinner in the _____ dining car. It was very beautiful and relaxing.
8 We had a _____ holiday. It was exactly what we wanted.

STUDY 1

Present perfect

We form the Present perfect with *have/has* + past participle. Regular past participles end in *-ed* in the positive form. Many verbs have an irregular past participle (see the list on page 175).

+	I/You/We/They**'ve** (= have) **finished/won.**	
	He/She/It**'s** (= has) **finished/won.**	
−	I/You/We/They **haven't** (= have not) **finished/won.**	
	He/She/It **hasn't** (= has not) **finished/won.**	
?	**Have** I/you/we/they **finished/won?**	
	Has he/she/it **finished/won?**	

We use the Present perfect to talk about the past and present together. It tells us something about the present.
I've met Daniel before. (= I know him now)
He's left the country. (= he is not in the country now)

Present perfect and Past simple with *for*

- We use the Present perfect with *for* to talk about an action or state which continues from the past to the present.
  I've been in New York for two weeks.

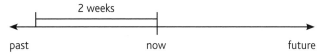

- We use the Past simple with *for* to talk about a past action or state in a period of time which is finished.
  I was in New York for two weeks.

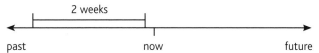

- We can ask about the period of time using *How long ... ?* with both the Present perfect and the Past simple.
  How long have you had that car?
  How long did you live in Canada?

PRACTICE 1

1 Write the Past simple form and the past participle for each of these irregular verbs.

		Past simple	Past participle
1	become	*became*	*become*
2	begin	_____	_____
3	come	_____	_____
4	grow	_____	_____
5	have	_____	_____
6	know	_____	_____
7	make	_____	_____
8	meet	_____	_____
9	say	_____	_____
10	spend	_____	_____
11	take	_____	_____
12	tell	_____	_____

2 Choose the correct answers.

1 I **have stayed / stayed** with my aunt last year.
2 My neighbours **have lived / lived** there for 25 years. They'll never move.
3 Your car is in really good condition. How long **have you had / did you have** it?
4 Gary **has started / started** his first business in 2001.
5 So far this year, we**'ve saved / saved** over £500.
6 I love this watch. I**'ve had / had** it for ten years.
7 Before my brother became a banker, he **has studied / studied** abroad for several years.
8 How long **have you played / did you play** the piano for when you were a child?

3 Complete the sentences with the correct form of the verb in brackets.

1 We _____ (be married) now for two years.
2 I _____ (live) in Africa for three years when I was a child.
3 I'm very tired because I _____ (not sleep) for 24 hours.
4 Kate _____ (work) here for nine months, but she's leaving next week.
5 _____ (Pelé / be) the best football player of the 20th century?
6 Lara and Martin first _____ (meet) eight years ago.
7 How long _____ (you / have) your ring? It's beautiful.
8 They _____ (not wait) very long before the bus came.
9 We _____ (stay) in Tenerife for our holiday four years ago.
10 I _____ (be) on the phone for over an hour now!

STUDY 2

Present perfect and Past simple with other time words

1 Time phrases with the Past simple

We use the Past simple to talk about actions or states which are finished. We often use the following time words:
- days, dates, times, years
  in 2002, on Friday, at 6:30, yesterday
- *last* and *ago*
  last weekend, five years ago
- questions and statements with *when*
  when I was ten years old

2 Time phrases with the Present perfect

- Often, there is no time phrase with the Present perfect. We do not know exactly when the action happened.
  She's lived in Spain, Egypt and Brazil.
- When we use time phrases with the Present perfect, they do not give a definite time.
  She's just had her baby. (= a short time ago)
  It's already sold a million copies. (= before now / expected)
  I haven't finished yet. (= before now; only in questions and negatives)
  He's never been abroad. (= not at any time)
- We also use the Present perfect with time phrases that refer to a time that is still in progress.
  I haven't seen him this morning. (= this morning isn't finished)
  Daniela has done very well so far. (= up to now)

PRACTICE 2

1 Put the word in brackets into the correct position in the sentences: (1) or (2).

1 Mr Ferris ¹_____ has ²_____ gone out. (just)
2 The gym opened about ¹_____ a year ²_____ . (ago)
3 Have you ¹_____ been to see that new film ²_____ ?(yet)
4 I've ¹_____ seen an elephant ²_____ . (never)
5 We ¹_____ have ²_____ seen this film three times. (already)
6 He came ¹_____ to England ²_____ . (last year)

2 Complete the conversations with the correct form of the verb in brackets.

1 A: Would you like a sandwich?
  B: No thank you, I _____ (already / eat).
2 A: Let's go to Egypt. I'd like to see the pyramids.
  B: I'd rather go to Morocco. I _____ (go) to Egypt last year.
3 A: Did you have any pets as a child?
  B: Yes, we _____ (have) two cats and a dog.
4 A: How long _____ (you / be) in the UK?
  B: Six months so far.
5 A: Why are you looking so happy?
  B: I _____ (just / pass) my exams!
  A: Congratulations!
6 A: Have you seen Paula recently?
  B: No. I _____ (see) her about six months ago.
7 A: What did Christine say when she heard the news?
  B: Mike _____ (not tell) her yet.
8 A: The children look very excited.
  B: Yes, they _____ (never / stay up) so late before.
9 A: Hello, this is Alan Young. Can I help you?
  B: Yes, I _____ (speak) to you half an hour ago.
10 A: _____ (you / read) the last Harry Potter book yet?
  B: Not yet, but I want to.

REMEMBER THESE WORDS

VERB PHRASES ABOUT AMBITIONS

to appear on television	to go round the world
to become famous	to go to university
to buy a house or flat	to have children
to earn €1 million	to learn how to drive
to get married	to start your own business
to go abroad	to write a book

THE INTERNET

a blog	to search
to download	a social-networking site
a hit	to upload
an online community	a video-sharing site
to post	a website

OTHER

an achievement	a film addict
an ambition	inspiration
to be confident	to inspire
to be interested in business	an internet user
a blog	a (multi-)millionaire
a computer game designer	to perform in public
confidence	to set your goals high
a dream	to sponsor
an ecologist	a volunteer

PRACTICE

1 Complete the sentences with a verb in the box.

> appear become buy earn get go have learn start write

1 My brother's ambition is to be a lawyer and _____ €1 million before he's 30.
2 A lot of young people nowadays want to _____ on television.
3 For my new job, I need to _____ how to drive a car.
4 I'm taking six months to _____ round the world before I go to university.
5 I don't want to work for a company anymore so I'm going to _____ my own business.
6 She wants to _____ famous by designing clothes for rich people.
7 They've decided to _____ married next year on a beach in Thailand.
8 I've decided to _____ a flat next year, somewhere near the city centre.
9 She got married when she was 40, but she didn't _____ any children.
10 I want to _____ a book about my travels in India.

2 Choose the correct answer.

1 All the information about dates and prices are on our *website* / *hit*.
2 When are you going to *search* / *upload* your holiday photos onto your computer?
3 I want to *blog* / *download* that film from the internet and watch it tonight.
4 The mini-film she put on YouTube has had thousands of *hits* / *websites*.
5 My friend writes a *blog* / *download* about funny things that happen in her life.
6 When you *upload* / *search* on the internet, you should just put in the essential words.
7 I waste so much time chatting to friends on *blogs* / *social-networking sites*.
8 There's a great *online community* / *hit* for support if you want to give up smoking.
9 He *posted* / *hit* information about his party on the internet and 800 people came!

08 STUDY, PRACTICE & REMEMBER

STUDY 1

Using articles

1 Use of *a* and *an*

We use *a* or *an* for the first time we mention something.

*I saw **a** beautiful vase in **an** antique shop the other day.*

2 Use of *the*

We use *the*:

* to refer to something/someone we have mentioned before.
  *I saw **a** beautiful vase in **an** antique shop the other day. When I went back, **the** vase wasn't there anymore!*
* to refer to a specific thing/person.
  ***The** man in **the** black coat is looking at you.*
* when there is only one of something (it is unique).
  ***the** Sun **the** Earth **the** Pope*
* with superlative forms.
  *The Nile is **the** longest river in the world.*
* with some place names.

Oceans and seas	**the** Pacific Ocean **the** Mediterranean Sea
Rivers	**the** River Danube **the** River Thames
Mountain ranges	**the** Rocky Mountains **the** Himalayas
Countries which are republics or unions	**the** United Kingdom **the** United Arab Emirates

* Other phrases with *the*:
  *at **the** bottom/top*
  *in **the** north/south/east/west*
  *in **the** centre/middle*
  *in **the** morning/afternoon/evening*
  *on **the** left/right*
  *on **the** coast/border*

3 Use of zero article

We do not use *a*, *an* or *the* (zero article):

* when we talk about things/people in general.
  Dogs make very good pets.
* with the names of people and nationalities.
  Michael and Jane are coming for dinner later.
  American people eat a lot of fast food.
* with many place names.

Continents	Africa Asia	Countries	Argentina Thailand
Cities	Madrid Bangkok	Lakes	Lake Superior
Mountains	Mount Fuji	Hills	Primrose Hill
Roads/streets	Oxford Street	Islands	Baffin Island

4 Other phrases with zero article

at home, at school, at university, at work, at night
in bed, in prison, in hospital
on holiday

PRACTICE 1

1 Add *the* to the following sentences where necessary.

1 I'm usually at _____ home in _____ evening.
2 Go past the gym, and _____ Oak Road is on _____ left.
3 It's a small town in _____ south of Turkey. It's on _____ coast, so it's very popular with _____ tourists.
4 While we were on _____ holiday in _____ Egypt, we decided to go on a cruise along _____ River Nile.
5 Is _____ Mont Blanc _____ highest mountain in _____ Europe?

STUDY 2

Quantifiers with countable and uncountable nouns

Countable nouns have a singular and a plural form.

mountain/mountains   table/tables   person/people

Uncountable nouns do not have a plural form.

traffic   scenery   nightlife

some, *any* and other quantifiers

With plural nouns and uncountable nouns	some, (not) any, no, a lot of, (not) enough	There are **some cakes** on the table. There is **a lot of traffic** today.
With plural nouns	(not) many, too many, a few	There were **too many people** in the room. I've got **a few pens** in my bag.
With uncountable nouns	(not) much, too much	He hasn't got **much money**. There's **too much noise** in here.

* *Some* means an indefinite number/amount (we don't know exactly how much/many). We use it in positive sentences.
  *I'd like **some** information, please.*
  We also use *some* in questions when we think the answer will be *yes*.
  *Did you buy **some** milk, like I asked you?*
  *Would you like **some** more tea? (= offer)*
* We use *any* before countable and uncountable nouns in:
  – negative sentences.
  *There aren't **any** Italian restaurants near here.*
  – questions where the answer could be *yes* or *no*.
  *Are there **any** shops near here?*
* *no* means the same as *not any*.
  *There's **no** food in the fridge. (= there isn't **any** food ...)*

- *A few* means 'a small number of'. We usually use it in positive sentences.

  *There are **a few** things I'd like to discuss with you.*

- We usually use *a lot of* (also *lots of*) in positive sentences to mean 'a large amount/number of'.

  *There are **a lot of** good places to ski near here.*

- We use *much* and *many* in negative sentences or questions.

  *I haven't got **much** time today. How about tomorrow?*

  *Are there **many** tourists at this time of year?*

- *Too much* and *too many* have a negative meaning. We use them to mean 'more than the right amount/number'.

  *I can't work here. There's **too much** noise.*

  *There are **too many** people in the queue.*

- *Not enough* also has a negative meaning. We use it to mean 'less than the right amount/number'.

  *There is**n't enough** time to go to the park today.*

  *There are**n't enough** chairs for everyone.*

PRACTICE 2

1 Choose the correct answer.

1 There's **too much** / **too many** sugar in this coffee.

2 **A lot of** / **Much** people come on holiday here every year.

3 I've got **some** / **any** bread if you want to make a sandwich.

4 I'm sorry, but there's **enough** / **no** time for us to stop.

5 Would you like **some** / **a few** more water?

REMEMBER THESE WORDS

CITY LIFE

carbon-neutral	public transport
a city centre	a recycling bin
a cycle lane	a residential area
green space	a shopping mall
a high-rise apartment block	traffic congestion
a one-way street	traffic lights
a pedestrian zone	

GEOGRAPHICAL FEATURES

a beach	a mountain
a coast	a mountain range
a desert	an ocean
a forest	a river
a hill	a sea
an island	a valley

OTHER

a capital city	remote
climate	situated
a continent	a solar farm
fresh water	spectacular scenery
a home town	temperature
in the (west) of	(un)inhabited
on the (north) coast	unspoilt
permanently	

PRACTICE

1 Complete the sentences with the words in the box. You do not need to use two of the words.

> residential shopping traffic cycle one-way city
> public high-rise recycling green pedestrian
> carbon-neutral

1 I don't mind cycling to work because there are lots of good _____ lanes in my town.

2 I don't have a garden because I live in a _____ apartment block in the city centre.

3 You can't drive in the city centre because the whole area is a _____ zone now.

4 Most of the _____ areas where people live are far from the city centre.

5 I like my town because there is a lot of _____ space and parks for people to walk in.

6 I don't use my car much because the _____ transport in my city is very good.

7 There are lots of good shops in a huge _____ mall near where I live.

8 I have three _____ bins: one for paper, one for plastic and one for food waste.

9 You have to be careful when driving in my city as there are a lot of _____ streets.

10 I don't like driving to work because there is so much _____ congestion.

2 Put the letters in bold in the correct order to complete the sentences.

1 We had a lovely holiday on a small _____ in the Caribbean. **d a l s i n**

2 Temperatures in the _____ sometimes get up to 48°C. **s e e d t r**

3 They go to the same _____ every year on holiday. **a c e h b**

4 Large companies are cutting down trees in huge areas of the _____ . **r o t s e f**

5 It took us five hours to climb to the top of the _____ . **n a n m o t u i**

6 I saw a good TV programme about fishing in the _____ in South East Asia. **e c a n o**

7 They moved to a small village on the _____ . **s o c a t**

8 There was snow at the top of the mountains, but not in the _____ . **a l v l e y**

STUDY 1

may, might, will definitely, etc.

1 *will definitely*

We use *will definitely* when we are sure something will happen. The negative of this phrase is *definitely won't*.

*We **will definitely** be out tomorrow evening.*
*I **definitely won't** get there before 6 o'clock.*

2 *will probably*

We use *will probably* when we are fairly sure something will happen. The negative of this phrase is *probably won't*.

*We **will probably** be out tomorrow evening.*
*I **probably won't** get there before 6 o'clock.*

3 *may/might*

We use *may/might* to say it's possible that something will happen. The negative of these verbs is *may not / might not*.

*We **may/might** be out tomorrow evening.*
*I **may not / might not** get there before 6 o'clock.*

PRACTICE 1

1 Put the words in the correct order to make sentences.

1 arrive / definitely / won't / 10 o'clock / before / We
2 for / There / not / food / everyone / might / enough / be
3 probably / spend / this year / at home / will / the summer / We
4 might / I / the children / later / take / swimming
5 not / time / be / There / enough / may
6 tomorrow / you / see / won't / I / probably
7 The / weather / tomorrow / better / get / may
8 definitely / a / will / be / It / game / difficult

2 Choose the option (a, b or c) that means the same as the phrase in bold.

1 **I promise I'll** think about it.
   a I'll definitely   b I might   c I'll probably
2 **It's possible we'll** buy a house abroad.
   a We'll definitely   b We definitely won't c We might
3 **I don't think they'll** change their minds.
   a They probably won't b They might   c They may
4 **There might** be too many people.
   a I'm sure there'll   b There may   c I'm sure there won't
5 **I'm fairly sure it'll** cost about $40.
   a It might   b It'll probably   c It'll definitely
6 **He might not** give me the day off.
   a I'm sure he won't   b I'm sure he'll   c It's possible he won't
7 **I'm sure the children will** be in bed when you arrive.
   a The children will definitely   b The children might
   c The children probably won't
8 **I definitely won't** lose it.
   a I'm fairly sure I won't   b I'm not sure I won't
   c I'm very sure I won't

STUDY 2

Present tense after *if, when* and other time words

1 'The first conditional'

if clause	main clause
If we have time,	*we'll go and see Sarah.*

- Notice that we use a present tense in the *if* clause and a future form in the main clause. This form is often called **the first conditional**. We use this for something that might happen in the future.
- We can also use other future forms or a modal verb in the main clause.
  If the weather's good, we're going to play tennis later.
  If you're very good, I might buy you an ice cream.
- We can change the position of the *if* clause and the main clause.
  I'll tell you if anything unusual happens.
  If anything unusual happens, I'll tell you.

2 *when, as soon as, before* and *after*

- We also use a present tense after *when* and *as soon as* to talk about things we are sure will happen in the future.
  When we get home, I'll show you our new kitchen.
- *when / as soon as*
  I'll phone you as soon as we arrive. (= I will do this immediately)
  I'll phone you when we arrive. (= it's not so urgent)
- *before / after*
  Remember to turn off all the lights before you go.
  After I graduate, I'll take time off to think about my future.

PRACTICE 2

1 Choose the correct answers.

1 I **tell / 'll tell** you if I **see / 'll see** him.
2 I **cook / 'll cook** dinner as soon as we **get / 'll get** home.
3 My parents **come / might come** to visit when they **come / will come** back from holiday.
4 I **give / 'll give** you my email address before I **go / 'll go**.
5 If she **passes / 'll pass** her exams, I **am / 'll be** very surprised.
6 I **phone / 'll phone** her when I **finish / 'll finish** my homework.
7 If I **go / will go** to the supermarket, I **buy / 'll buy** some milk.
8 He **emails / will email** tonight if he **has / 'll have** time.
9 If it **rains / 'll rain**, I **don't go / won't go** to the beach.
10 If he **gets / 'll get** the job, he **'ll move / move** to Shanghai.

2 Complete the conversations with the correct form of the verb in brackets.

1 **A:** Thanks for a lovely weekend.
  B: You're welcome.
  A: You and Liz must come and stay with me when you ¹_____ (be) next in Scotland.
  B: We'd love to.
  A: And I ²_____ (email) you the photos as soon as I ³_____ (get) home.
  B: Great.

2 **A:** Would you like to come to a talk on garden design tomorrow?
  B: OK. What time is it?
  A: 5:30 p.m. at the Sheldon Centre.
  B: OK. I ⁴_____ (come) before I ⁵_____ (go) to the gym.
  A: Great! I ⁶_____ (phone) you when I ⁷_____ (arrive).
  B: Sure. If I ⁸_____ (have) time, I ⁹_____ (ask) Angela, too.
  A: OK, great. See you tomorrow.

3 **A:** Have a great weekend in Athens, Ben!
  B: Thanks!
  A: Remember to send Grandma a birthday card before you ¹⁰_____ (go).
  B: I ¹¹_____ (do) it when I ¹²_____ (get) back.
  A: OK, but don't forget!
  B: I ¹³_____ (buy) a card as soon as I ¹⁴_____ (get) home.

REMEMBER THESE WORDS

MODERN EQUIPMENT

air conditioning	a microwave oven
central heating	an oven
a computer	a shower
a dishwasher	a vacuum cleaner
a flat screen television	a washing machine
a freezer	a wi-fi router
a fridge	

ADJECTIVES FOR DESCRIBING PLACES

an attractive house	an old-fashioned house
a comfortable room	a private garden
a dark living room	a quiet street
a large bedroom	a shady garden
a light kitchen	a small bathroom
a lively café	a spacious kitchen
a modern kitchen	a sunny room

OTHER

air freshener	a priority
a bottle of bleach	a rubbish bag
a cave house	running water
furniture	a shower curtain
messy	time-consuming
modern interior	wipes
to move house	

PRACTICE

1 Complete the sentences with the words in the box. You do not need to use two of the words.

central heating   air conditioning   oven   microwave oven   fridge   freezer   washing machine   dishwasher   shower   vacuum cleaner   flat screen television   wi-fi router

1 The floor is really dirty. Can you get the _____ , please?
2 You can keep milk fresh for up to a week in the _____ .
3 The _____ was very noisy, but it kept me cool all night.
4 I've got a new _____ , so I won't have to wash all the plates by hand anymore.
5 My _____ broke last night with all my clothes stuck inside.
6 I always keep plenty of ice cream in my _____ .
7 I can make a baked potato in about three minutes in the _____ .
8 The school is closed today because the _____ is broken and it's too cold.
9 Pieter spends so long in the _____ there's never any hot water for me!
10 David stayed at home all weekend because he was watching his new _____ .

2 Choose the correct answers.

1 The meeting room was *lively / spacious* – with plenty of room for everybody.
2 Most of the furniture was *old-fashioned / modern*, made over a hundred years ago.
3 We sat in the *shady / light* part of the garden under several large trees.
4 I've got a *private / lively* room at the top of the house – nobody else goes there.
5 This sofa is very *modern / comfortable* – I could stay here all day!
6 My office is very *attractive / dark* – there's only one small window and you can never see the sun.
7 Their new house is very *modern / shady* – it was built in 2012.
8 I live in a very *quiet / lively* road – there's almost no traffic.

10 STUDY, PRACTICE & REMEMBER

Past continuous

+	I/He/She **was travelling.**
	We/You/They **were travelling.**
−	I/He/She **wasn't travelling.**
	We/You/They **weren't travelling.**
?	**Was** I/he/she **travelling?**
	Were we/you/they **travelling?**

• We use the Past continuous to talk about actions in progress:
  – at a certain time in the past.
    I was driving home at 6:30 this evening.

```
driving home        6.30
        ～～～～～～
◄─────────────────────────────► now
past
```

  – when another (completed) action happened.
    I was driving home when I saw a friend of mine.

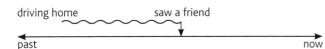

```
driving home            saw a friend
        ～～～～～～～～～│
◄─────────────────────────────► now
past                                      now
```

• We often use the Past continuous to describe the background situation in a story. For the main events, we use the Past simple.
  The sun was shining and everyone was getting ready for the party that afternoon. Then, my phone rang and …
• Sometimes the other action in the Past simple interrupts the action in the Past continuous.
  I was crossing the road when I slipped on some ice. (= I stopped crossing the road)
• When two actions happened one after the other, we use the Past simple for both actions.
  When I heard the crash, I ran to the end of the street.
• We use *when, while* and *as* to join the Past continuous and Past simple parts of a sentence.
  I saw Karl when/while/as I was waiting at the bus stop.

REMEMBER!
We do not use state verbs in the continuous form.
I knew her when we were children.
NOT *I was knowing her when we were children.*

1 Choose the correct answers.

1 He *drove / was driving* to work when a dog *ran / was running* out in front of his car.
2 I *met / was meeting* my old friend Harry as I *got / was getting* on the bus.
3 The lights suddenly *went / were going* out when we *cooked / were cooking* dinner.
4 While we *waited / were waiting* in the queue, someone *pushed / was pushing* past us.
5 As she *got / was getting* some money out of her bag, she *dropped / was dropping* her phone.
6 I *broke / was breaking* my leg while I *played / was playing* football last week.

2 Complete the conversation with the correct form of the verb in brackets.

I ¹_____ (walk) down the street about an hour ago when suddenly I ²_____ (see) an accident. A car ³_____ (drive) very fast along the road and there was this man in front of the car. He ⁴_____ (ride) a bicycle and he ⁵_____ (not hear) the car because he ⁶_____ (listen) to his MP3 player. Anyway, the car ⁷_____ (go) too close to him and he ⁸_____ (fall off) his bike. I quickly ⁹_____ (run) over to have a look. He ¹⁰_____ (lie) in the middle of the street, but he ¹¹_____ (not breathe). Fortunately, I ¹²_____ (remember) my first aid course. I ¹³_____ (call) an ambulance on my mobile and then while I ¹⁴_____ (wait), I ¹⁵_____ (begin) giving him the kiss of life. After one minute he ¹⁶_____ (start) breathing again.

used to

+	I/You/He/She/We/They **used to** walk to school.
−	I/You/He/She/We/They **didn't use to** walk to school.
?	**Did** I/you/he/she/we/they **use to** walk to school?

• We use *used to*:
  – for actions that happened many times in the past (habits).
    He used to wait for me at the school gates.
  – for feelings, thoughts, ideas, etc. in the past.
    I used to be afraid of the dark.
• Notice that the habit or state is probably not true now.
  We used to have a dog called Tilly. (= but we don't have the dog now)
  Or it may be true now.
  I didn't use to like sport at school. (= but I like it now)
• We can always use the Past simple instead of *used to*.
  We had a dog called Tilly.
  I didn't like sport at school.
• We do not use *used to* for actions that happened only once.
  I went to Spain in 2009.
  NOT *I used to go to Spain in 2009.*

PRACTICE 2

1 Complete the sentences with the correct form of *use(d) to* and the verb in brackets.

1 I _____ (play) the guitar, but I stopped about three years ago.
2 She _____ (not like) green vegetables, but now she loves them.
3 _____ (you / have) a dog when you were a child?
4 He _____ (go) to the gym three times a week, but he's too busy now.
5 I _____ (not speak) French at all, but now I'm nearly fluent.
6 _____ (you / watch) television a lot when you were a child?

2 Find and correct the five mistakes in the sentences below.

1 We used to live in Tennessee when I was young.
2 They used to go to Disneyworld in 1999.
3 Our parents often took us to the beach during the holidays.
4 I used to go swimming every week.
5 Did you used to have a bicycle when you were young?
6 My brother used to be afraid of spiders.
7 How did she use to meet Juan?
8 Philip used to start school a few months ago.
9 I used to get up at 10 a.m. every Sunday, but now I have small children.
10 He didn't used to like coffee, but he does now.

REMEMBER THESE WORDS

ACCIDENTS AND INJURIES

to be allergic to	to feel dizzy
to become swollen	to get a bee sting / to sting
to break your arm/leg	to get a rash
to burn yourself	to phone for an ambulance
to come round	to put a plaster / some ice /
to cut your finger	some cream on it
to faint	to stop the bleeding

FEELING ILL

to be sick	to have got a headache
to feel sick	to have got a sore throat
to have got a cold	to have got a stomachache
to have got a cough	to have got toothache
to have got an earache	my ear/hand hurts
to have got a fever	to sneeze

OTHER

an accident	hygiene
an allergy	an illness
bacteria	an immune system
a broken arm/leg	an injury
a disease	a remedy
an epidemic	to suffer from allergies
to feel breathless	a symptom
first aid	

PRACTICE

1 Complete the sentences with the correct form of the verbs in the box. You do not need to use two of the verbs.

be   become   break   burn   come   cut   get   suffer

1 I _____ my finger really badly while I was cooking. It didn't stop bleeding for ages!
2 That light is very hot. Be careful you don't _____ yourself on it.
3 I _____ a sting on my arm – from a bee or some other kind of insect.
4 After my sister fainted, it was about two minutes before she _____ round.
5 He can't eat cheese because he _____ allergic to all dairy products.
6 When I eat fish, my tongue _____ swollen and I find it difficult to breathe.

2 Which two of the symptoms often go together? Make logical pairs.

A
1 I feel sick.
2 I've got an earache.
3 I've got a cold.
4 I've got a cough.

B
a My ear hurts.
b I can't stop sneezing.
c I've got a sore throat.
d I've got a stomachache.

3 Put the sentences in the correct order to make a conversation in the doctor's surgery.

a What's the problem? *1*
b I think I'm allergic to my dog.
c No, I'm not.
d What are your symptoms?
e Thank you, doctor.
f Are you taking any medication at the moment?
g I've got a headache and I keep sneezing.
h Take an aspirin and go for a walk ... without your dog.

STUDY 1

like and *would like*

- We use *like* to talk about things we enjoy, and *love* to talk about things we enjoy a lot.

  *My little brother **likes** science fiction films.*

  *I **love** coffee.*

  If we put another verb after *like*, we use the *-ing* form.

  *I **like staying** in bed late.*

  *He doesn't **like lying** on the beach.*

  Some verbs we can use with the *-ing* form are: *like, enjoy, love, hate.*

  *I **enjoy running** on the beach before work.*

- We use *would like* to talk about things we want. *I would like* is more polite than *I want*.

  *I'**d like** a new tennis racket for my birthday.*

  If we put a verb after *would like*, we use the infinitive with *to*.

  *I'**d like to speak** to the manager, please.*

REMEMBER!

We often use *Would you like ... ?* for an offer.

Would you like some coffee?

Would you like to go to the cinema?

Notice that the answer is:

Yes, please. Or: *Yes, I'd love some. / I'd love to.*

NOT *Yes, I'd like.* Or: *Yes, I'd love.*

PRACTICE 1

1 Complete the sentences with the correct form of the verbs in brackets. Use either the *-ing* form or the infinitive with *to*.

1 I hate _____ (go) to the dentist.
2 I like _____ (cook) dinner for my friends at weekends.
3 I'd love _____ (get) tickets for the opera.
4 I enjoy _____ (walk) to work in the mornings.
5 I'd like _____ (do) some training in first aid.
6 I love _____ (travel) by public transport in unusual places.
7 I hate _____ (talk) on my mobile phone on the train.
8 I like _____ (make) new friends.

2 Choose the correct answers.

1 My husband *would like to / loves* cycling and swimming.
2 I'*d like / like* a new car, but I don't think I'll buy one this year.
3 He doesn't like *getting up / get up* early.
4 They hate *go / going* to the library.
5 She'*d like to / 'd like* speak to the President.
6 They enjoy *watch / watching* films with their friends.
7 We *like / would like to* cakes, sweets and chocolate.
8 I don't like *do / doing* the washing up.
9 They would like *to go / go* to Buenos Aires next summer.
10 I don't enjoy *visiting / visit* museums and art galleries.

3 Match the questions in A with the answers in B.

A

1 Do you like cheese?
2 Would you like something to drink?
3 Does she enjoy travelling by train?
4 Would you like an ice cream?
5 Does Jack like children?
6 Would you like to go to the cinema?

B

a No, she doesn't.
b Yes, I do.
c Yes, please.
d Yes, we'd love to.
e Yes, I'd love one.
f Yes, he does.

STUDY 2

conditional sentences with *would*

If + Past simple + *would(n't)* + infinitive without *to*

If clause	main clause
*If I **became** president,*	*I'**d build** more hospitals.*

We use conditional sentences with *would* to talk about imaginary, impossible or unlikely situations. The verb in the *if* clause is in the Past simple, but we are not talking about the past and we are not talking about a specific time.

*If I **had** a ticket, I'**d come** with you.* (= I haven't got a ticket)

*If you **lived** in the country, you'**d** soon **get** bored.* (= you don't live in the country)

Notice that:

- we can change the order of the *if* clause and the main clause.

  If you lived in the country, you'd soon get bored.

  You'd soon get bored if you lived in the country.

- we can use *were* instead of *was* after *I, he/she* and *it*.

  *If my brother **were** here now, he'd know what to do.*

  *If I **were** you, I'd go to the doctor's.*

- we often use *If I were you, I'd ...* to give advice.

  *If I **were you, I'd** look for someone else.*

- we can use *might* or *could* instead of *would*.

  *If you worked hard, you **might** pass the exam.*

  *If I borrowed Mum's car, I **could** give you a lift.*

1 Choose the correct answers.

1 If I *lived / live* in Canada, I'd go skiing every day.
2 If you *would borrow / borrowed* Tom's bike, you could come with us.
3 If I were you, I *go / 'd go* to bed early before the exam.
4 If we were rich, we could *buy / bought* a new flat screen television for the flat.
5 Claire would order spaghetti bolognese if she *were / would be* here.
6 *I / I'd* ask for directions if I spoke Russian.
7 If Petra were older, she *could go / went* with you to the cinema.
8 If I were you, I'*d take / take* the train into the city centre.
9 We *would drive / drive* to the coast if we knew the way.
10 If he wasn't afraid of spiders, he'*d go / go* to the zoo.

2 Complete the sentences with the correct form of the verbs in brackets.

1 If I _____ (have) a dog, I _____ (take) it for long walks every day.
2 She _____ (travel) round the world if she _____ (win) the lottery.
3 If I _____ (be) more intelligent, I _____ (study) to be a lawyer.
4 If my sister _____ (not live) in Australia, I _____ (see) her more often.
5 If you _____ (have) the opportunity, _____ (you / go) to the moon?
6 I _____ (live) in New York if I _____ (have) enough money.
7 If we _____ (have) a garden, we _____ (buy) a dog.
8 _____ (you / take part) in a survey in the street if someone _____ (ask) you?
9 If I _____ (win) the lottery, I _____ (not give up) my job.
10 They _____ (read) more books if they _____ (not be) so expensive.

3 Match the sentence beginnings in A with the sentence endings in B.

A
1 If Amanda understood Italian,
2 She would retire
3 We'd go out for dinner
4 I'd take you there
5 If he wanted a new job,
6 If I were you,

B
a I wouldn't buy that coat.
b if she had enough money.
c if I had a car.
d he'd look for one.
e she could read the newspaper.
f if it wasn't so cold.

REMEMBER THESE WORDS

ADJECTIVES WITH DEPENDENT PREPOSITIONS

afraid of
different from
full of
good at
interested in

keen on
similar to
suitable for
surprised about
worried about

SURVIVAL ITEMS

a battery
a blanket
bottled water
a compass
insect repellent
a knife
matches
a magnifying glass

a mirror
a rope
suncream
sunglasses
a tent
toilet paper
a torch
water purification tablets

OTHER

to go to the hairdresser's
a hobby
job satisfaction
on a camping holiday
on a desert island
a pet
physical work

a public performance
to research
a risk of heart disease
to sing in a choir
to sunbathe
a survey
to work in a team

PRACTICE

1 Choose the correct answers.

1 I'm really surprised *for / about* the exam results this year.
2 He is really different *from / for* her last boyfriend.
3 She is very keen *on / of* sunbathing while she's on holiday.
4 He's worried *to / about* being late for the train.
5 This coat is not suitable *for / to* winter weather.
6 Is anyone interested *about / in* taking part in the competition?
7 My brother is really good *of / at* making people laugh.
8 In my family, I'm most similar *to / with* my mother.
9 Her house is full *of / in* books.
10 I am really afraid *to / of* flying.

2 Read the clues and add letters to complete the words.

1 a shelter used for camping: t _ _ t
2 a cover for a bed, usually made of wool: b_ _ _ _ _ t
3 an instrument that shows directions: c _ _ _ _ _ s
4 a very strong, thick string: r _ _ e
5 something that provides a supply of electricity: b _ _ _ _ _ y
6 a small electric lamp that you carry in your hand: t _ _ _ h
7 special glass that you can look in and see yourself: m _ _ _ _ r
8 a substance that keeps insects away: i _ _ _ t r _ _ _ _ _ _ t
9 things you wear on your face when it is very sunny: s _ _ _ _ _ _ _ s
10 something you use to cut things: k _ _ _ e

STUDY 1

Present simple passive

We form the Present simple passive with the subject + *am/is/are* + past participle. Regular past participles end in *-ed*. For a list of irregular past participles, see page 175.

+	I **am made**.
	He/She/It **is made**.
	You/We/They **are made**.
−	I **am not made**.
	He/She/It **isn't** (= is not) **made**.
	You/We/They **aren't** (= are not) **made**.
?	**Am** I **made**?
	Is he/she/it **made**?
	Are you/we/they **made**?

- We use the passive when the person who does the action:
  - is not important.
    *This chocolate **is made** in Switzerland.* (= it's not important who makes it)
  - is unknown.
    *Hundreds of cars **are stolen** every week.* (= we don't know who steals them)
  - means 'people in general'.
    *His face **is recognised** all over the world.* (= people in general recognise his face)
- If we want to say who or what is the 'doer' of the action, we use *by*.
  *All my clothes **are designed by** Federico Pirani.*
- Active or passive? Compare the following examples:
  a *Martine **makes** all her own bread at home.*
  b *The bread **is made** in a large bakery outside town.*
  In sentence a, we use the active form because we are more interested in **who** makes the bread, so Martine is the subject (of an active verb).
  In sentence b, we use the passive form because we are more interested in the bread (not in who makes it), so the bread is the subject (of a passive verb).

PRACTICE 1

1 Choose the correct answers.

1 Coca-Cola *sells / is sold* all over the world.
2 It *drinks / is drunk* by millions of people.
3 94 percent of people *recognise / are recognised* it.
4 Rolex watches *cost / are cost* up to $20,000.
5 They *wear / are worn* by thousands of people.
6 They *show / are shown* different time zones.
7 Mercedes cars *come / are come* from Germany.
8 They *drive / are driven* by many rich and famous people.
9 The company *names / is named* after the owner's daughter.
10 Samsung products *make / are made* in South Korea.

2 Put the Present simple passive form of the verbs in brackets in the correct place in these sentences.

1 Thousands of mobile phones every year. (lose)
2 All the tickets over the internet. (sell)
3 A lot of the world's gold in South Africa. (produce)
4 The rooms every morning. (clean)
5 Millions of barrels of oil to Europe. (import)
6 Five hundred people in the new factory. (employ)
7 The cows at 6 o'clock every morning. (feed)
8 Cheese from milk. (make)

STUDY 2

Past simple passive

We form the Past simple passive with the subject + *was/were* + past participle.

+	I/He/She/It **was seen**.
	You/We/They **were seen**.
−	I/He/She/It **was not** (= wasn't) **seen**.
	You/We/They **were not** (= weren't) **seen**.
?	**Was** I/he/she/it **seen**?
	Were you/we/they **seen**?

- As with the Present simple passive, we use the Past simple passive when the action is more important than the person who did it.
- The Past simple passive is common when we are speaking formally, or in written reports.
  *More than thirty people **were injured** in the explosion.*
  *The idea **was developed** with a team of 15 designers.*
  *Great Expectations **was written** by Charles Dickens.*

PRACTICE 2

1 Complete the sentences with the correct form of the verbs in the box.

arrest   bite   build   design   repair   steal   take   damage
invite   write

1 The paintings _____ during the night.
2 This car _____ by a Korean company.
3 The three men _____ at about 6 o'clock this morning.
4 When _____ (this photograph)?
5 I _____ by a dog when I was a child.
6 The new shopping centre _____ by an American company.
7 _____ (your car) at this garage?
8 The Harry Potter books _____ by J K Rowling.
9 He _____ to a garden party at the palace.
10 The car _____ in the accident.

2 Put the words in the correct order to make questions.

1 was / built / this / When / house ?
2 were / Who / tea / invented / bags / by ?
3 about / you / Were / told / problem / the ?
4 computer / Was / your / on / left ?
5 much / How / was / money / stolen / from / wallet / your ?
6 *Sunflowers* / Who / painted / by / was ?
7 when / were / and / Where / born / you ?
8 credit / How / was / found / your / card ?

3 Complete the sentences with the Past simple passive form of the verb in brackets.

1 Razor blades _____ (produce) for the first time in 1901 by an American businessman, King Camp Gillette.
2 In 1928, penicillin _____ (discover) by Alexander Fleming, a Scottish scientist.
3 The first electric guitar _____ (make) in 1935 in Michigan, USA.
4 A new airport at Heathrow _____ (open) in London in 1946.
5 Car seat belts _____ (use) for the first time in 1959.
6 In 1970, the Nobel Prize for Literature _____ (give) to the Russian writer, Alexander Solzhenitsyn.
7 In 1982, the Best Actor Oscar _____ (win) by Ben Kingsley as Gandhi in the film *Gandhi*.
8 The Berlin Wall _____ (pull down) in 1989.
9 The Brazilian racing driver, Ayrton Senna, _____ (kill) in the 1994 San Marino Grand Prix.
10 In 2012 the Olympic Games _____ (hold) in London, England.

REMEMBER THESE WORDS

TYPES OF PRODUCT

accessories	electronic mail
chocolate bars	fast food
clothes	an internet search engine
coffee and pastries	soft drinks
electronic goods	sportswear
	trainers

PERSONAL ITEMS

aftershave	hair gel
a bracelet	lipstick
a comb	moisturiser
cosmetics	nail varnish
deodorant	a necklace
earrings	perfume
an eyeliner	a razor
a hairbrush	shaving foam

OTHER

to be disappointed with	to recommend something
to be made of (cotton/canvas)	a slogan
comfortable	a target market
fashionable	toiletries
highly recommended	value for money
a logo	well-designed
jewellery	

PRACTICE

1 Complete the sentences with the words in the box.

> accessories bars electronic engine fast pastries
> soft sportswear mail trainers

1 Why don't we go to the café on the corner for coffee and _____ ?
2 This shop sells jewellery, handbags and other _____ for women.
3 I'm changing my internet search _____ because it's too slow.
4 I eat _____ food like burgers and pizza about once a week.
5 Where can I get a wide range of _____ goods like computers and phones?
6 There will be snacks and _____ drinks during the break.
7 If you want to lose weight, you shouldn't eat so many chocolate _____ .
8 At the weekends, I usually wear _____ , not smart clothes.
9 I've started running, so I want to get a new pair of _____ .
10 I usually check my electronic _____ on my mobile phone.

2 Choose the correct answers.

1 You don't want to smell after playing football, so don't forget your *deodorant / cosmetics.*
2 He uses a lot of *hairbrush / hair gel* to keep his hair in the style he likes.
3 She was wearing a beautiful *necklace / bracelet* on her arm.
4 He cut himself with his *razor / aftershave* this morning.
5 My skin gets very dry, so I use *toiletries / moisturiser* every morning.
6 There was a good discount on the price of *earrings / lipstick* on the cosmetics counter today.
7 When he arrived, I could immediately smell his *aftershave / shaving foam.*
8 I always carry a *necklace / comb* in my handbag because my hair gets very messy.
9 I don't really like red *nail varnish / moisturiser.*
10 He bought her some very expensive, diamond *eyeliner / earrings* on holiday.

STUDY 1

Present perfect continuous with *how long*, *for* and *since*

+	I/You/We/They**'ve been working.**	
	He/She/It**'s been working.**	
−	I/You/We/They**'ve been working.**	
	He/She/It**'s been working.**	
?	Have you/we/they **been working?**	
	Has he/she/it **been working?**	

- We use the Present perfect continuous to talk about actions that started in the past and continue to the present.

  She's been working as a doctor for 40 years.

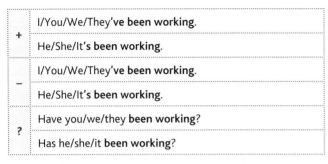

  40 years ago   now

- We use *for* and *since* to talk about periods of time from the past to the present.
  - We use *for* to talk about periods of time. It answers questions with *how long*.

    for 40 years   *for five hours*   *for six months*
    for a minute   *for 500 years*

    He's been teaching for ten years.

    10 years ago   now

  - We use *since* to talk about points of time. It answers questions with *how long*.

    since 1965   *since last year*   *since 2004*
    since Tuesday   *since 6 o'clock*   *since October*

    He's been teaching since 1996.

    Since 1996   now

REMEMBER!

We do not use the Present Continuous to talk about actions that started in the past and continue to the present.

I've been learning English since last year.
NOT *I am learning English since last year.*

- The following phrases often occur with the Present perfect continuous, but do not need *for* or *since*.

  all my life   *all morning*   *all day*   *all week*
  all month   *all year*

PRACTICE 1

1 Complete the sentences with *how long*, *for* or *since*.

1 _____ have you been waiting here?
2 I've been studying English _____ three years.
3 We've been coming here on holiday _____ 1998.
4 Jake has been looking for a flat _____ October.
5 He's been driving _____ about a year.
6 _____ have you been sitting there?

2 Put the time phrases in the box below into the correct column in the table.

> 1998   six years   ten minutes   last Sunday   a long time
> 7 o'clock   a minute   I was born   yesterday   a week

for	since

3 Complete the conversation with the Present perfect continuous form of the verb in brackets.

A: How long ¹_____ (you / play) football, Ben?
B: I ²_____ (play) all my life.
A: And how long ³_____ (you / train) young footballers?
B: I ⁴_____ (not /work) here very long. I started about six months ago.
A: I believe your son trains with you.
B: Yes, he ⁵_____ (come) here since January. He's really enjoying it and I think he's going to be good.
A: What about you, Carlos? ⁶_____ (you / cycle) all your life?
C: No, I haven't. I began when I was 15, so let's see, that means I ⁷_____ (cycle) for about six years now.
A: Is this your new bike?
C: Yes, I ⁸_____ (use) it since last month. You can see it's very light and it goes very fast.

STUDY 2

Present perfect continuous and present perfect simple

- In many cases, we can use the Present perfect simple and the Present perfect continuous with *for* and *since* with no real difference in meaning.

  I've been living in this house for over a year.
  I've lived in this house for over a year.

- But if a verb describes a state (for example *like*, *love*, *be*, *have*, *see*, *know*), we cannot use the continuous form.

  They've known each other for more than 50 years.
  NOT *They have been knowing each other for more than 50 years.*

- If we mention a number or quantity, we normally use the simple form.

  I've made six phone calls today.
  NOT *I've been making six phone calls today.*

1 Which of the sentences below can be changed into the Present perfect continuous?

1   How long have you known Steve?
2   I've played tennis for many years.
3   I've never liked romantic films.
4   It's rained since 6 o'clock this morning.
5   We've waited for nearly an hour.
6   I've been a teacher for ten years.
7   She's written 12 emails this morning.
8   He's been very excited all week.

2 Choose the correct answers.

1   **A:** How long *have you been knowing / have you known* Sally?
     B: For three months.
2   **A:** When *have you met / did you meet* Kristin?
     B: In July.
3   **A:** Hurry up! You *'ve been getting / have got* ready for ages!
     B: I'm coming!
4   **A:** That's a nice watch.
     B: Yes, I *bought / 've been buying* it when I was in Switzerland.
5   **A:** I like your ring.
     B: Thank you. I *'ve been having / 've had* it since I was six years old.
6   **A:** It's 10 o'clock. How long *has he played / has he been playing* that computer game?
     B: For three hours so far!
7   **A:** Pat *has written / has been writing* to eight companies this morning.
     B: Yes, I hope she gets a new job soon.
8   **A:** I *didn't see / haven't seen* you for ages. How are you?
     B: I'm really well, thanks.
9   **A:** How long *have you been living / did you live* in Turkey?
     B: For three years, from 2000–2003.
10 **A:** Katrina *has played / has been playing* basketball four times so far this week.
     B: Yes, she really likes it.

REMEMBER THESE WORDS

PERSONAL CHARACTERISTICS

affectionate	organised
ambitious	patient
easy-going	reliable
hard-working	sensitive
honest	sociable
open	sympathetic

GETTING A JOB

to apply online	to look for a job
computing skills	a part-time job
an education	personal details
to fill in an application form	qualifications
to go for an interview	a recruitment agency
a job vacancy	to write a CV
to log on to job websites	

OTHER

an 'arranged' marriage	a goodwill ambassador
audition	a happy marriage
common background	a 'love' marriage
divorce	shared values
to do things for myself	to share a flat / a flatshare
to earn a good salary	to start/run your own business
to fall in love	unemployed
a flatmate	

PRACTICE

1 Match the questions in A with the answers in B.

A 1 Are you sociable?
   2 Are you organised?
   3 Are you ambitious?
   4 Are you patient?
   5 Are you reliable?
   6 Are you easy-going?
   7 Are you sympathetic?
   8 Are you honest?
   9 Are you hard-working?
   10 Are you open?

B a Yes, I've never told a lie in my life.
   b Yes, I always do what I say I will.
   c Yes, I don't mind waiting if I have to.
   d Yes, I enjoy being with other people.
   e Yes, I never get upset about small things.
   f Yes, I want a better job as soon as I can.
   g Yes, I like planning and writing lists.
   h Yes, I'm good at listening to other people's problems.
   i Yes, I don't hide my feelings from other people.
   j Yes, I always put a lot of effort into my job.

2 Complete the sentences with the words in the box.
You do not need to use one of the words.

qualifications   apply   skills   details   CV   vacancies
on   recruitment   for   fill   part-time

1   Please _____ in the application form in black ink.
2   We need your personal _____ like name, address, date of birth, etc.
3   If you have access to the internet, you can _____ online.
4   I'm going _____ an interview next week, so I need to buy a new suit.
5   Please write down all your school exams, university degree and other _____ .
6   The people at the _____ agency helped me to find a job.
7   I got a _____ job to earn some money while I was at university.
8   There were no suitable job _____ that I could apply for.
9   I'm doing a computer course because I want to impove my computer _____ .
10 He wrote his _____ when he left university.

STUDY 1

Past perfect

We form the Past perfect with *had* + past participle. Regular past participles end in *-ed*. Many verbs have an irregular past participle. See the list on page 175.

+	I/You/He/She/It/We/They'd (= had) **finished**.
–	I/You/He/She/It/We/They **hadn't** (= had not) **finished**.
?	**Had** I/you/he/she/it/we/they **finished**?

- We use the Past perfect to show that one action happened before another in the past, and that the first action finished before the second action started.

  *He **had been** to the bank and he **was** on his way home.*

- We often use the Past perfect with *because* to explain a past situation.

  *Patrick **felt** ill because he'**d eaten** so much.*

- To show that two actions happened at the same time, we use the Past simple with *when*.

  *I **woke up** when the telephone **rang**.*

- If the sequence of events is clear from the context, it is not always necessary to use the Past perfect.

  *A robber **appeared** and **pointed** a gun at him.*

PRACTICE 1

1 Complete the sentences with the Past perfect form of the verbs in the box.

forget   not eat   go   do   try   leave   not phone   have
travel   spend

1 The children were hungry because they _____ all morning.
2 We couldn't get into the theatre because Lisa _____ the tickets at home.
3 She felt better after she _____ a rest.
4 Dan _____ into hospital the day before I arrived.
5 Abby was very worried because her son _____ .
6 We were tired because we _____ a long way.
7 I felt embarrassed because I _____ her name.
8 When Luke _____ his homework, he watched TV.
9 After Sharon _____ all the perfumes, she chose the most expensive one.
10 I couldn't get a bus home because I _____ all my money on a new coat.

2 Choose the correct answers.

1 When I **had got / got** downstairs, the phone **had stopped / stopped** ringing.
2 I **had been / was** sorry to leave, as I **enjoyed / had enjoyed** the evening very much.
3 Silvana **had been / was** very upset because she **had lost / lost** her purse.
4 When the exam **started / had started**, it became clear that I **didn't revise / hadn't revised** enough.
5 It **had been / was** a very long day, so I **had been / went** to bed early.
6 When I **saw / had seen** him, I realised I **meet / had met** him before.

STUDY 2

Narrative tenses

- We use the Past simple to talk about the main events in a story.
  *A man in Germany **had** a horrible surprise when he **checked** his email one morning.*

- We use the Past perfect to talk about actions which happened before the main events in a story.
  *When the bank **realised** their mistake, George **had spent** £85,000.*
  We use the Past continuous to talk about actions in progress at a certain time in the past. We often use it to describe the background situation in a story.
  *I **was walking** to work yersterday when someone rushed past me in the street.*

PRACTICE 2

1 Choose the correct answers.

1 A Venezuelan man [1]**was making / made** an expensive mistake when he threw away a black plastic bag; his wife [2]**had hidden / hid** all her jewellery in it. When she found out what [3]**had happened / was happening**, she [4]**phoned / was phoning** the rubbish company. The people there said that they [5]**were burning / had burnt** all that day's rubbish a few hours earlier.

2 While Frances [6]**was working / worked** in a bank, a man [7]**walked / was walking** in and demanded £100,000. After she [8]**had given / gave** him the money, he [9]**ran / was running** away. Unfortunately for him, he didn't realise he [10]**had left / left** his driving licence in the bank with his name and address on it.

3 Last week a 70-year-old German woman [11]**won / had won** €200 in a children's art competition by entering a picture she [12]**had painted / was painting** 60 years earlier.

2 Complete the paragraph with the correct form of the verbs in brackets. Use the Past simple, Past continuous or Past perfect.

Shivdan Yadav [1]_____ (live) in the Indian province of Rajasthan when he [2]_____ (take) his school leaving exams for the first time at the age of 18. He is now 56, and he still hasn't passed them. When he was 18, he [3]_____ (be) engaged to a local girl for several months. Shivdan only [4]_____ (want) to get married after he [5]_____ (pass) his exams. At that time, his father [6]_____ (agree) to postpone the wedding. After three years, however, he still [7]_____ (not pass) his exams, so his girlfriend [8]_____ (leave) him and married someone else. By the time Shivdan reached the age of 56, his ex-girlfriend [9]_____ (become) a grandmother, but he was still single.

REMEMBER THESE WORDS

MONEY

bank notes	an exchange rate
a bill	foreign currency
a cashpoint machine	a purse
change	a receipt
coins	a wallet
a credit card	

VERB PHRASES ABOUT MONEY

to borrow from	to pay a fine
to earn	to pay back
to inherit	to save up (to buy a …)
to lend to	to spend
to lose	to win

OTHER

to ask for assistance	a millionaire
to be greedy (about money)	on one hand
to be a waste of money	on the other hand
a billionaire	PIN (= Personal Identification
can/can't afford	Number)
financial success	to refuse
for and against	to scan
in total despair	a stockbroker
to insert	a tip
an internet auction company	to win a prize / a bet

PRACTICE

1 Complete the sentences with the words in the box.

bill   cashpoint machine   change   credit card   purse
exchange rate   foreign currency   receipt   wallet   coins

1 Excuse me, do you know if there is a _____ in this street?
2 When I got the _____ for the meal, I was shocked to see it was over €100.
3 He usually carries about £20 in cash in his _____ .
4 I've got quite a lot of _____ left over from my summer holiday.
5 Can you tell what the _____ between the euro and the pound is, please?
6 He never pays in cash – he uses his _____ for everything nowadays.
7 I need to take these jeans back to the shop, but I've lost the _____ .
8 Do you ever check that they have given you the right _____ in shops?
9 I bought her a new _____ for her birthday.
10 Do you have any _____ for the machine in the car park? I only have a $20 note.

2 Choose the correct answers.

1 I'm so lucky! I've just *won / earned* £100 in a competition!
2 She *borrowed / inherited* a lot of money from her old aunt when she died.
3 If you park your car there, you'll have to *spend / pay* a fine of £60.
4 I want to *save up / spend* enough money to buy an MP3 player.
5 Could you *lend / borrow* me £20 just until tomorrow, please?
6 He *spent / won* so much money at the weekend that he had to stay in all week.
7 After her promotion, she started *earning / inheriting* a huge salary.
8 I don't really like *lending / borrowing* money from my friends.
9 I put $30 in the pocket of my jacket, but I *won / lost* it on the way home.
10 He lent me £10 for lunch on Friday. I must *pay him back / spend* on Monday.

Audio script

UNIT 1 RECORDING 2

A = Announcer   J = Journalist

A: A new report into young adults' leisure time has some surprising results. John Crane reports:

J: In this digital age, many people think that young adults spent all their time on the computer. And a new government survey of how young adults spend their leisure time says that 87 percent of people in the UK between the ages of 16 and 24 use the internet every day. But it's still important for young people to go out with friends. And the most popular evening out is going to the cinema: 42 percent say it's their favourite way to spend an evening.

For people who don't go out, not surprisingly, television is more popular than radio. 82 percent say that they watch television for more than ten hours a week – mainly for films and news programmes – but only 23 percent listen to the radio.

Music is always a favourite topic, but it seems that many more people listen to music than can play a musical instrument. The survey reveals that 38 percent watch live music, but 30 percent of people between 16 and 24 can play a musical instrument.

Only 32 percent of young adults play sport; with football, swimming and cycling the most popular activities. But that means that more than two-thirds don't play any sport!

UNIT 1 RECORDING 3

1   The first computer game of *The Mario Brothers* was in 1983, with Mario and his brother Luigi.
2   The white player always starts in a game of chess.
3   Marbles are usually made of glass.
4   The game mahjong originated in China, probably about 2,500 years ago.
5   Snakes and Ladders is a board game. When you land at the top of a snake, you go down it, and when you land at the bottom of a ladder, you go up it.
6   Nobody really knows why there are 52 cards in a normal pack, but one idea is that there is one card for every week of the year.
7   In a sudoku puzzle, you complete a grid with numbers, using the numbers 1–9 once only in each square, in each line and in each row.
8   The pieces on a backgammon board are normally black and white.
9   In the English version of Scrabble®, the two highest-scoring letters are Q and Z, with ten points each.
10   There are 21 spots on a dice.
11   The World Dominoes Championships take place once a year.
12   An average game of Monopoly® lasts for one and a half hours.

UNIT 1 RECORDING 6

Born in Baltimore in the United States, Michael Phelps is one of the best-known athletes in the world today. He's a swimmer and Olympic champion, winning medals at the 2004, 2008 and 2012 Olympic Games. He has fans all over the world, as well as four million followers on Twitter, where he calls himself 'Phelps the Fish'. It's not surprising that Michael trains hard – he gets up at 5 a.m. and does at least five hours' training every day. But one thing that is surprising about Michael is his diet – he consumes 12,000 calories a day: that's six times the average for an adult male in his twenties. He says he sometimes eats burgers and other fast food. But because of his training regime he never has problems with his weight: he weighs just over 100 kg. 'Eat, sleep and swim,' says Phelps. 'That's all I can do'.

South Korean figure skater Yu-na Kim is one of the world's highest-paid athletes – she earns approximately $10 million a year. She skates for several hours every morning and in the afternoons she does other kinds of exercise. But she's not just a sportswoman; she also does a lot of important work to help people. She is a Good Will Ambassador for UNICEF, the World Children's Charity, and she often gives money to charities, including $27,000 to victims of the Japanese Tsunami in 2011. As she travels a lot, she has English classes three times a week. Yu-na comes from Bucheon, South Korea but she now lives in Los Angeles, California, with her mother, who is also her manager. And she finds time to makes several pop records every year! She is a big pop star in her home country of Korea.

UNIT 1 RECORDING 7

M = Marek   L = Laura

M: OK ... let's start. I'll interview you first ... Are you ready?

L: Yes ...

M: I'm going to time us on my phone ... We've got 60 seconds ... that's one minute, starting from ... now! So, what's your full name?

L: My full name is Laura Ines Rodriguez Ortega.

M: Wow! ... You've got a long name ... OK ... let me write that ... Laura ... Inés ... Rodriguez ... Ortega ... And have you got a nickname?

L: Yes, my friends and family usually call me Lalí.

M: Lalí ... L-A-L-I ... That's a nice name!

L: Thank you!

M: And, OK ... what next ... Yes, where were you born?

L: I was born in Buenos Aires ... in Argentina ...

M: Buenos Aires ... And when were you born?

L: When? ... Err ... on 18th December, 1990.

M: December ... 18th ... 1990 ... OK ... Err ...Well, tell me about your family.

L: OK ... I live with my father and mother and sister. Both my parents are doctors ... they work in different hospitals in Buenos Aires.

M: Oh really? They are both doctors ...

L: Yes, and my sister is two years younger than me. Her name is Patricia ... but everyone calls her Pati.

M: What do you do in your free time?

L: Mostly, I like doing a lot of sport in my free time. I mean, I play basketball ... I usually play about three or four times a week. And I sometimes go to the gym or go swimming. I really like keeping fit.

M: Oh, really ... that's great ... Oh! That's 60 seconds finished ...

UNIT 2 RECORDING 3

worked, watched, opened, invented, asked, stopped, travelled, started, lived, closed, walked, wanted, laughed, arrived

UNIT 2 RECORDING 4

1   Mother Teresa won a Nobel Prize for Peace in 1979, and Aung San Suu Kyi did the same in 1991. But the first woman to win a Nobel Prize was the Polish-born scientist Marie Skłodowska Curie ... for Physics, in 1903.

2   The Williams sisters – Venus and Serena – were two of the world's leading tennis players during the 2000s. Serena won her first US Open title in 1999, and Venus did the same a year later in 2000. They became the first sisters to both win the US Open.

3   British women aged 30 or more got the right to vote in 1918 two years before the United States but 21 years after New Zealand, the first country to give women the vote.

4   Iranian-born Anousheh Ansari became the first female 'space tourist,' on September 18, 2006. For her ten-day ride in the Russian Soyuz space capsule, she paid $20 million.

5   Russian cosmonaut Yuri Gagarin was the first human to travel into space in 1961, but there were only male cosmonauts until 1963 when 400 female cosmonauts applied to be the first woman in space. Only one woman made the flight – on 16th June 1963 – and her name was Valentina Tereshkova.

6   India had a female prime minister in the 1980s, but Indian presidents were all men until July 2007, when Pratibha Patil became the first woman to become President of India.

7   On 16th May 1975, the first woman reached the top of Mount Everest. She was a Japanese climber, Junko Tabei. Wanda Rutkiewicz was the first European woman to reach the top – in 1978; and Stacey Allison was the first American woman to reach the top – in 1988.

8   Kathryn Bigelow became the first woman to win an Oscar for Best Director for her film *The Hurt Locker* – a military action thriller, set in Iraq, starring Jeremy Renner.

UNIT 2 RECORDING 5

1 She was the first woman to win.
2 They were tennis players.
3 She was the first woman in space.
4 They were all men.
5 They were sisters.
6 He was from Russia.
7 They were from India.
8 She was a president.

UNIT 2 RECORDING 7

M = Mark   H = Helen

M: I remember the first time I went abroad, it was on a family holiday ... I was about six ... seven years old at the time ... we always had our holidays in England in those days ... but my parents decided to go to France on a day trip, so we went across to France on a ferry ... so there I was, I was with my mum, my dad and my brother ... I felt very excited because it was my first time on a boat ... finally we got to France ... and we looked around ... had lunch ... and to be honest, it wasn't very interesting, but I'll never forget one thing ... my father tried to speak French in the restaurant and they just couldn't understand him ... I felt really embarrassed ...

H: I'll never forget the last time I felt really scared ... It was about five years ago ... I suppose I was about 17 at the time. I was with a friend ... my best friend at the time ... Jenny, her name was. We went for a walk from her house through some fields and down to the beach. When we set off, everything was fine, but then we got to a field with a horse in it. Well, Jenny said it was OK ... I was a bit worried because I didn't like animals much, especially big ones like horses, but I believed her, so we went into the field. Then the horse came up to us and looked really angry. I was really scared ... and I stood still for ages ... But the horse didn't go, ... in fact ... it came closer and closer. In the end, we got out of the field, but I still feel sick when I think about it!

UNIT 3 RECORDING 1

1 You shouldn't send text messages to your friends.
2 You shouldn't listen to loud music.
3 You should make a list of things to do.
4 You should find somewhere quiet to study.
5 You shouldn't watch TV.
6 You should start work as early as possible.
7 You should take breaks sometimes.
8 You shouldn't use social networking sites.

UNIT 3 RECORDING 2

I = Interviewer   K = Kirsty

I: So, Kirsty, you live and work in Edinburgh ... You've got quite an unusual job, is that right?

K: Yes, well, that's right ... it's unusual, partly because I sometimes work at night, but mostly because part of my job is to scare people!

I: That is unusual ...

K: The thing is ... I'm a tour guide ... but I'm not the usual type. I'm a ghost tour guide ... so I show people the haunted places all around Edinburgh.

I: The haunted places?

K: Yes, the places where people say there are ghosts ... like the castle, and old buildings, ... you know, there is a lot of old history in Edinburgh ... Some of it is quite scary, but very interesting, and exciting too!

UNIT 3 RECORDING 3

I = Interviewer   K = Kirsty

I: So, how did you get the job?

K: Well, I'm really interested in history, and well ... I found out about this company. You don't have to have any special qualifications, but I think an interest in history is important, and you have to have a good memory. I can remember dates and other facts easily, so it's not a problem for me.

I: What other qualities do you think are useful?

K: I think you have to be a good story-teller ... and a good actor. I mean, you have to try and bring the history alive. I don't just talk about it – I try to get the visitors to become part of the history, and really believe it.

I: So do you have to wear a uniform or special clothes?

K: Er ... well, no, I don't have to wear a uniform but I wear special clothes from that period of history. Again, it's part of the acting to make it all as real as possible.

I: What's your favourite tour?

K: Well, I think my favourite is the tour we do at night. It's especially scary at night, because there are some parts of the tour where we turn out all the lights. It's completely dark ... you can't see anything at all! There are all sorts of noises. Some visitors get very scared ... but they all love it. It's very exciting ...

I: What kind of visitors generally come on these ghost tours?

K: All kinds of people ... a lot of children and young people obviously, but lots of older people, too. Local people ... and also a lot of foreign visitors, from Europe, America, Asia ... all over the world really.

I: Can you speak any other languages, apart from English?

K: Yes, I can speak French and Spanish, so sometimes I translate parts of my tour for visitors who speak those languages, but mostly it's in English. Unfortunately I can't speak Japanese ... that would be very useful, as a lot of our visitors are from Japan!

I: And, finally, are there any real ghosts ... ? I mean, have you ever seen one?

K: Well, no, I haven't seen a ghost, but I think I've heard one ...

I: Really? You've heard a ghost ... ? Who? Which one?

K: Well, it's a dog ... a famous dog in Edinburgh, called Greyfriars Bobby. He died in 1872 after sitting by his owner's grave for 14 years. After his owner died, the dog sat by the grave every day, for 14 years ... I'm sure I heard the ghost of that dog!

I: That's amazing! Your job sounds fascinating! Thank you ... so much.

UNIT 3 RECORDING 6

A = Annie   J = Jem   S = Silvia   J = Jarek

A: My name's Annie and I'm from New Zealand ... from a city called Christchurch. I'm still at high school and my favourite things at school are science subjects – especially biology. Outside school, I love all the usual things really ... like music, going to the movies ... but most of all I love my friends. I'm really interested in people and making friends. One day, ... er ... my ambition is to do something that can really help people, I'd like to study for that.

J: Well, I'm Jem and I'm from England. I'm 32 years old ... I'm an accountant but I don't like my job. When I was at school, I was good at maths, so I trained as an accountant. But now, I've realised that I want to do something more practical. I'm good with my hands – I like making things and solving problems. Also, I'm an independent person – I don't like working for a big company and I don't want to work in an office anymore. I'd like to work for myself and do something really useful.

S: My name is Silvia and I'm from Argentina. I'm at college right now, studying English and Italian ... I want to meet people from all over the world, that's one reason why I study languages. Also, my mum is Italian, so I've always been interested in different cultures. I like reading, too ... and meeting people ... Travelling and meeting people is something I love. I want to go to every continent, maybe learn some more languages, maybe Chinese or something.

J: Hi. I'm Jarek. I am 23 years old, from Krakow in Poland, and I am living in London at the moment and working as a barman. It's not a great job but it's a start – and it's giving me time to think about what I really want to do. Another good thing about living in London is that I can visit a lot of art galleries and interesting buildings. I love modern art and design, and also fashion. I'm not sure which direction to go in at the moment, but one day, I'd like to have my own company.

UNIT 3 RECORDING 7

A: Well, I think he should be a doctor or something like that ... Do you agree?

B: Hmm ... A doctor? Really ... ? Why?

A: Because he's good at maths ... and he wants to do something practical.

B: I'm not sure ... because he doesn't like working for a big company. He wants to work for himself. You know ... doctors often have to work in huge hospitals ... that's similar to working in a big company.

A: That's true ...

B: And, he wants to do something practical and useful, but he doesn't say anything about people. Being a doctor is about people really.

A: OK ... well, what do you think?

B: Perhaps he should be a plumber because he's good with his hands.

Audio script

A: Mm ... yes, I agree ... And he likes solving problems so he'll be a good plumber ... sorting out problems in people's houses ...

B: Yes. And he can work for himself ... and do something really useful. I think it's the perfect job for Jem.

A: A plumber is a big change from being an accountant, isn't it?

B: Yes ... that's what he wanted ... something completely different.

UNIT 4 RECORDING 2

August 23rd, January 10th, December 12th, March 19th, September 20th, May 22nd, June 14th, October 16th, February 28th, November 30th

UNIT 4 RECORDING 3

1   invite people into your home
2   make a cake
3   dress up
4   eat out
5   visit relatives
6   have a day off school/work
7   prepare a special meal
8   send cards to people
9   buy flowers
10 exchange presents

UNIT 4 RECORDING 5

Lucas – Brazil

One of the most important celebrations for me is New Year's Eve in Brazil, on 31st December. My mum is English and my dad is Brazilian ... so we live in England, but we usually go to Brazil for New Year ... I really love it! New Year is called *Ano Novo* in Portuguese – and people also use the French word, *Réveillon* ... I'm not sure why! The Réveillon celebrations in Brazil happen all along the coast, but I think they are especially fantastic in Rio de Janeiro. We stay in a friend's apartment in Rio – and it's usually boiling – often more than 30°C! Something I love about the New Year festivities is that everyone dresses up ... but always white, everyone wears white ... And everyone goes down to the beach in the evening, when it's dark. There are probably about two million people on Copacabana beach ... all dressed in white. It looks amazing ... And, there's a lot of music on the beach and people bring flowers and candles. You throw the flowers into the sea and also put the candles on the water, so that they float out away from the beach. It looks really lovely – with all the candles on the water. And the atmosphere is surprisingly peaceful at this point in the evening. The food is also a really important part of the evening, too. You can buy food that people cook on the beach during the evening. Typical food for New Year is a spicy chicken and rice dish which is delicious ... . Sometimes you can also find a tasty dessert made of maracujá which is a kind of fruit. At midnight, there is a big firework display which I love – it's really exciting. And then, of course, the party continues ... all through the night, until the next morning ...

Freya – Iceland

I think New Year's Eve in Iceland is one of the best times of the year. I'm from the United States but I'm married to an Icelandic man, Ivar. We live in the capital, Reykjavik ... the population is only about 200,000 but the people certainly know how to have a good time! New Year is on the 31st December, so it's the middle of winter ... and very cold! But I think it's a great time of year ... I really like the winter, and I especially look forward to New Year's Eve – it really is a major event in Iceland. During the first part of the evening, we stay home and listen to the radio ...

There is a ceremony broadcast from the cathedral, ... so we listen to that on the radio. Then we have dinner ... usually roast meat, and various tinned vegetables – tinned carrots, tinned peas, things like that. Traditionally, it's a real treat to have tinned vegetables! The part I like best is after that ... because after dinner, we go out. We go to the local park where there is a huge bonfire, and everyone who lives nearby meets there ... around the fire ... there's a really friendly atmosphere ... – it's great. You have to wear warm clothes of course, as it's freezing ... the temperature can sometimes go down to 10°C below zero. But ... the bonfire keeps you warm. People let off hundreds of fireworks throughout the whole evening ... It's illegal to let off fireworks at any other time of year ... so people buy lots and lots at New Year! It's really noisy and the sky is full of fireworks. Then ... at midnight, there is a big firework display over the city. I always think it looks like Reykjavik is on fire! When that's finished, we go to a nightclub in the town centre ... and often stay there until five or six the next morning ...

UNIT 4 RECORDING 7

For many people around the world, New Year is on January 1st, of course. But many people in the UK and the USA also celebrate Chinese New Year, which is at the end of January or the beginning of February. Christmas Day is on December 25th around the world but the date of Easter changes; it's usually between the middle of March and the middle of April.

There's no Independence Day in the UK, but the USA celebrates its independence on the 4th July, and International Women's Day is on March 8th in both countries. Father's Day is on the third Sunday in June in both the UK and the USA. Whereas Mother's Day is on different days: in the UK it's in March, but in the USA it's two months later, in May. Children – and many adults – in both the UK and the USA celebrate Halloween on October 31st.

UNIT 4 RECORDING 8

A   A: I wrote January 26th ... Australia day.

B: What happens on Australia day?

A: It's the day when the Europeans first came to Australia ... years and years ago ... and it's a public holiday, there are lots of concerts, fireworks ... and there's a big boat race in Sydney Harbour.

B: Sounds good.

A: Yeah, it's fun.

B   C: June 9th is a special day because it's my grandmother's birthday ... she's 70 actually and we're organising a special party for her ... and all her grandchildren are coming ... 12 of us!

C   D: So ... I'm looking at December ...What are you doing on December 24th ... ?

E: Well, I wrote December 24th because we're going to Austria for Christmas ... we're having a skiing holiday ... and we're spending Christmas there.

D   A: Why is March 12th important for you?

B: Because's that's my wedding anniversary ... I got married on March 12th five ... no six! ... years ago ...

A: And you're still happy.

B: Of course!

E   October 2nd is a very important day for me 'cos I'm starting university ... it's my first year ... it's really exciting ... I'm starting my economics course at Manchester University ... can't wait!

F   D: I wrote August 7th 2012 ...

E: Why August 7th 2012? What happened then?

D: ... because that's the day when I passed my driving test! Yeah!!

E: First time?

D: Er ... no ... third.

UNIT 5 RECORDING 2

1   A: Hello, I'm asking people about special clothes ... Could you tell me about some clothes or shoes which are special to you ... ?

B: Well, I've got some great trainers ... red Converse trainers ... you know ...

A: Red ones?

B: Yes ... I love them ...

A: When did you get them?

B: Erm ... I got them about five years ago, I suppose.

A: Why did you get them ... ? Did you get them for any special reason?

B: I was on holiday in the USA ... it was a great holiday with two friends ... I think I just bought them because I liked them ... you know, ... I went into the shop and saw them and I loved them immediately. I think it's because I like the colour ... but also I love the design. They're great and they remind me of that fantastic holiday we had together.

A: Do you wear them a lot?

B: Yes, I wear them all the time. And as I said, I bought them five years ago ... and they still look quite new ... I mean, they still look good ... yes, they're older but they're more comfortable than before ... They're the most comfortable shoes I've got ...

2   A: I'm doing a survey about special clothes ... What are the most special clothes or shoes you've got?

B: Erm ... I've got a dress ... it's blue and white checked ... It's one of the most special things I've got ...

A: When did you buy it?

B: I got it about eight years ago ...

A: And did you buy it for a special occasion or ... ?

B: Yes ... I did. I bought it because ... well, it was my friend's birthday and she had a picnic ... a kind of picnic party. So I bought it for that. And well, at this party, I met someone ...

A: Someone?

B: Yes, someone who later became my husband ... !

A: Really?

B: Yes ... we got married two years after that. So it's a very special dress for me!

A: How often do you wear it?

B: Well, I don't wear it now really ... I mean I was a lot thinner then ... so it doesn't fit me now ... I'm fatter than I was! But I still keep it ... because it reminds of that day ... one of the best days of my life!

3 **A:** I'm doing a survey about clothes which are special to people. Could you tell me about some clothes or shoes which are special to you ...?

B: OK ... I think something that I really love is my leather jacket ...

A: Leather jacket ...? When did you get that?

B: Well, ages ago ... erm ... I think about ten years ago ... maybe more ... ten or twelve years ago ...

A: Why did you get it? What is special about it for you?

B: Well, I thought it was the coolest jacket in the world! I loved it! It was my brother's jacket actually ...

A: Your brother's?

B: Yes, my brother's three years older than me. He had it for about three or four years ... and I thought he was really cool ... I wanted to be like him ... and I really wanted his jacket!

A: Did he give it to you?

B: Yes! I asked him so many times ... and in the end, he gave it to me ... I wore it all the time ... I never took it off really ... I mean, that was ten years ago!

A: Do you wear it a lot now?

B: It depends ... yeah, there are times when I wear it a lot ... and then, sometimes I don't ... it depends on what I'm wearing ... and what I'm doing ... but I still love it ...

UNIT 5 RECORDING 7

1 **A:** My daughter and her family came over for lunch yesterday ... it was so good to see them all ... especially my grandson, of course, little Harry ...

B: Ah, how lovely! ... How old is he?

A: Well, he's seven now ... but you wouldn't think it!

B: Oh really? How tall is he?

A: Well, that's just it ... he's very tall for his age. And a good-looking young boy ... looks just like his dad!

B: What colour are his eyes?

A: Blue ...

B: What's his hair like?

A: It's blond and curly... he really is lovely ...

2 **A:** So ... you said that he's tall, with dark hair and he was probably wearing a dark jacket and jeans ...

B: Yes ...

A: Now, did you get a good look at his face?

B: Well, yes ... quite good, I think ... I mean, it was all so quick, Officer.

A: OK ... well. Just think for a minute ... has he got a beard?

B: No, he's clean-shaven. I'm sure of that.

A: OK ... and as far as you remember, has he got a scar or a tattoo ... ?

B: No, he hasn't ... Well, I didn't see anything like that. As I said, it was very quick ... he just snatched my bag and ran ... so I didn't see him very well really.

3 **A:** Hey, Emma! Did I tell you about Daniel?

B: Well, no, not really ... tell me now. What does he look like?

A: He's tall, dark and handsome!

B: Really?!

A: Yes ... he really is.

B: And what's he like?

A: Well, he seems very nice. I mean, I only met him three weeks ago, but he's really kind to me ...

B: He sounds great ... Have you got any photos of him ... ?

A: Yeah ... look ... I've got one on my phone ...

UNIT 5 RECORDING 9

1 Well, he's quite tall ... he's got brown hair ... medium-length, brown hair ... and brown eyes. I think he's quite good-looking actually.

2 Yes, he's got a beard ... and a small moustache, too. He's tall and quite well-built ... and he's got curly hair.

3 She's got long fair hair. It's kind of curly – and long. I think she might dye her hair ... it's very fair. Yes, she probably dyes it.

4 Well, she isn't very nice. In the story, she's the nasty character ... you know, always horrible to people ... She's wearing glasses in this picture ... and she looks friendly, but she isn't really!

5 I think she's probably in her early twenties ... She looks young and she's wearing jeans and quite young clothes.

6 I think she's medium-height ... and she often wears very high shoes. But you can't see how tall she is in this picture because she's sitting down.

UNIT 5 RECORDING 10

A: ... so, OK ... the next question is ... number four ... Do you like clothes shopping?

B: Umm ...

A: What do you think? Yes ... No ... or Maybe ... ?

B: OK ... well, ... I like buying clothes ... I often go shopping for clothes with friends at the weekend, so I'll say ... 'Yes, it's my favourite hobby!'

A: Right, thank you. Question five ... Would you like to be a personal shopper?

B: A personal shopper?

A: Yes, you know, someone who helps other people buy clothes ... and helps them find clothes that suit them ...

B: Oh ... yes ... erm ... Well, I like shopping for clothes ... but only for myself really ...

A: OK ... so: Would you like to be a personal shopper? Yes, No or Maybe ... ?

B: Well, then ... I think it's 'No'... I don't really know what looks good on other people ... No. Not really.

A: OK ... number five ... 'No'. Moving on to Question six ... Question six is about tattoos ... What do you think about tattoos? Do you love them? Hate them? Or you don't really mind ...

B: Oh well ... that's easy! I hate them!

A: OK ... so, a definite 'No' for that one! Question seven ...

UNIT 6 RECORDING 1

L = Luke   D = Donna

D: So I hear you're going to have a holiday in New Zealand. Wow!

L: Yeah on a motorbike! From north to south ... nearly three weeks. I can't wait!!

D: Good for you ... So when are you planning to go?

L: Hmm I'm not absolutely sure ... when's the best time?

D: Well, don't go in our winter ... July, August time ... remember the winter and the summer are the other way round there!

L: Right ...

D: So December to January's probably the best time ...

L: Will it be hot in January?

D: It depends where you are ... possibly ... but you'll need some warm clothes ... especially if you're on a motorbike ...

L: OK ... maybe January ... it'll be nice to have some sunshine after Christmas ... oh, one thing ... How about visas?

D: Uh ... you've got a British passport, right?

L: Yeah ...

D: OK, so you won't need a visa ... you can stay up to six months.

L: Really? That's great.

D: Lucky you ...You'll love it! But anyway, tell me a bit more about ...

UNIT 6 RECORDING 2

1 You'll have a great time!

2 We'd like some more water, please.

3 She'd like to go home now.

4 Would you like another one?

5 They'll be here soon.

6 It'll be very crowded.

7 We'd rather go by car.

8 I'll see who it is.

9 Will you be here this evening?

10 You'll have to ask him.

11 I'd rather stay where I am.

Audio script

UNIT 6 RECORDING 3

A = Anabel   M = Maria

A: Wow ... this is so exciting! Where shall we go?

M: Well, let's look at the options ...

A: I'd like to go somewhere hot, I think. What about Dubai? Or Goa? I mean, I'd like somewhere which will give us a break from the cold winter here in January! What do you think?

M: Well, yes, that's a good point ... somewhere hot would be nice.

A: They are all quite far away, though. If possible, I'd rather go somewhere a bit nearer because we're only going for five days ... All the hot places are far away and it will take ages to get there.

M: True ... but I don't want to go somewhere cold. I mean, I don't want to go to New York ... look, it's minus three degrees! And Paris isn't much warmer ...

A: No, I don't like the cold much either ... but ... what do you think of the spa break in Spain?

M: Mmm ... That sounds lovely ...

A: Yes, it sounds great. It's not very hot, but at least it is relaxing. And it's quick to get there ... only three hours.

M: And it's a three-star hotel ... which is good. Would you like to stay in a hotel?

A: Yes, I'd rather stay in a hotel because self-catering is a lot of work ... 'Spanish Spa Special' then ... Do you agree?

M: Yes! Fantastic ... let's see if Caroline and Julia agree with us ...

UNIT 7 RECORDING 1

1 How long have you known him?
2 I've known him for three years.
3 How long were you a teacher?
4 I was a teacher for two years.
5 How long have you lived in Moscow?
6 We've lived in Moscow for six years.
7 How long did you live in London?
8 I lived in London for about six months.

UNIT 7 RECORDING 2

Ameet was always interested in business – he always had lots of brilliant ideas for making money and his ambition was to be a millionaire by the age of 25.

Kate studied for at least three hours every evening when she was 18. She wanted to become an ecologist and help save the planet.

Edward was always very quiet, and he never went out very much. He spent most of his time in his bedroom, playing games on his computer.

UNIT 7 RECORDING 3

P = Presenter   I = Interviewee

P: So ... it's five o'clock, ... so that means it's time for our weekly Internet Spot ... with David Taylor. David, what have you got for us today?

I: Well, today, I've got some amazing achievements ... some people who have achieved great things ...

P: On the internet?

I: Yes, that's right ... these people are quite different from each other, but have one thing in common ... They have used the internet in different ways to achieve fame and make money.

P: Ah ... that sounds interesting ...

I: Yes ... well, first, one of the most common ways of using the internet to achieve fame is to upload videos of yourself ... onto a website ... a video-sharing site like YouTube.

P: Thousands of people do that ... but not many of them become famous, do they?

I: No ... but some do! For example, a young American man, Tay Zonday, first became well-known in 2007 when he uploaded his song *Chocolate Rain* on the internet. Since then, his song has had over 68 million hits!

P: Wow! That's a lot ... but has he achieved anything else?

I: Yes, he has. He's made a lot of money ... He's been on many TV shows ... he's had some small acting roles ... and he's become a celebrity who people want to know about.

P: It's not just singers who can show their talent, is it?

I: No, that's right ... Blogging is very popular ... Some people have got book deals from their blog ...

P: Book deals?

I: Yes ... many people write blogs ... They post their ideas and thoughts on the internet ... and then publishing companies find talented writers by reading people's blogs ... and offer them a contract to make it into a book ...

P: Really? And they can become successful from that ...

I: Yes, absolutely ... I can think of one recent example: an English woman called Judith O'Reilly ... She moved away from London and went to live in the countryside with her family. She decided to write about her experiences in her new place ... living in a small village.

P: And she got a book deal?

I: Yes, a company read her blog, and offered her a book deal worth nearly €80,000!

P: That's a lot of money!

I: Yes! Obviously, she is a good writer ... and the internet is a good place to show off your skills ...

P: That's true ... but not everyone who becomes famous on the internet has a lot of talent ... for some people, it's just luck, isn't it?

I: Yes, like Matt Harding ...

P: What did he do?

I: He's one of my favourites ... he uploaded videos of himself dancing ... in lots of different locations throughout the world.

P: Dancing is a talent, isn't it?

I: In his case, no ... it isn't really! He dances really badly ... He just does a funny kind of dance for a few seconds in each place ... In his first video, he danced in 15 different countries. Then, some companies sponsored him ... so they gave him money to continue travelling and making his videos.

P: Really? That's good ...

I: Yes, in his third video, you can see him dancing in 42 different countries ... That one has had over 33 million hits!

P: He's certainly achieved something, then, even if he can't dance!

I: People love him ... His videos are some of the most popular, and he has appeared on all sorts of TV shows ...

UNIT 7 RECORDING 4

B = Bill   R = Ralph   D = Deb   P = Pawel   S = Swati

B: My surname is O'Driscoll, which is originally an Irish name, and I know that my family came over from Ireland sometime at the end of the 19th century and settled in the States and ... well, I've never been to Ireland. It's always been my dream to go back there and rediscover my family roots. Maybe find some of my long-lost cousins over there ... So that's my ambition: to rediscover the Irish side of my family ... yeah, I'd really like to do that.

R: Well, looking back, I'd say my greatest achievement was when I was about 18. I was very keen on football and I actually played one match for my local team where I scored three goals and I was the hero for a week or two. I still look back on that with a lot of pride ... As for my dream ... one thing I'd love to do is to visit the Taj Mahal in India. I suppose I'm getting a bit old now, but you never know – one day!

D: Well, I've always wanted to own a car. I don't have a car at the moment because I can't afford one ... also because I can't drive ... but anyway, it's my ambition to own a car one day – but not just any old car. It has to be a Ferrari ... and a red Ferrari at that. I don't know why ... I suppose I ought to learn to drive first ... but that's what I really want, yeah, to own a lovely red Ferrari.

P: I'd really love to buy an enormous house which is in the middle of the countryside, or in the mountains somewhere, but you know, really miles from anywhere ... and it has to have lots and lots of space, enough space so that I can invite all my friends and all my family for a big party ... and then they can all go away and I can just enjoy the peace and quiet ... that's my ambition.

S: Yes, well, I think one of the best things I've achieved is getting into university, where I'm studying medicine now, and my ambition is to really help people in some way ... Not necessarily to be a famous surgeon or anything like that, but to make some medical discovery that really helps people. A drug that can cure some disease or something like that ... so that my name is remembered ... I think that would be a really great thing to do.

UNIT 8 RECORDING 1

T = Thomas K = Keith A = Ali E = Eveline V = Vanitha A = Adrian

T: There are a lot of one-way streets in Amsterdam – but they have planned the roads well and there are cycle lanes everywhere. Almost everyone has a bicycle so it feels safe and clean.

K: York is a beautiful, historic city so they made nearly all of the city centre into a pedestrian zone. People really enjoy going shopping there now.

A: Traffic congestion is a real problem in Los Angeles. Many people use their cars because public transport isn't very good.

E: Berlin is a really green city. There is a lot of green space and there are seven types of recycling bins. We are proud that Berlin airport has the first carbon-neutral petrol station.

V: Bangalore is really crowded – and growing all the time. They've built new shopping malls and there are lots of new residential areas, with huge high-rise apartment blocks.

A: Like many other cities, Cape Town is trying to be as 'green' as possible. The electricity for many of the traffic lights in the city now comes from the sun – using large solar panels.

UNIT 8 RECORDING 2

1 Asia is bigger than Europe.
  True. Asia makes up 30 percent of the world's land mass, and is by far the biggest continent.
2 New York is the biggest city in the world.
  False. New York City has a population of over 8 million people and is certainly the biggest city in the United States. But there are many other cities (including Tokyo, Mexico City and São Paulo) which are bigger.
3 Mount Fuji is in China. It's the highest mountain in Asia.
  False. Mount Fuji isn't in China; it's in Japan. And at 3,776 metres it's the highest mountain in Japan. But there are other mountains in Asia, such as Mount Everest and K2, which are more than 8,000 metres high.
4 The Queen of England lives in Buckingham Palace, London.
  False. The Queen of England has several homes including Buckingham Palace, but her official home is Windsor Castle.
5 The Mediterranean Sea is bigger than the Pacific Ocean.
  False. The Mediterranean Sea has an area of just two and a half million square kilometres compared to the Pacific Ocean's 166 million square kilometres.
6 The Moon is smaller than the Sun.
  True. The sun is of course much bigger than the moon: approximately 400 times bigger, in fact!
7 The Alps are a mountain range in Scotland.
  False. The Alps are a mountain range in Europe, the highest in fact and they run through France, Switzerland, Germany and Italy ... but not Scotland.
8 The Mississippi River is in the United States.
  True. The Mississippi River passes through the cities of St Louis, Memphis and New Orleans. It's the longest river in the United States.

UNIT 8 RECORDING 4

Well, I finally decided to move to Canada about nine months ago and live here permanently. I'm really excited because I lived here for a few years when I was a child, and also a few times as an adult ... and I've now decided to stay. Something I love about Canada is the space ... I mean, it's huge! It's actually the second biggest country in the world, if you include all the land and the water ... but it only has 0.5 percent of the world's population. So that means, there is a lot of space for everyone!!

I love being in the outdoors and in Canada, the countryside is beautiful and there's so much to do outside. First, there are so many lakes and rivers ... It's incredible, but Canada has about 20 percent of all the fresh water – in lakes and rivers – in the whole world! I love going walking in the mountains and going fishing ... It's so beautiful. There are also thousands of miles of coast, as Canada has three oceans as its borders ... the Pacific Ocean along the west coast, the Atlantic Ocean along the east coast, and the Arctic Ocean in the north. As well as the USA as its land border, directly to the south, of course.

When I was a child, I lived in Ottawa ... the capital city. It's not the biggest city in Canada, but it's where the government is. Toronto is the biggest city ... and that's where I live now – it's a really lively and multi-cultural place ... The official language in Toronto and Ottawa is English, but in some places in Canada, the official language is French ... like in Montreal for example.

The summer is very nice in Canada, but I like the winter best. There are some great places to ski ... and I also love the national winter sport ... ice hockey. I'm in a team with some friends, ... and I watch the professional matches as much as I can. I love watching the Canadian national team ... Everyone wears the national colours ... red and white ... and it's a great atmosphere!

So, yes ... I suppose that Canada is most famous for the beautiful countryside and outdoor activities ... but, you might not know that there are some famous Canadian popstars ... Nelly Furtado, for example ... and Avril Lavigne ... and also Justin Bieber ... Most people think they are American ... but they're not ... they're Canadian.

UNIT 9 RECORDING 3

M: You know the problem: you're expecting visitors ... and your house looks like a disaster site! What to do?
W: It's time to stop worrying. Here's the solution – we're going to tell you how to clean a house ... in just three minutes!
M: Here's what you'll need ...
W: a big black rubbish bag ...
M: some wipes ...
W: a bottle of bleach ...
M: and some air freshener.
W: Got those? Good. So, we're ready to go. How to clean a house in three minutes.
  First of all, get your big black rubbish bag and run round the living room picking up all the things that shouldn't be there. Put the rubbish bag in a room where your visitors won't go – a bedroom, for example.
M: Go back into the living room. Use the wipes to clean surfaces like tables, bookshelves and the television.
W: Now for the bathroom. Put some bleach down the toilet.
M: Look around the bathroom. Pick up anything that is making the bathroom look messy and put them in the shower ... but don't forget to close the shower curtain!
W: Run into the kitchen. Take any dirty pots and plates and things that you haven't washed up and put them into the oven.
M: Go round all the rooms with some air freshener. When people smell lemon they automatically think 'Hmm ... clean!'
W: Finally, close the doors of all the rooms you don't want people looking inside!
M: And there you are. Now, relax, put on your best smile and ...
W: You're ready to greet your visitors!

UNIT 9 RECORDING 4

1 It's very difficult for people to find the right type of place to live ... houses and flats, you know, ... there isn't enough cheap accommodation around here. So I think the flats idea is the best solution. Besides, if they build new flats, it will help other businesses in the area. I'll be very pleased when all the work is complete ... it's a horrible building site at the moment.
2 I'm sure they'll ask local people for their ideas before they make a decision ... I think it's exciting! After the old power station goes, the area will be more attractive. Personally, I think the hotel scheme is the best one for the area. Unemployment is quite high around here and there will be more jobs for local people if they build a new hotel on the site.
3 If they decide to put a cinema here, it will create very serious parking problems. There aren't enough parking spaces for local people as it is. And the roads will have too much traffic ... As soon as more people want to come to the town centre, the traffic will be terrible. I don't think the people who are developing this site think about the local people ...
4 Well, I'm not sure, really I'm not. Before they make a decision, they will have to ask local people what they think. Not everybody wants the same thing. The area will change completely if they put a new shopping centre there. We have plenty of small shops around here, and a shopping centre will make things very difficult for local businesses.

Audio script

UNIT 9 RECORDING 5

1 If they build new flats, it will help other businesses in the area.
2 I'll be very pleased when all the work is complete.
3 I'm sure they will ask local people for their ideas before they make a decision.
4 After the old power station goes, the area will be more attractive.
5 As soon as more people want to come to the town centre, the traffic will be terrible.
6 The area will change completely if they put a new shopping centre there.

UNIT 9 RECORDING 7

A: The beach is really beautiful ... and I think the Blue Parrot could be very attractive and popular ... with a few changes ...
B: A lot of changes ... I think! Everything needs changing ... the decor, the food, the waiter ...
A: Yes, well ... you're probably right! So, firstly, how about changing the colour on the walls?
B: Yes ... definitely ...
A: It will look a lot better if we change the colour ... I think we should paint it all white ... It will look much cleaner and more spacious. What do you think?
B: Well, I don't think we should have only white, because it might look really boring. I think we should include some different colours ...
A: Hmm ... OK, maybe ... what other colour?
B: Well, what about blue? You know, the name is the Blue Parrot ... I think we should include some blue to make it more interesting ...
A: Yes, OK then ... so blue and white walls ...
B: Actually, maybe we should have more colours ... you know, make it more tropical ... How about having each wall a different colour: one white, one blue, one yellow, one red.
A: Errr ... no! I don't think it's a good idea to have too many colours. We want the café to be relaxing and attractive ... Let's keep it simple, with just white and blue ...
B: OK ... maybe you're right ... And what about the food ... ? We need some really delicious things on the menu ...
A: Yes ... you're right ... well, maybe we could have ...

UNIT 10 RECORDING 1

1 If you cut your finger, the first thing you should do is try to stop the bleeding. You can do this by pressing on the area. You could also put your finger in cold water – then keep it up above your head. Obviously, if it's a bad cut, and quite deep, you should see a doctor or go to hospital.
2 Well, if you burn yourself, don't put butter or oil on it. That is the worst thing you can do actually. You should cool the burn down, so put it in cold water ... for about five or ten minutes. If it's a bad burn, you should cover it loosely with a clean cloth ... don't put a plaster on it ... and then go to hospital.
3 If someone faints, you shouldn't pour cold water over their face, and you certainly shouldn't shake them and try to wake them up! You should just leave them to come round, and of course, yes, make sure they are comfortable and not in a dangerous place.
4 If you think someone has broken their arm, then the first important thing is – don't move them. I mean, make sure they are warm, comfortable and out of danger, but don't move them if at all possible. Then, phone for an ambulance as quickly as possible.
5 If a bee stings you, you shouldn't put a plaster on it ... Just put some ice on it or put it under cold water. Normally, that's all you need to do ... Sometimes people have bad reactions to bee stings, though, so if you feel dizzy or breathless, or anything, you should certainly phone a doctor quickly.
6 If you get a rash after eating strawberries, it may mean you are allergic to them, so stop eating them and the rash should soon disappear. Don't put cream on it, but if it gets worse rapidly, you should speak to a doctor as soon as possible, as you might have a serious allergy.

UNIT 10 RECORDING 2

J = Jason   R = Rachel
J: I'm just phoning to say that I'm really sorry but I can't meet you for lunch today ...
R: Oh, that's a shame. Are you OK? What happened?
J: Well, it's a long story! Marco and I were walking home from work through the park ... on Friday afternoon ...
R: Yes ... ?
J: I was walking along when I felt something sting my hand. I've never been stung by a bee before, and I'm telling you, it really hurt!
R: Oh dear ... but ...
J: Well, it wasn't just the pain ... As I was standing there, my hand started to become swollen and red. And then ... I started to feel a bit dizzy and breathless ...
R: Oh no!
J: Marco realised that I was allergic to the sting and called an ambulance. Anyway, to cut a long story short, I went to hospital, and they gave me something and I was fine ...
R: That's good ... but ...
J: Well, I was fine at that point ... and then we left the hospital. It was quite late by this time, so we decided to get the bus home.
R: OK ... good idea.
J: Yes, but while we were waiting at the bus stop, something flew into my eye ... a piece of dirt or something ...
R: Mmm?
J: Well, it was really painful and I couldn't see anything, and my eye became swollen ... and as we were still outside the hospital, we went back in!
R: That was lucky ...
J: Yes, except ...Well, the nurses sorted my eye out, and after about an hour, we left, ... again. Of course it was really late, and I was tired ... and on the way out, I fell over on the pavement outside the hospital and ... well, ended up in hospital again ...
R: With ... ?
J: With a broken arm!
R: What?! You broke your arm! That's terrible! I can't believe it! ...

UNIT 10 RECORDING 5

A: Well, the three finalists are Lorraine, Gareth and Amanda. So, who do you think should win the prize?
B: OK ... well, let's see ... Lorraine broke her arm ... Gareth got stuck in a drain ... and Amanda lost her camera ... Umm ... I think Lorraine should win ...
A: Do you? Why's that?
B: Well, because she broke the same arm twice! That's really unusual! And she was talking to the insurance company at the time ... that's quite funny ...
A: Hmm ... true ... that is funny ... but I don't think her story was the funniest really ... I mean, the prize is for the funniest or most unusual thing that happened, isn't it? What about Amanda? Her story is really funny!! She buried her own camera, and then lost it!!
B: Yes ... that's crazy ... there wasn't anyone on the beach to steal her camera and then she lost it anyway! But it's not really an accident ...
A: No, but it's a mishap ... she probably made a claim on her travel insurance ... for a lost camera.
B: Mmm, maybe ... I don't know ... Gareth's story is funny ... He dropped his phone ... and ended up stuck in a drain ... What do you think?
A: Yes, that's funny too ... though maybe he didn't think so!

UNIT 11 RECORDING 2

W: Well, I think that going to the hairdresser's is definitely something you either love or hate.
M: Do you?
W: Yes, I know that some people think it's really boring, but personally I love going to the hairdresser's. For me, it's just a perfect way to spend my time ... I like sitting there with my magazine ... What about you? Do you like going to the hairdresser's?
M: No, I hate it! I only go when it's absolutely necessary ...
W: Oh well ... that one seems to be a 'love it or hate it' thing, doesn't it? Let's see ... what else? Flying. I think that's definitely a 'love it or hate it' thing. People usually have strong opinions about it, don't they? Do you like flying?

M: No, I don't. You know, one of my oldest friends lives in the United States ... and I'd love to visit him one day, but the problem is ... I'm really afraid of flying. I hate sitting in a small place for all that time ... the whole thing is just awful! What about you?

W: I'm the same. I hate flying too ... I'm just too scared. I'm sure it's fine really, but I don't like it at all. We both hate flying then ...

M: Yes ... and something else I really hate is sunbathing ... You know, when you're on holiday ... just lying in the sun. It's so boring!!

W: Oh really? I love it ... I think I enjoy sunbathing for two reasons: I like lying down, because well, it's relaxing, isn't it ... ? And I love reading ... so put the two together and it's perfect for me! I'd like to live somewhere hot and sunny so I could go to the beach and read books every day!

UNIT 11 RECORDING 5

1 Would you like to come to our house on Saturday?
2 How about going to see a film next week?
3 Would you like to go out for a meal?
4 How about going out for a meal?
5 Would you like to have an ice cream?
6 How about having an ice cream?
7 Would you like to go for a drive?
8 How about going for a drive?

UNIT 11 RECORDING 6

W: So what do you think? If you went to live on a desert island, what would you take?

M: Well, firstly, I'd take a tent. Definitely.

W: Really? I don't think so. Why?

M: Well, if you didn't have a tent, you wouldn't sleep properly. You know, a tent would keep you dry if it rained ... and it would keep you warmer ... Actually, I'd take a blanket, too ... I mean, it would probably be really cold at night ...

W: A tent and a blanket? Are those your first two choices ... ? So you could sleep properly?! What about food and water ... those would be more important, wouldn't they?

M: Well, yes ... they're important, too ... My third choice would be bottled water ... obviously you would need water to survive ...

W: Bottled water? You would have to take a lot ... I don't think it would be possible to take enough ...

M: Hmm ... I don't know ... and I'm not sure about the food ... there's nothing on the list about food ...

W: Well, if you were on a desert island, you would have to find your own food ... I suppose.

M: Yes, that's true. A knife would be useful ... to prepare food ...

UNIT 11 RECORDING 7

M: So, the survey is about the most important things in life ... Let's see what you think ... First, which of these is the most important thing in life for you: is it 'A: having a lot of money', 'B: being in love', 'C: becoming famous', 'D: making a difference to other people's lives' or 'E: other' ... you know, something else ...

W: Umm ... let's think ... well, it's certainly not 'becoming famous' ... I'm really not interested in that ... And it's not 'having a lot of money'. I mean I want to have enough money ... but I don't particularly want 'a lot' ... um ... I like making a difference to people's lives ... I'm a nurse, and it gives me a lot of satisfaction to help people. Yes, I'll say: 'd'.

M: OK, great. Thanks for that. Next one: If you could choose the perfect number of children, what would it be: none, one, two, three, four or five plus ... you know, five or more children?

W: Well, I definitely don't want five or more children! But I think one day, I'd like to have one or two children ... err ... let's say, two, because then they wouldn't be on their own.

M: OK. And question three: If you could choose any pet, what would it be: 'A: a cat', 'B: a dog', 'C: a fish', 'D: none', 'E: other'?

W: This one's easy for me ... I hate having animals in the house ... In fact, I'm allergic to a lot of animals, and I haven't got time to look after them. So, my answer is 'D: none'!

UNIT 11 RECORDING 8

A: Perhaps surprisingly, only 10 percent of people chose 'having a lot of money' and 'becoming famous' as the most important thing in life. The most popular answer was 'being in love', which nearly 50 percent of the people who answered made their first choice. Popular answers in the 'other' column included 'having a big family' and 'being successful in your job'.

B: The number of people who said they wanted five or more children was more or less the same as the number of people who said they didn't want any children – about 10 percent in each case. The most popular choice for the perfect number of children was ... two, with nearly 40 percent of people choosing that number.

A: In choosing the perfect pet, there were some surprising answers in the 'other' category, including a butterfly, a frog and even a giraffe – but easily the most popular answer, with almost 45 percent of the votes, was a dog.

B: Though many people have the idea of moving to the country when they get older, only 13 percent of people in the survey chose this as the perfect place to live. The most popular answer – with nearly 40 percent – was living 'in a city', with living 'in the suburbs' and living 'in a town' some way behind. The most popular 'other' answer was ... 'in a forest'!

A: The question 'Would you ever marry for money?' brought some surprising results. The most popular answer – with 45 percent of the votes – was 'yes, possibly', with about 30 percent not sure and 25 percent saying definitely not!

B: For question 6, there were many different opinions. The answer people least agreed with was d, - 'Money, a big car, a big house ...You can have it all!' with only 8 percent saying they agreed with it. Easily the most popular answer – with 30 percent of the votes – was 'The most important thing in life is to be happy ... but to be happy, you need to give as well as receive.'

UNIT 12 RECORDING 1

1 What colour was the nail varnish?
2 What was between the perfume and the deodorant?
3 Was there a hair brush in the picture? What colour was it?
4 Was the comb the same colour as the razor?
5 What make was the perfume?
6 How many lipsticks were there?
7 What was below the aftershave?
8 Was there a necklace in the picture? What colour was it?
9 Was the bracelet next to the eyeliner or the necklace?
10 What was above the shaving foam?

UNIT 12 RECORDING 4

Today, I've come to talk to you about a great new product, which I think will be extremely popular and will become a best-seller very quickly. We have developed an amazing new fizzy drink called FizzFive! It's a drink that's both fizzy and healthy, too! Feel alive with FizzFive!

The idea for FizzFive was developed by myself and three friends after we found that no fizzy drinks in the shops were healthy. We have taken several years to develop this drink and we now believe that it is ready for the market. Previously, there were plain, natural, healthy fruit drinks, and there were unnatural, unhealthy fizzy drinks. We wanted something which was both – fizzy and healthy. So, we decided to make a drink that contains real fruit and vitamins and is totally natural – but fizzy, too. And we believe that's exactly what FizzFive is. ... Feel alive with FizzFive!

FizzFive comes in five different flavours: orange, apple, lemon, grape and pineapple. It contains five different vitamin groups. It increases your energy by five times. In summary, it tastes good, it makes you feel good ... and it's fizzy! ... Feel alive with FizzFive!

The drink was tested on various different people and we believe it will be popular with all age groups. However, we feel that the main target market will be young people who like fizzy drinks but also understand about the importance of health. We think the packaging is very important so the bottle is colourful and appealing to young people.

Now, what we need is some help and investment from you to help us to launch this fantastic product in the market. We'd like to ask you for £55,000 to help get FizzFive into the shops and start selling. We know it will be a winner and will make money for ourselves and you. Feel alive with FizzFive! Thank you very much for listening!

Audio script

UNIT 13 RECORDING 1

M = Maddie   T = Tom

M: So Tom ... we've got these emails from three people here ... and we need to decide which one is best ...What do you think?

T: Yes ... well ... let's see. Fabio sounds like a nice person – he's easy-going and he likes people. That's a good start ...

M: True ... and he is earning money, ... but he's been living with his aunt for three years and before that, I suppose he was living with his parents. It sounds like he might not be very good at doing the housework and things ...

T: Mmm ... you could be right ... Well, ... Anicka says she can cook, and sounds quite reliable ... but four to eight hours of piano practice!! That could become annoying!

M: Oh, I don't know! I think it might be nice ... she's been playing since she was three, so I'm sure she's really good ...

T: Well, ... let's see ... what about Liam?

M: Liam ... hmm ... well, it's hard to tell I think ... I mean, he sounds hard-working and everything, and would probably share the housework, as he says ... but I don't think he would be very easy to share with ... and the flat would be full of computers!

T: Yes, but ... it could be good to have someone to fix our computers! And also, if he keeps himself to himself, well ... that's quite good, too ...

M: Oh, no ... I'd like someone a bit more sociable ... like Fabio ...

T: OK ... well, let's think then. Not Anicka ... I'm not sure I could stand the piano ...

M: OK ... if that's how you feel ... Fabio or Liam then? ... I think Fabio ...

T: But, as you said, he might not be very good at housework and things ...

M: Well, I think that's OK ... I'd prefer someone sociable ... and I don't really want the flat full of computers ...

T: OK, then ... Let's go with Fabio ... but we'll have to make some rules about cooking and cleaning and things ...

UNIT 13 RECORDING 2

1 I have been waiting. I've been waiting.
2 You have been working. You've been working.
3 He has been working. He's been working.
4 It has been raining. It's been raining.
5 We have been waiting. We've been waiting.
6 You have been sitting. You've been sitting.
7 He has been coming. He's been coming.
8 I have been looking. I've been looking.

UNIT 13 RECORDING 4

M: OK ... so, I think it's going to be quite difficult to decide who the best candidate is, don't you? They all look strong to me ...

W: Yes ... I suppose so. They are all excellent in their world ... you know, a top sportsperson, a top businesswoman, and everything ... but there are some qualities that you really need to become a Goodwill Ambassador ...

M: Some qualities?

W: Yes, you know, some personal characteristics are very important ... I mean, Don Barris says he is very shy ... so I don't think he would be a good ambassador ... because you have to be sociable. You have to talk to all sorts of people and speak on TV and things ... I don't think you can be shy to do that.

M: Mmmm ... true. Who do you prefer then?

W: Well, I prefer Pete Power because ...

M: Pete Power ... ?

W: Yes ... I prefer Pete Power because he is really well-known all over the world. He sounds like he is ambitious and sociable ... and people really like popstars ...

M: I don't agree with you ... I mean, yes, he is well-known, but he hasn't got the right experience ... He's been working in the music business and also TV, but he hasn't done any work with people who need help ... or anything like that ...

W: That doesn't matter ... I think he will be the best at getting people interested ... because people like him ... so they would listen to him ...

M: Yes, but what about Tracey Valentine? I think she will be the best ...

W: Tracey Valentine? ... but she's unknown outside Fredonia ...

M: I don't think that's a problem. She would be able to represent the people very well. She knows a lot about the country and problems that people have ...

UNIT 14 RECORDING 2

$6,000, 290, 6.32, £50 million, 620, 98.5, 5 billion, 8.2, 49.8

UNIT 14 RECORDING 3

1 The boss of a company called one of his employees into his office. The young man had started work at the company a few weeks before and he sat down nervously. 'When you started working here a month ago, your salary was $50,000,' said the boss. 'Two weeks later, I doubled your salary to $100,000. Now I'm going to pay you $250,000 a year. What do you say to that?' 'Thanks, Dad,' said the young man.

2 The American comedian Jack Benny was famous for being mean. One day, he had been to the bank and he was on his way home, when a robber appeared and pointed a gun at him. 'Your money or your life!' hissed the robber. There was a long silence. 'What's the matter with you?' said the robber. 'I said: 'Your money or your life!' 'I'm thinking about it,' said the old man.

3 A man asked a millionaire friend of his how he had become so rich. ' As a young man, I was very poor,' he said. 'I spent my last $100 on a second-hand car. I spent the next week repairing it. Then I sold it for $200. With the $200, I bought two second-hand cars. I spent the next two weeks repairing them. Then I sold them for $400. It wasn't much but I had made a profit of $200.' 'What happened next?' asked the friend. 'My wife's father died and left me $10 million,' said the millionaire.

UNIT 14 RECORDING 5

A man in Germany had a horrible surprise when he was checking his email one morning. Thomas Vogel, aged 22, found he had bought items worth nearly €1 million from an internet auction company. Thomas said he hadn't heard of the company before and didn't know anything about the €800,000 house, the €100,000 car or the €25,000 small plane he had bought. The internet company insisted he paid for the items, however, as it seemed that he had bought the items in his name.

UNIT 14 RECORDING 6

My name is Henry Adams, from San Francisco in the United States of America. A few years ago, through bad luck, I found myself in London without money, food or accommodation. I was in total despair. Suddenly, a voice said: 'Come in here, please'. A servant showed me into a luxurious house, where a man I had never seen before was finishing his breakfast. I hadn't eaten for days and the sight of all that food was almost too much for me. Without a word, the man handed me an envelope. When I got outside I saw that the envelope contained a letter ... and something amazing. A bank note for £1 million!
'I can see you are an honest man,' the letter read. 'The money in the envelope is yours for 30 days. At the end of the month, come back to the house. I have a bet on you.' The letter had no signature, no address and no date.

Immediately, I ran into the nearest restaurant and ate hungrily. When I had finished my meal, I handed the million-pound note to the waiter. 'Can you change this for me please? I don't have anything smaller.' Of course, the restaurant couldn't change the note – but because I was clearly a rich man, they said I could pay the next time. Over the next few days, I bought a new suit and found a room in an expensive private hotel. No one could change the note, but they gave me what I wanted as they believed I was a millionaire. Soon I became famous. People invited me to all the best parties ... and I met Portia Langham ... the most beautiful woman I had ever seen. I fell in love with her within two minutes and told her my story. 'When I go back to see the man at the end of the month ... will you come with me?' She said yes. A month later, I returned to the house. The servant showed me in, and the man asked me the question. 'Do you have the million-pound note?' 'Here it is,' I replied. 'So I win the bet!' the man shouted. 'Father! I knew it.' 'My darling daughter!'

I couldn't believe my eyes or ears. The man was Portia's father ... and he had made the bet to prove that an honest man could live for a month without money. Portia and I are now married. I never bought anything with the million pounds, which is now on the wall of our home in London. But the note got me something far more important than money.

- *Your turn! Plan, talk, write about a first time story* ☺

- *'I'll never forget the first time I ....*
- *'I was .... years old at the time.*
- *'I was in ...*
- *'I was with my ....*
- *'I felt very .... because ...*
- *'At first, I was nevous/worried....*
- *'Then, ...*
- *After that,*
- *'A few days/months later, I ...'*
- *'In the end, ...*

ESL Writing: Write it Right!

Speaking Practice

- Complete the sentences to make them true for you, then share with your group. Use the past simple or the past continuous where appropriate:

1. I .... when I decided to move to the UK.
2. I .... at 5 pm yesterday.
3. I .... when I slipped and hurt my ....
4. While I was shopping in town a few weeks ago, I ....
5. I .... when I met my partner.

The day that changed my life ...(Sonia)

I'll never forget the day I <u>met</u> my husband.

I was 21 years old and I <u>was living</u> in a small village with my parents in the North of England. I <u>was working</u> in the local shop and wondering why I never finished school. It was 35 years ago!

One day, while I <u>was walking</u> my dog in a field it <u>started</u> to rain heavily. There were no cars around so I tried to hurry home. I <u>was running</u> when I <u>fell</u> and <u>broke</u> my leg!

I was in pain and I couldn't get up. I felt nervous and really scared! *Suddenly*, as I <u>was lying</u> on the floor in pain, a young man came running towards me. He <u>was carrying</u> a big umbrella and <u>asked</u> me what happened to me. In those days, we didn't have mobile phones so we couldn't call for help. Instead, he tried to get me up on my feet and help me walk.

We were 2 miles away from the village. My leg <u>was hurting</u> so much so <u>I asked</u> him to carry on without me, But he refused and lifted me up and carried me in his arms all the way to the nearest hospital, then took my dog back home!

He came back to visit me and brought me some soup. While I <u>was eating,</u> he <u>told</u> me he <u>lived</u> in Central London and that he <u>was visiting</u> his aunt for the weekend. We <u>talked</u> all evening. He <u>made</u> me laugh and forget about the pain. My parents <u>arrived</u> and thanked him for helping me.

A few days later, he called me ask me out on a date. My parents couldn't say no! We went out on many dates after that as he came to see me every weekend.

One weekend, as we <u>were having</u> dinner at an Italian restaurant, he <u>gave</u> me an engagement ring and <u>asked</u> me to marry him. I screamed with joy and said 'yes!!!'. Everybody in the room clapped and gave us their best wishes. I was so happy and I couldn't wait to tell my parents that I got engaged!

After a beautiful wedding, we <u>moved</u> to London, to the big city. *In the end*, I went back to college and qualified as a social worker. My life changed for the better and I *finally* had a job I was proud of and a man I loved more than life itself! I am so grateful I broke my leg on that day ☺

Your turn!

❑ Write about an accident you or a member of your family had. Plan this in pairs.

➢ What were you doing?

➢ What happened?

➢ How did you feel?

➢ What happened in the end?

The last time I had an accident was 20 years ago. when I was Teenager.

I was crossing the Road. I didn't look here and there. Suddenly a car came quickly and hited me. I Jumped in the air and felled down.

My family was with me, thatswhy luckely, They called a Ambulance.

After some time I arrived the hospital and had a few tests. but fortunately I hadn't any serious accident. Although I had some sliched on my car.

4

Complete the gaps **with past simple and past continuous verb forms**. Check, then make the sentences true for you:

- ❑ I ----------- *(watch) Tv at 8 o'clock last night.*
- ❑ I ---------- *(go) to the cinema last Saturday.*
- ❑ I ----- *(live) in the countryside when I ----- (decide) to move to the UK.*
- ❑ When I ----------- *(call) my mum the other day, she ------ (cook) dinner.*
- ❑ While I ----------- *(study) at secondary school, I ------ (do) a lot of sports.*
- ❑ I ---------- *(feel) very nervous during my last flight.*
- ❑ I --------- *(spend) a lot of time on the internet when I -------- (buy) my first sma phone.*

The last time I had an accident *was 3 years ago.* It was a scary experience *but* I am a lot better now.

I was driving to work *when* a dog *suddenly* crossed the street in front of me! *At first,* I tried to avoid hitting it *but* I lost control of my car and drove straight into a tree. *After a few minutes,* people came to help and safely got me out of the car. I couldn't stand up *because* I hurt my back quite badly. So somebody called an ambulance.

30 minutes later, I arrived at the hospital and had a few tests and a scan. *Fortunately,* I didn't break any bones and I felt a little stronger after a couple of hours. *Eventually,* I called my husband who quickly came to pick me up. He was angry *because* I didn't call him sooner, *but* he was very concerned and caring that evening *and* he asked my children to be good and to help me around the house.

During the next few weeks, I was in a lot of pain and I couldn't stand up for long periods of time. I had to take painkillers every 3 hours and to sleep on a hard surface. I *also* had physiotherapy three

Times a week. It was a very hard time for me   and I couldn't look after my family properly.

Luckily, my family and friends helped me a lot. My best friend drove my children to school and back everyday. She was very nice to them too. *Sometimes,* she even made them sandwiches for their lunch. My mum was also very helpful. She did the housework for me on Sundays and cooked for my family every evening.

After 3 months, I got better and I was able to look after my family again. *I felt happy* and wanted to thank my mum and my best friend for all their help. *So* I invited them for a barbecue and gave them each a present and a bunch of flowers. They were very pleased.

Read the article and answer the questions below:
1. What is the article about? --------------------
2. How many paragraphs? What is each paragraph about? ---------------------------------
3. What linking words are used to connect ideas? --
4. Which linking words are used to connect two or 3 simple sentences and form ONE long sentence?

3

feed the animals at the zoo/a monkey jump on his face.
walk home from work/ a thief steal her bag.

- He *was feeding the* when *a monkey jumped on his face*
- She *was walking* when *a thief stranded stole*

Practice 1

Cycle , fall off their bikes,   sail, catch fire,   walk down the street/walk down a fashion runway , get out of the car, trip   , lose her shoe,
 lose his/her balance.

Injuries: What happened to these people?
(twist, cut, burn, get a bruise, injure)

He broke his arm

- **Have you had any similar injuries over the past few years?**

---

run, hurt, fall, put away, break, slip

He ---------------------- down the stairs when
he ------------ and ------------- his leg.

She -------------------- the dishes when she -----------
and --------------- her back.

Verb list

VERB	PAST SIMPLE	PAST PARTICIPLE
be	was / were	been
beat	beat	beaten
become	became	become
begin	began	begun
bend	bent	bent
bite	bit	bitten
blow	blew	blown
break	broke	broken
bring	brought	brought
build	built	built
burn	burned / burnt	burned / burnt
burst	burst	burst
buy	bought	bought
can	could	been able
catch	caught	caught
choose	chose	chosen
come	came	come
cost	cost	cost
cut	cut	cut
dig	dug	dug
do	did	done
draw	drew	drawn
dream	dreamed / dreamt	dreamed / dreamt
drink	drank	drunk
drive	drove	driven
eat	ate	eaten
fall	fell	fallen
feed	fed	fed
feel	felt	felt
fight	fought	fought
find	found	found
fly	flew	flown
forget	forgot	forgotten
forgive	forgave	forgiven
freeze	froze	frozen
get	got	got
give	gave	given
go	went	gone / been
grow	grew	grown
hang	hung	hanged / hung
have	had	had
hear	heard	heard
hide	hid	hidden
hit	hit	hit
hold	held	held
hurt	hurt	hurt
keep	kept	kept
kneel	knelt	knelt
know	knew	known
lay	laid	laid
lead	led	led
learn	learned / learnt	learned / learnt

VERB	PAST SIMPLE	PAST PARTICIPLE
leave	left	left
lend	lent	lent
let	let	let
lie	lay	lain
light	lit	lit
lose	lost	lost
make	made	made
mean	meant	meant
meet	met	met
must	had to	had to
pay	paid	paid
put	put	put
read	read	read
ride	rode	ridden
ring	rang	rung
rise	rose	risen
run	ran	run
say	said	said
see	saw	seen
sell	sold	sold
send	sent	sent
set	set	set
shake	shook	shaken
shine	shone	shone
shoot	shot	shot
show	showed	shown
shut	shut	shut
sing	sang	sung
sink	sank	sunk
sit	sat	sat
sleep	slept	slept
slide	slid	slid
smell	smelled / smelt	smelled / smelt
speak	spoke	spoken
spend	spent	spent
spill	spilled / spilt	spilled / spilt
spoil	spoiled / spoilt	spoiled / spoilt
stand	stood	stood
steal	stole	stolen
stick	stuck	stuck
swim	swam	swum
take	took	taken
teach	taught	taught
tear	tore	torn
tell	told	told
think	thought	thought
throw	threw	thrown
understand	understood	understood
wake	woke	woken
wear	wore	worn
win	won	won
write	wrote	written

Pearson Education Limited
Edinburgh Gate
Harlow
Essex CM20 2JE
England
and Associated Companies throughout the world.

www.pearsonelt.com

© Pearson Education Limited 2013

The right of Sarah Cunningham, Peter Moor and Araminta Crace to
be identified as authors of this Work has been asserted by them in
accordance with the Copyright, Designs and Patents Act 1988.

First published 2013
Sixth impression 2018

ISBN: 978-1-4479-3690-9

Set in Bliss Light 10.5pt/12pt
Printed in Slovakia by Neografia

Acknowledgements
*The publishers and authors would like to thank the following people and
institutions for their feedback and comments during the development of
the material:*
Kirsten Colquhoun, EC Cape Town, South Africa; Jane Fairbairn,
Kingston College, Kingston, UK; Deborah Friedland, Oxford, UK;
Neil Hamilton MacLeod, Kansai Gaikokugo Daigaku (Kansai Gaidai
University), Osaka, Japan; Tim Goodier, Eurocentres, London, UK;
Stephen Greene, Tailor-Made English, Curitiba, Brazil; Joanne Johnson,
Institució Cultural del CIC, Barcelona, Spain; Antony Jones, Carrara,
Australia; Paul Martin, International House, London, UK; Chris Rogers,
Trebinshun House, Brecon, Wales; Michael Terry, Merit School,
Barcelona, Spain; Lech Wojciech Krzeminski, Maria Curie-Sklodowska
University, Lublin, Poland.

The publisher would like to thank the following for their kind
permission to reproduce their photographs:

(Key: b-bottom; c-centre; l-left; r-right; t-top)

Alamy Images: Ken Adams 8t, AfriPics.com 106t, China Images 30-31,
Kathy deWitt 114bl, 122tl, Paul Doyle 34cl, Fancy 110tr, Tim Gainey
13bl, Jason Gallier 95, Mike Goldwater 72b, Juice Images 6tr, Kevpix
87tl (Inset), Loop Images Ltd 31tl (Inset), Alan Mather 27, Hilke
Maunder 72t, moodboard 20br, Prisma Bildagentur AG 31bl, Philippe
Roy 54t, rudy k 49r, TongRo Image Stock 32cl, Westend61 GmbH
53b; **(c) Telegraph Media Group:** 65t; **Courtesy of Comic Relief
UK:** 34tr; **Comstock Images:** 100/E; **Corbis:** Adnan Abidi / X01847 /
Reuters 19tl, Bettmann 16bl, 17b, 18b, Chen Gang / Xinhua Press 64c,
Dan Herrick / ZUMA Press 12, Hugo Philpott / Reuters 32-33, Image
Source 96-97, Juice Images 53t, Kim Ludbrook / epa 36l, Sonja Pacho
64l, Paul J Sutton / PCN 11r, Philippe Lissac / Godong 10tl, Ted Spiegel
19b, Troy Wayrynen / NewSport 11l, John Van Hasselt 19cl; **Digital
Vision:** 74b; **DK Images:** 100/B, Gary Ombler 100/H; **Fotolia.com:**
Africa Studio 88c (Inset), Yuri Arcurs 24b, 26, 52t, 120tc, arquiplay77
101, 134, Arto 88cr, Peter Atkins 37cr, babimu 124tr, Bernard Bailly
8cl, Mario Beauregard 98tl, Beboy 52bl, 57tr, 70t, Ionescu Bogdan
8-9, Elisabeth Coelfen 120tr, DeVIce 67bl, elenabdesign 111c,
EyeMark 68-69, Sean Gladwell 8cr, Joe Gough 67br, Graffiti 50-51t,
graja 124cr, Gramper 8br, grandaded 8bl, Svetlana Gryankina 100/P,
Joseph Helfenberger 81, iofoto 97tr, Irochka 21c, Dejan Jovanovic
111r, karandaev 110br, Natalya Korolevskaya 82tl, Diana Kosaric
54b, ksena32@ukrpost.ua 104bl, Andrey Kuzmin 88c, Kwest 74t,
xiangdong Li 32cl (Apple), luchshen 130, Lucky Dragon 100/F,
Maridav 114t, michaeljung 59, micromonkey 116bl, Yang MingQi
8bc, Felix Mizioznikov 92tr, Monkey Business 97tc, morchella 100/N,
Natika 105bl, Christopher Niemann 60tl, nikitos77 84cr, omicron 84br,
Philippe Perraud 57br, pirotehnik 100/J, Vadim Ponomarenko 7tr,
Noel Powell 63bl, pressmaster 7tl, rabbit75_fot 14-15, raphotography
98tc, Alexander Raths 94, Radu Razvan 100/L, satin_111 36r, Scanrail
100/I, Tolubaev Stanislav 98tr, sumnersgraphicsinc 88cl, tele52 111l,
Aleksandar Todorovic 57cl, yalmedfa 86-87t, zirconicusso 100/O;
Freud Communications: 107cr; **Getty Images:** 15t (Inset), 38t, 43tr,
49l, 74tr (Inset), AFP 120bl, DAJ 32cr, Erik Dreyer 60cl, Krzysztof
Dydynski 78t, Gamma-Rapho 98cl, Steve Glass 10b, Bernard Grua
70bl, 72c, Thierry Grun 104-105, Elke Hesser 48bl, David J Spurdens
60bl, 69tl (Inset), Kactus 23, Andreas Levers 105tl (Inset), MCT
14bl, Michael Ochs Archives 96bl, 122bl, Popperfoto 79br, Redferns
17t, 123tl, Smith Collection 60tr, Thinkstock Images 58, WireImage
65c; **Photo courtesy Google UK:** 107tr; **Image courtesy of The
Advertising Archives:** 108tl, 108cl, 108bl, 108br; **Imagemore Co.,
Ltd:** 39t; **Imagestate Media:** John Foxx Collection 22; **innocent**

ltd: 107bc; Kraft Foods UK: 107bl; **Mary Evans Picture Library:**
Classicstock / H. Armstrong Roberts 16tr; **MindStudio:** 28, 63tr;
Monsoon Accessorize Ltd: 107cl; **Peter Moor:** 44tl, 44cl, 44bl; **Nike:**
107tl; **Pearson Education Ltd:** Tudor Photography 100/G; **PhotoDisc:**
7c, Martial Colomb 57tl. Life File. Emma Lee 39c, Ryan McVay
66br, Siede Preis Photography 13-129; **Photoshot Holdings Limited:**
65b, UPPA 34cr, 106bl, 110bl; **Press Association Images:** Andrew
Matthews / EMPICS Sport 10tr, Lionel Hahn / ABACA USA / Empics
Entertainment 18t, Mark Cuthbert / UK Press 42tr, Stephen Pond /
EMPICS Sport 98bl, Tammie Arroyo / UK Press 43br, Timothy Allen
/ Comic Relief / PA Archive 35t; **PYMCA:** © Mr Hartnett @PYMCA.
com 50tr, 51tl, 51tc; **Rex Features:** 64r, c.ABC Inc / Everett 47,
Everett Collection 62tr, Ilpo Musto 123tr, Ken McKay 25, 35b, Geoff
Moore 118, Sipa Press 9r; **Shutterstock.com:** 78bl, 83, Varina and Jay
Patel 90t, Andresr 29b, Kiselev Andrey Valerevich 29c, Yuri Arcurs
121tl, Mircea Bezergheanu 116cl, Bomshtein 113br, cheyennezj 113tl,
Coprid 100/A, Dushenina 13br, ene 100/C, Fine Shine 60c, gameanna
42bl, 45br, Mayer George Vladimirovich 82b, Vadim Georgiev 21bl,
Natali Glado 122tr, goldenangel 88bl, Goodluz 37br, Gts 38c, V. J.
Matthew 75, Marcio Jose Bastos Silva 116tl, Alexander Kalina 45tr,
Karuka 100/M, Vitaly Korovin 100/D, leungchopan 99, luckypic 113tr,
Robyn Mackenzie 45c, Malyugin 103, Brian Maudsley 90cl, Katarzyna
Mazurowska 82tr, dora modly-paris 45tl, Monkey Business Images
33br, Sharon Morris 90cr, Piccia Neri 84cl, nilovsergei 32cr (Rose),
nito 57cr, oliveromg 102b, Tomasz Parys 37cl, Picsfive
60cr, Tomislav Pinter 100/K, Popkov 7bl (Tina), prapass 84tr, Rambleon
124tc, Alexander Raths 20cr, StockLite 29t, Supri Suharjoto 7bl (Jay),
v.s.anandhakrishna 63tl, Rui Vale de Sousa 121tr, vanessaweber 63br,
Denis Vrublevski 124bl, 125tl, walshphotos 66cr, winnond 38b, Yellowj
84tl, yo-ichi 117; **SuperStock:** age fotostock 24t, Belinda Images 88t,
Blend Images 102t, Cultura Limited , Fancy Collection 40, 116tr, Flirt
32bl, 37t, Image Source 96tl, imagebroker.net 13cr, Juice Images 112,
Minden Pictures 54c, Radius 77t, Transtock 66bl, Yuri Arcurs Media
/ SuperFusion 48br; **Survival International:** Anvita Abbi 19cr; **The
Kobal Collection:** 20th Century Fox 127t, Film 4 / Celador Films /
Pathe International 127b, Nordisk Film 43cl; **The Red Consultancy
Ltd:** Courtesy Samsung 107tc; **TopFoto:** The National Archives /
Heritage-Images 79t; **Whitbread:** 107c; **www.imagesource.com:** 6bl

Cover images: *Front:* PhotoDisc: Siede Preis Photography

All other images © Pearson Education

In some instances we have been unable to trace the owners of copyright
material, and we would appreciate any information that would enable us
to do so.

Illustrated by: Julian Mosedale p28, p46, p52, p90, p119, p135; Fabio
Leone (Bright Agency) p128; Clementine Hope (NB Illustration) p92,
p133, 137; Dominic Bugatto (Three In A Box) p80; Juice Creative p76,
p133, p137; In House p20, p23, p40, p58, p77, p94, p112, p130, p132,
136.